Donna,

Well, Sis, here it is - my first book! I enjoyed writing it and I hope people enjoy reading it!

Love Ya,
'Nay

(4-1-12)

Another Chance

Another Chance

Renee Lohr

authorHOUSE®

AuthorHouse™
1663 Liberty Drive
Bloomington, IN 47403
www.authorhouse.com
Phone: 1-800-839-8640

First published by AuthorHouse 11/30/2011

ISBN: 978-1-4685-2393-5 (sc)
ISBN: 978-1-4685-2394-2 (hc)
ISBN: 978-1-4685-2392-8 (ebk)

Library of Congress Control Number: 2011961950

Printed in the United States of America

Chapter 1

She stared at the phone on the end table by the couch, knowing she had to make the call. After being in New York City for three weeks, it was time to let someone know she was back. The one person she really wanted to call wasn't a good choice at the moment. She tenderly rubbed her very pregnant stomach when the baby started to kick. "I know . . . I know" she murmured, "I'll do it." Taking a deep breath, she walked to the phone and picked it up, dialing a number she hadn't used in a long time but never forgot. When the ringing started on the other end, she almost pressed the *OFF* button. But the call was answered after the third ring and she quickly asked to speak to Sara Collins.

"May I ask who is calling?"

She had to clear her throat twice before she could speak clearly: "Amber Wilson."

"Just a moment, please."

With her heart pounding, Amber sat on the couch as she waited for Sara. Would Sara even talk to her?

"Amber? Amber . . . is it really you?"

Tears of relief and happiness filled Amber's eyes. "Hello, Sara."

"Where the hell have you been?"

Amber had to ask her question before she lost her nerve. "Can I see you?"

There was a moment of silence, then Sara asked, "You're here in Manhattan?"

"Yes . . . and I would like to see you . . . I need to talk to you . . . today, if that's possible."

Another silence. Amber was afraid Sara would tell her to get lost after what she had done. But Sara said, "Oh, Amber . . . I would love to see you and talk . . . we need to talk . . . but I have to be in court in an hour."

Sara was an assistant District Attorney . . . a good one, who won many of her cases.

"But how about this afternoon . . . around two? Hopefully court will be over with by then and we can have a late lunch. Could you meet me at Alexander's? Um . . . could I have a number to get in touch with you just in case?"

Gratefully, Amber gave her phone number. "I'll see you at two. Thanks so much for meeting me, Sara. I have so much to tell you."

"Oh, Amber . . . why did you . . . Okay, you can explain all that to me later. I have to go . . . It's so good to hear your voice again."

"I'll see you later." Amber was close to tears as she shut off her phone. Replacing it in it's cradle, she then rubbed her stomach again, something she did often as she spoke to her baby. "Wait till Aunt Sara sees me . . . I don't know if I can explain everything."

* * *

Amber had figured it would be at least a fifteen minute ride from her apartment to Alexander's Restaurant. But she had forgotten about New York City traffic. It seemed that every light was red and so, twenty-five minutes later, the cab pulled in front of the restaurant. Amber worried that Sara didn't wait for her. Her mind wasn't totally on what she was doing as she paid the driver. When she reached to open the door, he said, "Hey, lady! Don't you have anything smaller than a fifty? My last fare took about all my small bills for change!"

"Sorry." Amber opened her wallet for a twenty dollar bill. As they exchanged bills, she told him, "Keep the change." She didn't want to waste any more time. But she suddenly stopped be-forgetting out of the cab, and turned her head to look at the thirty-something driver. "Um . . . "thank-you for returning my money." That rarely happened in the big city.

His rather plain face lit up when he smiled. "I just figured you could use it for the new little one. I know . . . I have four with another on the way!"

Amber had to return the smile. "Congratulations . . . and thank-you again."

She stepped out of the cab.

* * *

Alexander's was crowded. Amber scanned the large room to find Sara, hoping she was there and had found a table. Men in business suits and families with small children were among those at the popular restaurant. She spotted a hand waving from a table toward the back of the room. With a smile, Amber made her way around tables and chairs. Sara had stood to greet her. Amber noticed that her pretty auburn hair was cut in a cute shorter style. She also noticed the look of shock and surprise when Sara saw her large stomach. But that didn't stop them from hugging, with Amber bending some to accommodate Sara's shorter frame. They parted with tears on their faces.

"Oh! Look at you!" Sara gushed. "Let's sit. We have menus already."

"Have you been waiting long?"

"Not too long. Just long enough to start on a much needed cup of coffee."

"Sorry I'm late. I forgot how the traffic is around here."

Sara smiled. "How could you forget?"

After a smile and a roll of her eyes, Amber asked, "How was court?"

Sara shrugged. "It went well. We got what we wanted . . . But hey! I'm not here to talk about my work. I want to know about you!"

A waitress with bright red hair appeared. "More coffee?"

"Yes, please" Sara replied.

As she refilled the cup, the waitress asked Amber, "Would you like something?"

"A large lemonade, please."

"I'll be right back."

As the waitress walked away, Sara's eyes met Amber's before glancing at her stomach. "It's Ricky's, isn't it?"

Tears burned Amber's eyes as she nodded. "Yes" she whispered.

"How far along are you?"

"Eight months."

Sara clasped Amber's hand. "What happened? Why did you leave? Where did you go?"

The waitress reappeared and placed the glass of lemonade in front of Amber before pulling a pad and pen out of her apron pocket. "Would you like to order now?"

Sara ordered a small salad with Russian dressing and a side of French fries. Amber ordered a turkey club sandwich. "Light on the mayo, please."

When they were alone again, Sara frowned slightly. "Is that sandwich all you're eating?"

"Don't you remember the size of a club sandwich? All I've been doing is eating. You'd think I was eating for two." A slight smile tugged at Amber's lips at her weak attempt of humor but then tears filled her eyes and a few spilled over and slid down her face before she wiped them away. "I miss him *so* much, Sara."

"You're eight months pregnant . . . that's how long you've been gone. Is that why you left?"

"I didn't know I was pregnant when I left."

"Then why did you go?" Sara leaned forward. "You walked out of Ricky's life . . . as well as mine and A.J.'s. He wasn't the only one hurting after you disappeared."

"I am sorry, Sara . . . so very sorry. I didn't think I could handle his job any longer. I knew he was a detective when I met him but it really didn't hit me until I moved in with him. It was the middle of the night phone calls because of a murder . . . guns, fighting, domestic disputes . . . whatever . . . I worried about Ricky, about his safety . . ." Amber wiped more tears from her face. "You know how it is, Sara . . . you married into it with A.J.. And look at your job . . ."

Sara sat back slowly, looking at Amber.

With a shrug, Amber said, "I ran away . . . I just ran away, leaving the best thing that *ever* happened to me . . . as well as a couple of great friends. I regretted it every day . . . I had a lot of time to think over the last eight months. I was two months along before I knew I was pregnant. I wanted so much to make things right but the longer I waited, the harder it was to do." After taking a drink of lemonade, Amber pleaded, "Please understand, Sara."

Their food arrived and conversation halted.Even after the waitress walked away, both Amber and Sara were lost in thought,eating in silence. Both women had plenty of questions but didn't know where to start. The room around them was filled with conversation and laughter but the two women could have been alone for all they noticed. Sara finally broke the silence between them: "I know that Ricky doesn't know about the baby. Were you planning on telling him?"

"Yes . . . as soon as possible. I know I should have told him sooner but with the way I left . . . I was too afraid of what he would say . . . or that he wouldn't even talk to me. There were so many times I picked up the phone . . . I even called once but didn't get to talk to him." Amber sighed. "I made a promise to my dad that I would tell Ricky . . . but I just didn't tell him as fast as he wanted. me to." She sighed again. "Would he have listened to me?"

"You could have called me. A.J. and I were so worried about you."

Amber heard the hurt in Sara's voice and it made her feel worse. "I'm sorry . . . I can't tell you how sorry I am. I *should* have called you." She met Sara's sad eyes.

Looking away, Sara ate the last French fry on her plate. "I take it you stayed with your dad."

"That's where I was." Amber had to clear her throat and blink back fresh tears but then smiled. "I made him and my brother suffer right along with me!"

Sara smiled then. "How is your dad? And Jake?"

Amber had to swallow the lump in her throat before answering. "Jake's doing okay."

"How does he feel about becoming an uncle?"

"He's thrilled! He told me he was thinking it was never going to happen!" Amber's hand rubbed her stomach. "Jake is *too* happy! He's bought and bought for the baby . . . I told him he had to stop!" Sadness crept back into her eyes. "He also told me . . . quote, unquote . . . that he's going to kick me square in the ass if I don't tell Ricky about his child *real* soon." Leaning toward Sara, she gently grasped her arm. "I can't stand it any longer . . . I have to ask . . . how is Ricky? I know he has to be furious with me."

Sara took a few long moments to reply. "Your leaving hurt him *so* much, Amber. He kept to himself for awhile but finally accepted my invitations to our place every so often. And now . . . he's seeing someone."

Amber had guessed that much after the night she had finally called Ricky and a female voice had answered his phone. After asking for him, Amber was told he was in the shower and could the woman take a message. Her answer was "No", saying she would try again some other time . . . which she never did. She had hoped it had been one of his sisters. But hearing that what she had guessed was true, it felt as though Sara had kicked her in the stomach. Even though Amber had tried to prepare herself for that possibility, to actually hear it was almost too much to bear. "Have you met her?" she quietly asked, sitting back in her chair.

"Well . . . she's a detective that works with A.J. and Ricky. She transferred to their precinct about two months after you disappeared."

Her hand automatically went to her stomach. "About the time I found out I was pregnant."

This time Sara's hand gently griped Amber's. "They started to date about two months after she joined the squad. They've had to keep it quiet because it's against regulations to have personal relationships within the squad."

"But you and A.J. know."

"Remember . . . A.J. is his friend as well as his partner."

"What's her name?"

"What good . . ."

"*What's* her name?"

"Deana. Deana Roberts."

Amber seemed to think about that detail for a moment. She then asked, "Is she pretty?"

"Amber . . . don't." Sara's voice sounded forceful.

Swallowing hard but failing to stop the tears, she wiped them off her cheeks. "I have to see him, Sara. Do you think he will talk to me?"

"Oh, god, Amber . . . I really don't know. Look, I'll talk to A.J. tonight to see what he thinks."

"He probably won't speak to me, either. What's he going to think about me being back *and* pregnant with his partner's baby?"

Looking at her friend, Sara replied, "He loves you to pieces but he was very angry with you with the way you left." She sighed, giving Amber's hand a gentle squeeze. "I have your number. I'll call you after I talk to him."

Amber nodded, afraid she would start to cry if she spoke. After a few moments, she felt it was under control and attempted a smile. "All I do is cry! I'm thirty-four years old and pregnant! It's been very rough on the hormones!"

With a smile, Sara said, "I've read that's normal."

With an un-ladylike snort, Amber exclaimed, "I'm beyond normal!"

The remark gave the friends a much needed laugh.

Glancing at her watch, Sara muttered, "Oh-oh" and looked at Amber. "I have to go back to my office . . . I have paperwork to finish."

"I'm so glad you came, Sara."

"You don't know how happy I am you called." She gently gripped Amber's hand. "I wonder where our waitress disappeared to . . ."

It was then the two noticed that the room was just about empty and tables were being cleaned off by the waitresses. Sara caught the attention of the redhead and asked for the check.

"Lunch is on me" Amber told her friend. "I asked to see you."

"But I asked you to meet me for a late lunch." Sara took the check and looked it over. "It's not even worth fighting over" she said with a grin.

Amber slowly stood. "I sat too long." Then, she winced when the baby kicked, not once but twice. Her hand rubbed the sore area.

"Are you okay?"

"The baby's kicks get harder and more frequent . . . and not always in the same spot!"

After handing the waitress a twenty dollar bill, Sara asked Amber, "Do you know if you're having a boy or a girl?"

Shaking her head, she replied, "I know that seems to be the way to go these days but I don't want to know ahead of time. I want to be surprised . . . I want a healthy baby."

"And you'll have one." Giving Amber a hug, Sara said, "I'll call you tonight . . . just when depends on the conversation with my husband."

"Depending on his mood, right?"

"You know how he is."

That brought a chuckle from Amber. "But I love him anyway."

"I'll be sure to tell him that!"

But her smile disappeared as she said, "I hope he's not too mad at me."

"Don't cry. He softens up when it comes to you."

"He used to."

After giving her a big hug, Sara said to Amber, "I will talk to you later."

As she turned to leave, Amber cried, "Wait!"

"What's wrong?"

"Is Ricky happy? Does this Deana make him happy?"

Looking at Amber for a long moment, Sara debated on what to tell her. She took both of her hands in hers. "He's better than he was. He smiles and talks more. I probably shouldn't say this this because I don't want to get your hopes up but I don't see between them what you had with him. I know he cares about her but he doesn't love her. Now, he needs to know about this baby. I know he'll do what's right . . . he'll take care of it . . ."

"But I don't need his . . ." Amber started to say.

"Hey! One step at a time! Wait to see if he talks to you.Now, I *have to go*! Wish me luck with my hubby!" Sara then hurried toward the door.

Watching her, Amber silently wished her all the luck in the world.

She knew she would need it.

* * *

Chapter 2

Around five o'clock, Amber made something to eat then washed the dishes she used. Looking at the clock, she chuckled, knowing she would be eating again in a couple of hours, remembering what she had said to Sara about eating all the time. Getting comfortable at the kitchen table once more, Amber reached for the deck of playing cards she had been playing Solitaire with quite often since she had been back. When she placed the Queen of Hearts on the King of Spades, her mind drifted back to when she first met Ricky . . .

It was Valentine's Day . . . over a year ago. She was in the drugstore, checking out the different sample cologne sprays. She didn't plan on buying any because the prices were more than she cared to spend. But it was fun sampling each one. As she was spraying her wrist, someone bumped her arm from behind, causing her to spray up her coat sleeve. Amber had to turn her head to keep it out of her face.

"I am *so* sorry! Are you okay?" A man's voice apologized. "I wasn't watching where I was going."

Amber looked up into the face of a man about 6'3" tall, with short dark hair and the darkest eyes she had ever seen. She stammered her response: "Um . . . yes, I'm fine. No damage . . . I think!" Sniffing at her sleeve, she raised it for him to smell. "What do you think?"

He looked at her, then leaned toward her arm. "Not bad. What fragrance is it?"

The sample bottle read White Musk.

With a smile, he said, "I like it. Let me buy it for you."

Totally stunned, Amber exclaimed, "Oh, no! You don't have to do that!"

"But I did bump into you and now you're wearing more than you planned on."

"True but . . ."

"No buts."

Looking closely at him, she asked," You really like it?"

The stranger laughed. "Well, it's a little strong but probably worn in a normal dose it would really be nice." He held out his hand. "Rick Davis."

She looked at his hand then at his face before placing her hand in his. "Amber Wilson."

His fingers gently squeezed hers. "Nice to meet you, Amber Wilson." With a smile, he added, "I have to admit that this is a first for meeting someone like this."

"Me, too." Smiling, she said, "It's nice to meet you, Rick."

"Are you sure you're all right? You didn't get sprayed in the face?"

Shaking her head, she replied, "I'm fine. No spray in the face."

"How about the coat? Does it need dry cleaning?"

"This thing? No dry cleaning. I can toss it in the washing machine."

His dark eyes looked at her a long moment before he smiled and said, "Okay, then . . . You take care, Amber Wilson."

"Thanks . . . You, too, Rick Davis."

Her knees felt like they were made of jello when she walked away from him. "Please don't give out on me!" she silently pleaded. Amber couldn't believe what had just happened! What a hunk! Those eyes! And that smile!

Amber went to the check-out line after collecting what she needed. Carrying shampoo, conditioner, Q-tips and a box of tissues, she waited in line, though her mind wasn't exactly on what she was doing. When it was her turn, she placed the items on the conveyor belt and looked up to see Ricky at the next register. He must have felt her gaze because his head turned and he smiled at her before turning his attention back to the cashier. The young girl that waited on Amber started talking about a new shampoo she was using but Amber's mind was on the man at the next register. She tried to smile at the right time to the girl's chatter. She paid for her items then glanced once more at Ricky (who's back was to her) before picking up her bag and leaving the drugstore.

Amber didn't get too far up the sidewalk before she heard her name being called from behind her. She stopped and turned to see Rick walking in her direction. With his long legs, it didn't take long for him to reach where she stood. "Happy Valentine's Day" he said, holding a bag out to her. Puzzled, Amber looked inside to find a bottle of White Musk spray cologne.

"Oh, Rick . . . I can't accept this . . . really, I can't."

"And why not? It's just a gift . . . between friends." He smiled. "Call me Ricky. My friends call me Ricky."

It wasn't often that Amber was at a loss for words. She had never imagined anything like this happening to her! But she knew she couldn't accept the gift. "Thank-you but I can't . . . Ricky." She tried to give the bag back.

But he put his hands and the other bag he held behind his back. "You have to. I have no one else to give it to . . . and it's definitely not my scent!"

Amber had to smile. "I'd worry if it was!"

"So, you'll take it."

After a slight hesitation, she gave in. "Okay . . . I will. Thank you. This is very nice." Her green eyes met his dark pair. "I'll think of you every time I wear it."

"I hope so." The husky sound of his voice caused her heart to pound even harder. "Enjoy." He held out his hand to her.

When Amber placed her hand in his, his long fingers wrapped around hers and held firmly but gently.

"I haven't had a Valentine's gift in a long time" she heard herself say.

"No? A pretty girl like you? What's wrong with the guys you know?"

Amber came close to making light of his comment about her being pretty but decided to bask in the compliment. "Maybe because I don't let them too close."

Ricky stepped closer. "Like this?"

"Um . . . yeah." It was suddenly difficult to think . . . and breathe.

He was close enough that Amber wanted him to kiss her! She tried to keep from licking her suddenly dry lips.

"I repeat . . . Happy Valentine's Day." When he spoke, his warm breath moved her hair on the top of her head.

She had to clear her throat, then, "Thank-you . . . again. The same to you."

He still held her hand. She wanted to follow him home but instead, slowly pulled her hand out of his grip. "'Bye, Ricky."

"'Bye, Amber. Take care."

Forcing herself to walk away, Amber silently pleaded, "Please, ask for my number! Say you want to see me again!"

But he let her keep walking.

* * *

". . . and he *just* bought you a bottle of cologne?"

"*Yes*! Maggie, I couldn't believe it! I've never seen him before!"

"Is he a pervert . . . or a stalker?"

"Oh god! I hope neither! But, oh . . . you should see him! *Whoa*! What does he want with me?"

"Will you stop putting yourself down? You *are* pretty! And decent . . . nice . . . loveable . . . and more!"

"No wonder I have you for a friend" Amber teased. Maggie Ackerman was her boss, as well as the closest thing she had to a friend since moving to The Big Apple.

"Unless, of course, he's just looking for some unsuspecting female to treat well . . . then rape her and Lord knows what else."

"Oh . . . wouldn't that be just my luck? But he's so good looking and seems so nice . . ." Amber sighed loudly. "I probably won't see him again, anyway."

* * *

A week later, Amber stopped for a few groceries on her way home from work. It wasn't one of her favorite things to do but she did love to eat! As she checked over the red seedless grapes, a man's voice sounded very close to her when he said, "I like your cologne." Startled, she turned to find Ricky standing on the other side of her grocery cart.

"Hi!" she greeted, surprised . . . and happy . . . to see him.

"Hey . . . how are you?"

Smiling, Amber replied, "Couldn't be better." And right then, she meant it!

He returned the smile but seemed to struggle with what he wanted to say. Finally, he said, "I never asked for your number . . . and I couldn't find it in the phone book."

He had tried to call her! "Yeah . . . I'm unlisted."

"Well, then . . . would you like to join me for something to eat?"

"Now?"

"Too short notice?"

"Well . . . I . . . um . . ." She glanced at the contents in her shopping cart.

"Oh, not right this minute. Don't hurry . . . I have some things to pick up, myself. Um . . . how about we meet at the front of the store when we're done shopping and then figure things out from there?"

"Sounds good."

Ten minutes later, Amber walked toward the front of the store. She had to fight the urge to hurry along . . . she didn't want to seem too eager! Ricky waited near a check-out, looking at a magazine. "Been waiting long?" she asked, stopping along side his cart.

"Only a couple of minutes" he replied, returning the magazine to it's place on the rack. "Did you happen to look outside?"

Looking toward the store front, where it was basically all windows, Amber saw it was snowing outside, with the flakes falling large and fast. "Wow! Um . . . maybe we should get together another time."

He shrugged his shoulders. "Or . . . we can buy a pizza and take it back to your place." His eyes met hers. "What do you say?"

She felt no qualms about him going to her place. Amber had a good sense of judging people . . . she trusted her instincts. But she asked, "Are you sure? It looks nasty out there."

"I've driven in this . . . I've lived here awhile . . . unless you don't want company."

"I didn't say that . . . okay, let's get a pizza."

Ricky picked up a fresh-made sausage and mushroom pizza to put in the oven. Amber selected an all-ready made tossed salad. "I have dressings at my place."

"How about dessert?"

"Do you like dessert?"

"I *love* dessert!"

"Well then . . . let's check it out."

A store-made coconut cream pie with lots of whipped cream and a cherry on top was their top choice, with a pumpkin and a chocolate dream pie coming in a close second and third.

"Enough food?" Ricky asked.

"Plenty" was her reply.

Their supper was put in Ricky's car. As the snow continued to fall, they attempted to clean off their cars but the wind did not help. They finally gave up.

"I'll follow you" Ricky told her. "Which direction are we headed?"

Amber pointed east from the store. "Two blocks up."

"See you there."

As she slowly drove along the unplowed street, Amber thought about how she was taking a guy to her place that she had only seen twice . . . and knew nothing about. But she liked him. There had been only one time that she had been wrong. She had married a man she was so sure she was in love with, only to divorce him two years later. And if Jake had any idea what she was doing now, he would throttle her before asking questions. She loved her big brother but there were times he could be a little too protective. Pulling into the parking area behind her apartment building, Amber saw the headlights of Ricky's car behind her. They would have an enjoyable evening . . . there was nothing wrong with that. She was thirty-three years old, old enough to do what she wanted. Who knew where the night would lead? But who was Ricky Davis? What did he do for a living? Hopefully he was single. She'd had enough of married men . . . one of the reasons Amber had divorced her husband was because she alone wasn't enough for him but yet she turned around and did what he had done to her . . . to other wives. Ricky *had* to be single . . . he was tall, dark and handsome and he seemed to have a good personality . . . So, Amber . . . *why* was he single?

A knock on the car window startled her.

"Hey! That's not fair! It's cold out here and warmer in that car!"

Nice going, Amber! "Sorry" seemed so lame when she got out of the car. "I guess I didn't want to get out."

"I don't blame you" Ricky replied, as she took the grocery bags out of her car. His hands were full so he couldn't help her.

He walked beside her to the building.The wind and snow made it difficult to talk without raising their voices. Amber managed to unlock the back door to the building without dropping anything. Ricky looked around as she unlocked the door. "It's well lit out here but are you out here much after dark?"

"Not any more than I have to be" she replied, stepping inside. "I'm usually home before dark, unless I have to make a stop after work, like tonight." When Ricky pulled the door closed once they were both inside,

Amber added, "I can't wait till it's daylight till nine o'clock at night!" She stamped her feet to knock some of the snow off her boots. "The elevator is this way."

"What floor do you live on?" Ricky asked, after stamping snow off his feet.

"Third."

"I'm thankful for elevators when there's a lot of groceries" he said with a smile.

After pressing the button for the third floor and the door slid shut, Amber sat her bags on the floor of the elevator. When they started to move, Ricky asked, "Do you shop at Arnie's often? I've never seen you there before."

"I shop there most of the time, usually on my way home from work."

"I stop there every so often."

She looked up at him. "I've never seen you. there." *I would have noticed you if you were!*

"No, I just shop at your local drugstore and help you choose your cologne."

His eyes met hers and they both laughed.

The elevator stopped and the soft sound of a bell chimed as the door slid open. "Lead the way" he said, then followed her two doors to the right of the elevator.

"Home sweet home" Amber told him, again setting her bags on the floor to unlock the door.

"Nice place" Ricky commented as he stepped inside.

"Thanks." It was an efficiency apartment, with one large room and a bathroom. In the kitchen area was a small wood table and two chairs. In the 'living room' was a couch, recliner, a coffee table, two end tables, lamps, pictures, and some knick-knacks. The couch pulled out to become Amber's bed.

"This is cozy" Ricky told her, looking around the apartment.

"Thanks again" she said. "I had better turn the heat up."

But she first removed her coat, hanging it on a coat tree near the door. Taking off her boots, she placed them near a register not far from the tree. Ricky did the same then gathered up all the bags while Amber turned up the thermostat.

"Where do you want these?" he asked, holding the grocery bags.

"Over there on the counter." Following him into the 'kitchen', Amber said, "I'll turn the oven on. It'll help warm up the place *and* bake the pizza!"

"I hope it doesn't take too long!" Laughing, Ricky rubbed his hands together. "Okay . . . let's see . . ." He took the pizza out of the bag and looked for baking instructions. "Can they make this print any smaller?" he grumbled. Then, "Here it is! 450 degrees, Amber."

"That will take a few minutes to heat up" she said as she turned the oven dial. "Coffee?" she then asked.

"Sounds good."

"Okay . . . give me a minute to get it started . . ." she murmured, mostly to herself, as she reached for the coffee can in the cupboard.

The two of them sat on the couch to wait for the coffee to finish perking. Amber sat with her feet under her at one end, facing Ricky. "Um . . . is it too soon to ask what you do for a living?"

He smiled. "Trying to make conversation?"

"How did you guess?" she asked, with a laugh.

"I'm a detective."

That was an answer she hadn't expected. "A *what?* . . . *You're* a cop?"

"Do you have something against law enforcement officers?"

"No . . . but I did wonder if I should be bringing a man to my apartment that I don't really know, even if he did buy me some nice cologne." She knew her cheeks had turned red.

"And, to clarify things, I am no longer a *cop* . . . I am a detective."

"You used to be a cop . . . does becoming a detective make you safer to be with?"

Ricky didn't reply but, his eyes never left her face. He looked amused.

"Please tell me it would be better if I shut up now before I put my foot in my mouth even farther."

He laughed. "Okay, then . . . tell me what you do for a living."

"I work at *T's For You*, a tee shirt shop over on . . ."

"I know where it is . . . it's not a big place but it seems to do a lot of business."

Amber smiled with pride. "We do keep busy!"

"What do you do there?"

"Oh, let's see . . . we silk-screen shirts with our own designs or at times somebody brings in something they specifically want . . . one of the guys also does air-brushing. We sell tank tops and sweatshirts, too."

"How many work with you?"

"There's seven of us. My boss, Maggie . . . who became a good friend . . . gave me the job when I went in looking for one. Her and her husband, Matt, are great people . . . as friends and bosses. I do like my job . . . and adore the people I work with." Her eyes met his. "Can you say that?"

His dark eyes lingered on hers a long moment before answering, "No, I can't. I mean, don't get me wrong . . . I work with some good people . . . my partner is my best friend . . . but of course, the nature of my job is much different from your's . . ."

"I understand . . . that was a dumb question to ask you."

"No it wasn't." He smiled. "I'm glad you like your job. Not many people say that."

"How true. Um . . . the coffee's ready. How do you like yours?"

"Black."

"Me, too." Amber stood and went into the kitchen. As she reached into the cupboard for cups, she heard the click the oven makes when it reached the temperature needed. "Okay! We can have something to eat soon!" She checked to see how long it would take the pizza to bake. "Twenty minutes!" she moaned. "I don't know if I can wait that long!"

Ricky appeared beside her. "Don't forget that we also have salad and pie."

"The pie!" She looked up at him. "How about dessert first?"

With a laugh, he said, "As tempting as that sounds, I think I'll eat salad first."

"You're right . . . what was I thinking?"

"That you're hungry. What can I do to help?"

Minutes later, they were seated at the table, drinking coffee and eating salad.

"So, where do you work?" Amber asked him.

"Over at the 27th Precinct. I've been there three years, after transferring from Brooklyn."

"How long have you been a cop? I mean, detective?"

He smiled. "Ten years . . . well, four as a detective."

"What made you decide that line of work?"

He shrugged. "It's just something I've wanted since I was a kid."

"So, now you work at the 27th . . . that's not that far from here. No wonder you shop at Arnie's at times." Amber frowned. "I can't believe I've never seen you in there before."

"You shouldn't do that."

"Do what?"

"Frown. You have a nice smile."

Her cheeks felt warm as she smiled at his compliment and looked down at her half-empty salad bowl.

"Amber, look at me" Ricky softly told her.

When she didn't, his long fingers gently rested under her chin to raise her face till their eyes met. Amber sat mesmerized as she watched his face slowly move toward hers and his lips softly touched hers. Ricky pulled back just enough to look into her eyes before kissing her again, this time with a little more pressure. Her eyes closed with the second kiss as she enjoyed it, wanting more. But when his lips were no longer there, she opened her eyes to find him sitting back in his chair, watching her.

"Okay?" he softly asked.

Amber nodded, refraining from licking her lips to taste him again . . . though she still felt the warmth of his kiss. "That was nice" she quietly told him with a smile.

"It was" he agreed, returning the smile.

"What if the snow gets too much and you can't go home?" *Did I really ask that?*

Ricky didn't look away when he replied, "We'll take it from there."

A heat rushed through her body, a feeling she hadn't experienced in a very long time. Amber didn't look away from his gaze, liking what feelings he aroused in her . . .

The oven timer went off.

Neither of them moved.

Ricky finally said, "The pizza's done."

Amber chuckled, pushing back her chair. "I know."

"I'll help."

As she reached to silence the buzzer, Ricky opened the oven door. He took the two potholders Amber had taken out of a drawer. Setting the pizza pan on top of the stove, Ricky closed the oven door as she murmured, "Gotta shut the oven off." Their bodies were close to each other and as she reached in front of him, her hand brushed against his solid abdomen. Her breath caught and as she brought her hand back, it happened again. Not moving for what seemed minutes, she finally looked up to meet his gaze. Without breaking eye contact, their bodies turned toward one another. The tips of his fingers stroked her cheek before his hand moved behind her head and gently moved her face toward his as his mouth descended upon hers. His kisses were brief at first, as if taste-testing. Once, twice, three times . . . again and again . . . each kiss was a little longer than the last. Amber enjoyed what he offered . . . it had been awhile since she had been with anyone. Oh, she had dated but it had been a few months since the last date and she didn't go to bed with anybody . . . not for lack of trying on their part . . . she grew tired of it, since none of the men she went out with seemed worth it . . . but with Ricky it was different. When his hands clasped each side of her face, her lips parted for his tongue. Their bodies pressed against each other, fitting well . . . with his erection against her. With a moan, she adjusted her body so her pelvic area could press against his hard length. Sliding his hands down to her bottom, he gripped her and held her closer. His kisses became more intense . . . and Amber answered. For a brief moment, his mouth left hers so his teeth could nip at her earlobe and her throat and then he moaned before taking her mouth once again.

The buzzer sounded, causing them to step abruptly away from each other. "What the . . . ?" Amber couldn't focus. Breathing hard, her body still tingled from Ricky's mouth and the feel of his hands . . . and erection. Finally, she reached and shut off the noise. "I must have reset the timer instead of shutting it off." Looking up at Ricky, she said, "I guess I wasn't thinking straight with you standing so close."

His breathing still came hard when he smiled. Gently smoothing back some of her light brown hair from her face, Ricky told her, "I'm glad I have that effect on you."

She wanted to be back in his arms but instead said, "I guess we had better eat this pizza."

Ricky hugged her briefly before kissing her forehead. "Let's eat."

After eating two slices of pizza each, they sat at the table with pie and coffee. Conversation with Ricky was easy. They talked about many subjects and had opposite opinions on some things. But he listened to what she had to say and asked questions without seeming nosy. Making each other laugh was easy.

Awhile later, he asked where the bathroom was. When he joined her again, Ricky commented, "Somebody must like sunflowers and butterflies."

Amber smiled. "And how did you come to that conclusion?"

"Well, from what I've learned from my detective work, I deduced that conclusion since I saw sunflowers on the toilet lid, as well as a bouquet of artificial sunflowers in a vase on the toilet tank. As for the butterflies, the border you have going around the middle of the walls looks great. For a small bathroom, you did a good job." He grinned as he spoke.

"Thanks. Sunflowers are my favorite. Didn't you notice that the placemats have sunflowers on them? Up home, one of our neighbors had a big farm and on the field behind us, for many years, he grew sunflowers. What a sight that field was when they were all in bloom! And when the sky was blue . . . it made the picture so much prettier!"

"And how do the butterflies come in?"

"My parents planted flowers all over and for some reason, in this certain area, there were always butterflies around . . . different colors and sizes. I used to sit and watch them for hours . . . trying to see how close I could get before they fluttered away."

Ricky watched her as she talked and then asked, "You're a country girl. What are you doing in a place like Manhattan?"

Her shoulders shrugged. "I wanted to try something different . . . get away from home."

"Are you happy here?" "Hmmmmm . . . yeah." And she smiled.

His fingers grasped hers and his eyes met hers. "I'm glad you made the move."

Her heart pounded at his words. "Me, too."

As the night grew later, Amber happened to glance out one of the two windows she had in her apartment. "It stopped snowing."

Ricky followed her gaze then looked at his watch. "It's almost eleven thirty." His eyes met hers. "I should get going. We both have to go to work in the morning."

She didn't want him to leave. After what had happened between them earlier, she would have liked him to spend the night. But he was right . . . work in the morning. Her alarm went off at six forty-five.

Standing, they both picked their dishes up off the table.

"You don't have to do that" Amber protested.

"I know." Ricky carried the dishes to the sink.

She smiled before following him. "Want to take the pizza with you? You bought it."

"Okay, but just a couple of pieces."

"And there's pie . . . you had better take some pie, too! There's almost a whole pie to be eaten."

Ricky reached for her, pulling her close. "Tell you what . . . I'll come back and help you eat it. How about that?"

"I'd like that."

He looked down at her, his eyes searching her face before zeroing in on her mouth. Covering her mouth with his, his tongue slid in. He groaned as she sucked it. Holding her as close as he could, his hands moved to her bottom again to press her against his growing erection. They kissed until they needed to breathe.

"Any more of that and you won't be going anywhere" Amber stated, breathing hard.

"I shouldn't have done that." He watched her lick her lips. "I'm not happy the snow stopped."

"You can still stay." Her body ached for him.

"No, I had better go. The snow would have given me a reason to stay but . . . let's wait for a night when we don't have to get up early the next morning."

Disappointed, yes, but Amber had to agree with him. His suggestion sounded better than a few hours in bed and then having to get up to go to work.

"I've got to go." He briefly kissed her mouth before backing away to dress for the outside.

As she watched him, Amber still wished he would stay and quench the thirst he had started in her. "Drive careful" was all she could think of to say.

"Have to."

Amber smiled.

Ricky reached out to touch the corner of her mouth with an index finger and then stroked her lips. "You have such a kissable mouth" he murmured. "I don't want to stop when I start."

"I don't want you to stop" she whispered.

He sighed loudly, pulling back his hand. "You don't make this easy, Amber. No, not tonight." Turning toward the door, he stopped suddenly to look back at her. "Can I have your number?"

"Sure." Her heart pounded a little faster as she found paper and a pen.

"I'll call you soon" he told her, putting the paper in his coat pocket. Looking at her a long moment he said, "If I touch you again, I won't be leaving."

Couldn't he hear her heart pounding against her chest? "It's your choice."

Moments later, Ricky shook his head. "I can't . . . it wouldn't be fair to either of us." Stepping once again toward the door, he stopped to look at her. "Talk to you soon."

"Good."

And then he was gone.

Amber looked at the closed door before slowly walking over to lock it. He said he would call her. He said they would have a night together. Walking to one of the windows, she watched him as he walked quickly toward his car. He must have taken the stairs. She could picture his long legs running down the steps. She saw him wipe the snow away from the door handle and then open the door. He disappeared for a moment, appearing again with a snow brush in his hand. She saw the exhaust blow a cloud in the cold air behind the car as the engine tried to warm up. Would he come back just for sex? Ricky brushed the snow off his car, looking up at her and waving before getting into the running car and driving out of the parking lot. He wouldn't be back just for the sex. Amber felt something different when with him . . . she had a feeling he felt it too . . .

The ringing telephone brought Amber back to the present. Her eyes blinked a couple if times, as if just waking from sleep. Placing what cards she still held in her hand on the table, she struggled to get her pregnant body out of the chair, hoping to get to the phone before the ringing stopped. "Hello?"

"I can't believe you're back. Where have you been, Amber?"

Smiling broadly, she exclaimed, "Oh, A.J.!"

* * *

Chapter 3

"I repeat . . . where have you been?" he asked in his no-nonsense voice. "I missed you and I was worried sick . . . and also madder than hell at you for taking off the way you did!"

Sara's voice could be heard in the background: "Be careful . . . don't upset her."

But it was as if his wife hadn't spoken: "And now I hear you're pregnant with Ricky's baby?"

Blinking back tears, Amber waited a few moments to get her emotions in check before she spoke. "Are you going to yell at me or talk to me?"

There was a long pause before she heard his chuckle. "That's my girl. You haven't forgotten how to set me straight."

"Believe it or not, I have missed you. I wanted to call you but I was afraid you would yell. I can't say 'I'm sorry' enough to you and Sara . . . and I really don't know how to explain . . ."

"Sara told me about your conversation this afternoon." A.J. sighed loudly. "Ricky was very hurt and angry after you left him. Sara told you about Deana . . . he's been seeing her for a few months. I really have no idea how he'll react to you being back . . . and wanting to see him." He sighed again. "And I get to tell him that you're having his baby. Oh . . . dammit, Amber!"

"I didn't mean to lay this all on you but I didn't know what else to do."

"I'm trying to understand why you never called . . . but as mad as I was at you, I'm damn glad to hear your voice."

Amber had to smile. A.J. was tough on the outside but under that shell he was loveable. As long as she had known him, he was never one to mince his words. If it was on his mind there was no doubt he would say it out loud. It was a relief he was talking to her.

"I want you to know that Deana is a good person and has been good for Ricky . . . but she's not you. I don't know what's going to happen after he hears about you . . . but I'm glad you're back."

"Thank-you" she whispered as tears slid down her face.

"I'll talk to him, hopefully tomorrow. And then I'll call you by this time tomorrow night."

"I know it's a lot to ask of you."

"It's okay. He's my friend . . . and I love you both. I'd rather he heard it from me instead of you calling him."

After a few minutes of small talk, Amber shut off her phone, with another promise from A.J. that he would call her as soon as he talked to Ricky.

She tried to get up off the couch but it wasn't an easy task. And the baby kicked a couple of times. "Okay, okay! I'll sit for awhile!" Sitting back, Amber rubbed her stomach while talking quietly to her baby. "I hope your daddy will talk to me. I guess I can't blame him if he doesn't." Resting her head against the back of the couch, Amber whispered, "Why didn't I listen to your grandfather sooner?" Closing her eyes, her thoughts went back to the night Ricky came back to her apartment It was Saturday, four days after she had given him her number and he hadn't called. Amber let out a long sigh. She really liked him and was so sure the feelings were mutual. Boy, had she ever pegged him wrong! "Life goes on" she muttered, then surveyed her apartment. When she felt depressed, she cleaned. Glancing out the window, she saw it was snowing, with the wind blowing it sideways. Amber tried not to think of how it snowed the night Ricky was there. With that, she threw herself into her work.

Under the three couch cushions she found potato chip crumbs and popcorn. "Oh, Mom would not have been happy seeing this!" Amber muttered before turning the vaccuum cleaner on. After a few minutes, she thought she heard something over the noise but dismissed it. But she heard it again and shut off the noise. The phone was ringing. "It might be Jake" she said out loud, since she hadn't talked to him in over a week.

Going into the kitchen, she grabbed the phone. "Hello?"

"Amber . . . it's Ricky."

Her heart pounded at the sound of his voice. "Hi . . . how are you?"

"Good, thanks. Hey, look . . . I'm sorry I didn't call sooner but we've had this case at work and it's kept us working late the past three nights. I didn't think you would want a call between midnight and one . . . so, I didn't call."

"It must have been some case."

"Yeah . . . we wrapped it up last night. I was home a little after eleven but I went straight to bed. I just got up a little while ago."

Amber looked at the clock on the microwave. It read one fifteen. "You must have been tired."

"I was. I . . . um . . . called to see if there was any pie left."

He did remember! "There sure is. I haven't had any more since that night."

"Good. Well, I know this is very short notice but I was wondering if you would join me for something to eat. And then . . . if it's okay with you . . . we can go back to your place for what's left of the pie."

"Well . . ." Amber didn't want to sound too eager. ". . . let me check my calendar . . ." she teased. "Let's see . . . yes . . . tonight is good."

He chuckled. "Lucky me."

No . . . lucky me! "You do know it's snowing again, don't you?"

"It's not a blizzard."

"Okay . . . so, how should I dress?"

"Casual. Since it's snowing and cold, jeans will be good . . . and a warm sweater. And Ill be at your place at six thirty, if that's good with you."

"See you then."

* * *

By six twenty, the apartment was clean and Amber was dressed to go. Checking herself in the full length mirror on the bathroom door, she smiled, pleased with her blue jeans, a black pull-over and a charcoal gray cardigan sweater. She was ready. No . . . wait! She wasn't totally ready! Finding the bottle of White Musk cologne on a shelf in the bathroom, Amber lightly sprayed around her neck and then on the inside of each wrist. Now, she was ready for Ricky.

At six twenty-five, the phone rang.

Her first thought was that it was Ricky and he was calling to cancel their date. But Caller ID showed it was her brother. "Jake!" Amber said into the phone.

"Hey, sis! What's up?" "Hey, it's good to hear from you . . . but I can't talk right now."

"Why not? You got a hot date?"

"Yes."

There was silence for a moment before Jake spoke again. "Really? I was joking when I asked you that."

"Well, I wasn't when I answered you. I'll call you tomorrow, Okay?"

"Yeah . . . but who is he? You never said anything about dating anyone."

"It's our first date . . . more or less."

"What do you mean by that?"

There was an expected knock on the door.

"Look, Jake . . . I've got to go. My date's here."

"What's his name? Where are you going?"

"Out to supper. 'Bye, Jake!"

Amber opened the door with the phone still in her hand. Her heart fluttered a few times seeing Ricky standing there, even if he was bundled up for cold weather. She stepped back and motioned him inside, talking into the phone, "I'll call you tomorrow, Jake!" And she shut off the phone before Jake could say anything more. "Hi" she greeted Ricky. "That was my brother. We haven't talked in awhile."

"You mentioned him in our talk the other night. He lives up north, right?"

"Right . . . near Lake Placid. Well, let me get my purse and we can go."

When she dropped her phone into her purse and returned to Ricky, he was waiting with her coat, ready to help her put it on. Amber was impressed. The only other man who had ever done that for her was her father.

"Have you been outside?" he asked. "The wind has gotten colder and stronger. Do you have gloves?"

"In my pockets" she replied, pulling them out. "After growing up in God's country up north, I always come prepared when it comes to winter . . . Oops! My scarf!" With a grin, she took it off the coat tree and wrapped it around her neck. "Now I'm ready." Amber then noticed how Ricky was watching her. "What? Did I forget something else?"

He didn't say anything. He just stepped toward her and leaned to brush his lips over hers. But it turned into a kiss and that kiss led into another . . . and another. He finally stepped back and his eyes met hers. "Let's go eat. The sooner we can get back for that dessert the better."

Dessert? Did he mean the pie? Amber didn't think so. Her body felt very warm all of the sudden. She either had to take her coat off or get outside. "Yes, let's go."

But the moment the elevator door slid shut, Ricky pulled her into his arms and kissed her. The kiss lasted for three floors. The kiss was still going on when the door opened. Reluctantly, they stepped away from one another and turned to step out of the elevator. There stood another couple waiting to get on.

Amber felt her face grow warm as she greeted the couple. "Hi,Ginger . . . hi, Fred."

"Nice to see you, Amber" Fred returned. He and his wife exchanged knowing smiles before they entered the elevator. The couple, in their sixties, nodded at Ricky before the door closed.

"Did I hear their names right?" Ricky asked. "Their last names aren't Rogers and Astaire, are they?"

With a laugh, Amber replied, "They get asked that a lot. What are the odds of a couple having the same first names as a famous dancing couple but their last name is Warner?"

* * *

"Where are we going?" Amber asked after Ricky drove for about fifteen minutes, toward the docks.

"I hope you like seafood."

"Shrimp is my favorite with haddock a close second."

"How about lobster or crab?"

Amber's answer was a wrinkled nose.

Laughing, Ricky replied, "Well, I guess that answers that!" He then turned into a parking lot. "I don't know why I didn't ask you before if you like seafood."

She smiled and said, "You seemed to have other things on your mind."

"I guess I did." He pulled into a parking spot not far from the door. "Must be the weather is keeping people away. On Friday and Saturday nights, this parking lot is normally so packed it's hard to find a place to park." He turned the engine off then looked at Amber as he unhooked his seatbelt. "I did enjoy the other night."

"Me, too." Her eyes moved to his mouth. He was such a fantastic kisser!

As if he read her thoughts, Ricky quietly said, "I want to kiss you but I know there's no stopping at only one."

"Like Lay's potato chips, huh? You can't eat just one?" "Something like that . . . but kissing's healthier."

Amber couldn't resist licking her lips. Ricky watched a she did.

"Let's just try one" she softly suggested, a she unhooked her seatbelt.

After a moment's hesitation, he leaned forward. "If we don't watch it, we'll be necking like a couple of teenagers . . . necking up a storm . . . steaming up the windows . . . sounds tempting, doesn't it?"

Amber took a shaky breath as his mouth descended toward hers. She returned the kiss until his tongue slid into her mouth. Pulling back, she whispered, "We'd better go inside." But what she really wanted was to forget about eating and go back to her apartment.

Ricky exhaled a long breath. "You're right. Let's go."

Getting out of the car, he walked around to open Amber's door. As they walked toward the door of the restaurant, she asked, "Have you been here often?"

"A few times. The food is good." "I've never heard of this place."

As he held the door open for her, he asked, "How long have you lived here?"

"Seven months."

"I don't know how you never heard of Sly's Fish Fry. You *must* be new in town!" he teased.

A sign near the door read: Please Seat Yourself. Ricky pointed toward the last open booth near the back and Amber nodded. His hand rested against her lower back as they walked to their seats. A waitress was right there as they sat opposite each other, placing menus in front of them. Looking at Ricky, she smiled. "Hey! How are you? Haven't seen you around in awhile."

"Yeah, I know. I've been busy. How about you?"

"I just keep working. Tonight's been a little slow so far . . . it has to be because of the weather. The booths are the only seats in here that are filled." She glanced at Amber. "You two must be hungry to be out in this cold."

"Ricky told me that this is a good place to eat."

The young blond laughed. "He should know . . . he's been here enough. Now, can I get you two some coffee?"

"Sounds good" Ricky told her.

"Two coffees coming up." She stopped to look at Amber. "Milk? Sugar?"

"No thanks."

"Oh . . . straight black like he drinks." She walked away.

Amber watched her then said to Ricky," Somebody has a crush on you."

He shrugged. "Jen's a nice girl. She's working to buy a car, she told me awhile back."

"Hope they pay well and the tips are good."

Ricky only smiled then opened his menu.

Amber opened hers, thinking, "Well, end of *that* conversation!"

When their meal arrived, Amber's eyes became huge when she looked at her plate. She had ordered a haddock sandwich with fries and cole slaw. "I think I should have gotten just the sandwich" she commented, amazed at how much of the fish stuck out from each side of the roll.

With a chuckle, Ricky said, "I should have warned you. I never thought . . . we could have shared my fries . . . there's more than enough." He had ordered a seafood platter and the large plate was piled with fried shrimp, clams, scallops and a large piece of haddock. "I'll share my shrimp."

"I'll take one. They look huge."

"Be careful . . . they're hot."

Stabbing one with her fork, Amber cut off a piece and put it in her mouth. "You're right . . . it is hot."

His eyes met hers as he said, "Remember . . . save room for dessert."

Suddenly, her body felt very warm. Amber took a long drink of water.

About half-way through their meal, Amber commented on how fast the room was filling up. The five booths and six tables in the front room where they sat were all occupied. Ricky told her that there were more tables in a room to the back.

Their time together passed smoothly. Conversation flowed easily between them. Jen appeared and asked if they wanted any dessert. Time seemed to stop when his eyes met Amber's. Ricky finally stammered, "No, thanks, Jen. We have to go."

Jen saw the look that had passed between the two. "Lucky girl" she muttered to her self as she turned to get their bill.

After paying, Ricky helped Amber with her coat before sliding his on. As they walked toward the door, Amber noticed when one woman saw Ricky and smiled before leaning toward the man who sat beside her, his back to them. The woman sat back in her chair, again smiling at Ricky, who noticed her that time.

"Well, I'll be damned!" he exclaimed, walking toward their table. "What are you two doing out in this weather?" He clasped the man's left shoulder. "Don't you know it's cold outside?"

The man turned in his chair. "We have to eat, just like you do." He peeked around Ricky and said, "Hello" to Amber. When he stood, Amber thought he was was an inch or two taller than her 5'9" frame. His body was stockier than Ricky's lean frame and his hair was thinning and turning gray. He looked older than Ricky, maybe in his mid to late forties. But his face was handsome, with a smile that warmed Amber. She liked him instantly.

"Oh, sorry!" Ricky exclaimed. "Amber, this is my partner, A.J. Collins, and his wife, Sara. Sara, A.J . . . this is Amber Wilson."

"Ah! Now I get to put a face with the name" A.J. commented, shaking Amber's hand.

"Oh?"

"Well, your name was mentioned a few times this past week, especially during this last case we had. He wanted to get home at a reasonable time to call you but it never worked out that way for him." A.J. grinned.

"Well, it's nice to meet you, Amber" Sara said. Her shoulder-length auburn hair was styled, her green eyes sparkled and there was a dimple to the left of her mouth when she smiled.

Believing in first impressions, Amber liked this woman. With a smile, she replied, "I'm glad to meet you, too, Sara."

Their food arrived, steaming.

"Well, we'll let you eat while it's hot. That chowder looks good, A.J." Ricky said.

"The best New England Clam Chowder in the City."

"I'll have to try it sometime. So, well, A.J., see you Monday . . . and good to see you, Sara." He leaned to kiss her cheek. "Take care."

"You, too. And Amber, we'll have to get together sometime."

"I'd like that."

Placing his hand on Amber's back, Ricky said, "Enjoy your meal, you two. Catch you later."

"Drive careful" A.J. called after him.

Ricky waved his hand as he and Amber made their way to the door. He held his keys in his other hand.

The wind blew strong and cold. Amber pulled her hood up. Noticing a car idling, it took a moment before she asked, "Is that your car?"

"Car starters were a great invention."

"You aren't kidding." Just then, Amber's right foot slid out from under her. At the same moment, she grabbed for Ricky's arm as he reached to catch her before she landed in the snow.

"Are you okay?" he asked.

"Yes, thanks. Klutsy me." Was her heart pounding because of the close call or because Ricky was touching her?

Tucking her hand under his arm, he told her, "Hold on. We're almost there."

Reluctantly, she let go of his arm when they reached his car. He opened the door for her and after closing it, hurried to get in on his side.

Not speaking, Ricky looked at Amber as he reached back for his seatbelt. Then with a moan, he forgot about the seatbelt to place his fingers under her chin and raise her mouth to his. The kiss was intense from the moment his mouth covered hers and his tongue entered, tasting everywhere. But it ended as quickly as it started. Breathing hard, he watched her as he finally buckled his seatbelt. Ricky saw her fingers fumble when trying to hook her seatbelt but it did catch. He listened a moment to her quick breathing before putting the car into reverse and backing out of their parking spot. The car's backend slid somewhat as they drove out of the parking lot.

* * *

Chapter 4

After the elevator door closed, Ricky showed restraint by not touching Amber anywhere except her lips. His kisses were soft, tender . . . and each kiss became longer than the previous one. "You smell great" he finally whispered.

She had to smile. "You think so? Some stranger bought it for me."

"He has good taste." The kiss that followed was slow and so full of promises.

They didn't realize their ride had stopped till the door opened. The kiss ended and they both looked up, half expecting someone to be looking in at them . . . but noone was there.

"Come on . . . we have some pie to eat." Ricky put an arm around her as they walked toward her apartment.

"Do you want coffee to go with that?" Amber unlocked the door.

"Sure do."

After starting the coffee, Amber took the pie out of the refrigerator, knowing pie wasn't what she really wanted right then. "Do you honestly have room for this?"

"I reminded you to save room for dessert" he replied, stepping behind her and sliding his arms around her middle.

"Can't you feel how stuffed I am?" she moaned, as her head fell back against his shoulder. "I feel like I ate a whole school of haddock!"

Ricky chuckled softly as he nuzzled her ear. "So . . . no room for dessert?"

Not for pie! She was content with the nipping and tugging his teeth were doing to her ear. But it ended all too soon when he kissed the side of her face and whispered, "Coffee's ready."

She put plates and forks on the table while Ricky poured coffee. When he looked at the pie, he commented, "I forgot how big that pie was."

They sat and talked while eating pie and drinking coffee. At one point, Ricky watched as she attempted to put a forkful of pie into her mouth and for some reason, it didn't fully make it into her mouth, leaving a gob of whipped cream on her top lip while the remainder fell back onto her plate. Laughing, Amber reached for her napkin.

"No . . . don't . . ."

The napkin stopped halfway to her mouth as she looked at Ricky, wondering why.

He got out of his chair and pulled her out of hers, so that she stood inches from him. "Let me." Taking the napkin out of her hand, he let it drop and it fell to the floor. Amber looked puzzled until he leaned forward and his mouth lowered to where the whipped cream was on her lip. His mouth covered the spot and she felt his tongue lick at the cream. He then gently sucked at the spot, removing the rest of the cream, before covering her mouth with his and his tongue slid inside. With a moan, Amber sucked on his tongue, tasting the whipped cream. She had been married, had been with other men but had never experienced anything as erotic as what had just happened.

His arms held her tightly against his body while her arms moved up around his neck and her fingers were in his hair. Sliding down her back, his hands grasped her backside to press her against how hard he had become. Moaning against his tongue, Amber's body strained against his length, wanting more. It was his turn to moan. His hands let go of her to slide between their bodies to touch her breasts. Amber inhaled sharply when his fingers brushed over her nipples, causing the tips to grow into hard buds. Pulling his mouth away, Ricky pushed her shirt, then her bra up to uncover her, watching as he caught the hard tips to roll them between his thumbs and forefingers. It was a big turn-on as she watched him watching what he was doing to her before arching back to allow him better access. His mouth suckled at one breast, then the other. The sensation just about brought her to her knees.

Suddenly, he stopped. Amber looked up, wondering why. With his labored breathing, he asked, "Where's your bed?"

Bed? What a time *not* to have a bed available! Her body ached in want for him. It took a moment to be able to catch her breath to speak: "My bed . . . we have to make my bed." After kissing his mouth one more time, she panted, "The couch . . . the couch has to be pulled out."

He yanked her to him, covering her mouth with his, his tongue stroking hers. He took her hand and pressed it against his erection, to feel it as it throbbed against the front of his jeans. Amber moaned at the size of him. Wanting more than just a feel through the denim material, both her hands moved to his zipper. But he stopped her, holding her hands against his throbbing member. Again releasing her mouth, he grunted, "Let's make the bed."

Not wanting to waste any more time, Amber forced herself away from him to get to the couch, with Ricky right behind her. He yanked two of the three cushions off and tossed them in the general direction of the one she removed. Reaching for the handle to fold out the couch, he said to her, "Get some blankets." Against the wall near the bathroom door, was a large decorative cupboard that Amber kept sheets, blankets, pillows and some clothing. She didn't even look at what she was grabbing in her rush. Far from a neat job, they quickly threw a sheet over the bed, then a blanket and pillows. Another blanket and sheet fell to the floor near the end of the bed. Ricky turned to her, reaching for the hem of her shirt. Pulling it off over her head, he saw that her bra was still pushed up over her full breasts. He leaned to pull a nipple into his mouth. As he sucked, his hands moved behind her to unhook the bra. Moments later, he stood and pushed the straps over her shoulders and down her arms, where the black bra fell to the floor. Their eyes met and their breathing matched . . . fast and hard. Ricky wasted no time in pulling his shirt over his head.

Amber's eyes traveled down, soaking in the sight of his broad chest, with the dark hair that spread across it and narrowed down to the top of his jeans. His chest heaved with each breath but then inhaled sharply when her fingers caressed his nipples. "*Damn*" Ricky hissed. "*Jesus*!" he gasped when her tongue replaced her fingertips.

Her hands slid down his chest to the front of his jeans. Breathing faster, she looked up to see that his eyes had become darker as he returned her look. Amber stepped back, wanting a look at his erection when it was freed from the confines of his jeans. First, the button . . . then the zipper. Reaching, her fingers slid into the waistband at each hip and pushed down. Her heart pounded faster when she realized he wore no underwear. His jeans dropped and his erection stood tall and thick. Wasting no time, her hands wrapped around his swelled member. He sucked in his breath as she moaned at the size of him.

"I know you want it as much as I want you" Ricky's voice sounded husky. "But I want to see you."

Reluctantly, her hands let go of him and moved to unbutton and unzip herself. He watched until she started to remove her clothes. "Let me" he said, reaching toward her. After easing her jeans over her hips, they fell to her feet and he soaked in the sight of the black thong she wore. Liking what he saw, Ricky's eyes slid up to her breasts before returning to her hips. She wasn't skin and bones, which made him happier. He liked a woman with a little meat on her bones. Reaching again, his hands settled on her hips as his mouth took hers once more. As their tongues mated, he slid his hands down over the bare skin that her thong didn't cover and held her tightly against him. The only thing between them was the patch of thin silky material that was her thong. And it didn't help that Amber pressed herself against his erection that throbbed for her. One of his hands moved from her bare behind to slide between their bodies and down between her legs. Reaching under the material, his fingers touched and stroked before they slid into her. "Oh-h-h-h, damn, Amber . . . *you're so wet*!" he whispered.

She moaned, pressing against his hand, wanting him . . . needing him.

The thong came off and they fell into bed. Ricky had brought protection . . . Amber thought it took too long to put on. But, it was definitely worth the wait.

It had been quite awhile for Amber. And the men she had been with . . . none of them came close to Ricky. He filled her like no other. Meeting his every thrust, her hips raised for him to plunge deeper. Her climax was nothing she had ever experienced before. Wave after wave rushed over her and before she finished, Ricky joined her.

Time seemed to stop. It took awhile for their breathing to quiet and for Ricky to feel like he could finally move his body off of Amber's to lay beside her. He slid his arm under her head and her body rolled against his. He quietly asked, "Are you okay?"

After a soft chuckle, she replied, "I'm better than okay."

"Oh, man . . . me, too." He kissed the top of her head.

They dozed for awhile and when they woke, were ready for each other again. But this time was different. They took their time, exploring and enjoying each other more. Amber never realized that there were so many ways for a man to use his hands, mouth and tongue. Her climax was no less than the first with him . . . and she made sure he was happy, too.

They slept again. Amber woke first and looked at the lighted alarm clock on the end table. It was 2:20 in the morning. She had to use the bathroom but it wasn't easy to get off the bed. Ricky had an arm and leg across her body. His breathing told her that he was still asleep. Gently, she moved his arm but when she touched his leg, his body stirred.

"Amber?" he asked, sleepily.

"Sh-h-h-h . . . I'll be right back."

"Hurry" he mumbled, pulling the blanket over his shoulders.

The apartment was cool; her naked body felt the difference after getting out from under the blanket and away from Ricky's warm body. She rushed to the bathroom. On the way back to bed, Amber picked the extra blanket up off the floor and spread it over him. Crawling over him to get back into bed, she was happy when his arm slid around her, pulling her close to him.

"Glad you're back" he told her.

"Did you miss me?"

"You bet. But now you're back in bed with a cold body. We'll have to fix that."

A rush of heat swept through her body at the thought. "I'm all for fixin'."

He kissed her then said, "But now *I* have to go. See what you started?" He chuckled before planting another kiss on her lips. "I'll be right back."

"I'll keep the bed warm."

"Good woman." He playfully swatted her bare bottom before tossing back the blankets and walking toward the bathroom.

Amber watched him with the help of the streetlight outside in the parking lot. She was very happy and wondered how long it would last. He was the type of guy she would like to have in her life.Would he stay around? She was sure Jake would like him. That was important to her, especially after marrying the guy nobody liked but she stayed with him, hoping to prove them all wrong. But, oh, they were so right. Amber was twenty-two when she divorced the guy. Now, after eleven years, she found someone she really liked . . . someone who talked to her, listened to her, made her laugh and treated her like she wanted to be treated. And he was fantastic in bed! She had no idea it would be so good! When she heard the toilet flush, Amber told herself not to count her chickens before they hatched. He might not be back after he left her apartment the next day.

Ricky hurried back and slid under the blankets Amber held up for him to get into bed. "Ah . . . much better!" His arm moved around her to hold her close. "Miss me?"

"Oh . . . you know it. Oh! You're cold!" She slid an arm across his chest, trying to warm him. Her voice was suddenly husky sounding. "Can we fix it?"

"You don't have to ask twice . . ." His mouth sought hers. He moved her body to lay on his as he worked her mouth.

He was hard by the time her body was on his. Her body quivered as the junction between her legs adjusted around him. But that wasn't what she wanted . . . she needed him inside her. Their tongues played with each other for awhile but then Amber pulled her mouth from his to raise her body over his face so that he was able to lick her nipples and suck at each breast. Being wet enough, her lower body slid up and down against his erection . . . till neither could take any more. Amber sat up to lower herself onto him, feeling him throb as he slid deep inside.

What a ride she had! Amber tried to meet Ricky's eyes but as their movements increased, her head went back and her hands slid over her breasts. Watching her, Ricky was turned on even more when she touched herself. His hands reached to cover her hands, while his fingers caressed her nipples, which were hard buds by that time.

It wasn't long before Amber came. She heard Ricky cry out, then felt him explode inside her. Collapsing on him, she felt his arms slowly slide around her back as he held her. Even after she came down from her high and her breathing was normal again, Amber stayed locked in his embrace. Slowly, she slid off, to lay beside him. "*Ohmygod*" she sighed, her head on his chest.

"Yes" he agreed, rubbing her arm as he kissed the top of her head.

Her eyes closed and she dozed for a few moments before realizing that he was no longer touching her. She looked up at him to find him staring up at the ceiling with both of his hands beneath his head.

"Ricky?"

He didn't say anything; didn't look at her.

"Ricky?"

His eyes met hers, looking serious. "I didn't use a condom that time."

Sitting up, Amber said, "I'm on the Pill."

Not speaking for a few moments, Ricky then sputtered, "And that's supposed to . . ." His voice trailed off.

"And that's supposed to what?" What was his problem?

After a couple of silent, long moments, he reached out to touch her cheek. "Nothing . . . come here."

After a few more long moments, as she looked down at where he lay, Amber finally curled beside him.

"Sorry" he said. "I just don't want to get you pregnant right off the bat. I'd like us to get to know each other a little better."

"Do you plan on getting me pregnant?" The question surprised her as she blurted it out.

He softly laughed, pulling her into his arms. "Let's just take one day at a time, okay?"

From what he's saying, he's planning on being around . . . for awhile anyway!!

"Is Ricky short for Richard?" *Where did that question come from?*

"No . . . my given name is Enrique."

"Enrique . . . I like the sound of that. What nationality is it?"

"Spanish. My mom was from Puerto Rico and my dad was the white boy from the Bronx, as my mom used to say."

"*Used* to say?"

Ricky softly sighed. "I lost them both within a year. My dad died of a heart attack and mom had ovarian cancer." He was quiet for a few moments before saying, "That was ten years ago."

"I'm sorry." Her voice was soft as she spoke.

His response was taking her hand and kissing the backs of her fingers.

She smiled, looking at him. He made her happy. *Enjoy the moment, Amber.*

"So . . . what else should we talk about?"

"Well . . . Okay . . . Mr. Enrique Davis, what is your middle name?" *Did I really ask that??*

"What?"

"It was the first thing that popped in my head."

Ricky laughed. "Okay . . . well, it's Scott. That was my dad's name." A pause, then, "What is your middle name, Amber Wallace?"

"Lynn. It was my mom's name."

"You lost your mom, too?" "Yep . . . whan I was fifteen. She was in a car accident."

"I'm sorry. Fifteen had to be a tough age to lose your mom."

"You aren't kidding. Ask my dad and my brother . . . they had to deal with me!"

With a laugh, Ricky said, "Oh, I can sympathize with them! I have two older sisters!"

"You have two sisters? What are their names?"

"Linda and Laura."

"No Spanish names?"

"My dad won with my sisters' names . . . then he had to settle for his name as my middle name."

"*Enrique* . . . so *sexy* sounding" Amber purred.

"Nobody ever made it sound so sexy . . ." Rolling her onto her back, he kissed mouth . . .

* * *

Sunlight filled the room when Amber opened her eyes. Looking at the clock, she was surprised to see the time was 10:43. The last time she had looked at the clock it was 3:22 A.M.!

Ricky's fingers skimmed down her arm. "Hey, there is life."

Smiling sleepily, she asked, "How long have you been awake?"

"About fifteen minutes. I've been watching you sleep."

Stretching, she said, "Oh! That must have been interesting."

He chuckled. "I thought it was."

"Why? Was I drooling or snoring?"

Another chuckle. "A little of both."

"Haha . . . How did you sleep?"

"When I slept? Like a rock. How about you?"

"When I slept?" She then laughed. "Anyway, I haven't slept that good in a long time."

"Glad to be of service." He kissed her. "Good morning."

"Good morning." Returning the kiss, she then said, "I have to get up." Climbing over his body again, Amber suddenly felt awkward being naked in front of him, even after the night they had. Wrapping one of the blankets around her, she hurried over to the thermostat. "I hope it warms up fast." Looking back at Ricky, she saw he was sitting up, with the other blanket pulled around his waist. It was time for a better look at the man who took her where no other man had. His broad shoulders and muscled arms looked delicious in the daylight. Her heart pounded at the sight of his broad chest and tight abdomen. It wasn't a dream . . . this man *was* in her bed. She couldn't stop the smile that spread across her face.

"And what are you smiling about?"

"You . . . last night . . . need I say more?"

"No, that tells me plenty." He returned her smile.

"I'll be right back and make some coffee." Amber headed for the bathroom.

She returned, wearing a long bathrobe. Ricky stood at one of the windows in his briefs. "My car is out there somewhere."

"We got more snow?" she asked, walking to him.

"Like we needed more."

Amber felt that familiar heat as she moved closer to him. He looked so good, no matter what he had on! Didn't she have enough of him the night before? Standing beside him, she looked out the window. There had to be another four to five inches of snow. "It's a good thing that your car isn't white. You'd have to wait till the snow melted to find it."

"Ha-ha" he commented, putting an arm around her shoulders and kissing her cheek.

"And you're lucky that today is Sunday and nobody's around. Any other day people are roaming around out there and someone would call the cops when they saw a sexy tall guy wearing only his skivies standing in a window. You'd be arrested for indecent exposure, bud."

"Oh . . . I'm sleeping with a comedian. Give me that mouth." He placed his fingers under her chin to raise her mouth toward his. "How about a little less talk and a little more action?" Ricky softly suggested before their mouths met. At first, it was slow and gentle but as their passion grew, he turned their bodies for a better fit.

After the long, heated kiss ended, Amber stepped back, shaky and breathless. "Whew!" she gasped. There was no missing the effect the kiss had on Ricky, and she had to tear her eyes from the front of his briefs. "I think we had better refuel first. How about some coffee and breakfast?"

It wasn't his first choice but he said, "Sure."

What was left of the pie was still on the table. "So much for that" Amber said, looking at it.

"We ate some of it."

"Yeah . . . we did."

"Should we save what's left?"

Amber hesitated a moment before answering, "No, we'd better get rid of it. I know it wasn't that warm in here overnight but I'd rather not chance it."

"Yeah . . . we can always but another one . . . the thicker the whipped cream the better."

A sudden heat was centrally located in her body at the memory of what he did with a little whipped cream . . .

Amber decided to start the coffee before cleaning the table. Without a word, Ricky picked the pie up off the table and carried it to the waste basket near the refrigerator. Spotting a napkin on the floor by the table, Amber bent to pick it up, remembering how it happened to end up there. As she stood, the tie had loosened on her robe She looked toward Ricky, who had just dropped the pie into the garbage and had his back to her. "Hey . . ." she quietly called to him. When he turned, she fully opened her robe. "Want to shower before breakfast?"

* * *

It was in the shower that Amber gave Ricky his nickname of 'Ricco', a name she would call him only when they were alone.

* * *

"I'll call you" Ricky told Amber as he got ready to leave. It was almost 7:30. They had been together since the evening before . . . and were reluctant to go separate ways

"Good."

He pulled on his boots.

"Want some help cleaning off your car?" she asked.

There was a slight hesitation before Ricky answered. "That's tempting but stay in here where it's warm."

"Hey, remember where I grew up.This is nothing compared to winters up north."

Chuckling, he grasped her arm and pulled her close. "Stay in here and be warm. Thanks for the offer, though." Ricky kissed her. After their mouths finally parted, he looked down at her mouth as his thumb stroked her bottom lip. "What is it about this mouth of yours? I can't stop kissing it. Not that I want to . . ." His mouth reached for hers again. When he pulled back, they were both breathing faster. "I've got to go." Putting on his coat, his eyes were on Amber. "I'll see you sometime this week." His next kiss was short but sweet. "I enjoyed my weekend. Aren't you glad we waited? We weren't rushed . . . 'Bye for now . . ." Another kiss and Ricky was out the door.

Amber locked the door behind him before going to the window to watch him. Her fingers caressed her lips, remembering his words about her mouth. She watched as he started his car, then brushed the snow off. Her heart warmed a little more when he cleaned the snow off her car. He'd be back . . . he said he would. *But she couldn't stop thinking about the guys that she had sex with and they never returned* . . . Ricky waved to her before getting into his car. Watching the tail lights disappear, her hand pressed against her mouth. *Please come back* . . .

The phone rang again, waking Amber. Luckily, it was on the couch beside her. Not checking to see the caller's name, she answered, thinking it was A.J. calling back. "Hello?"

"Hey, Sis! Did you have that baby yet?"

* * *

Chapter 5

"Jake! How are you?"

"Me? I'm good. How about you? You sound like I woke you up."

"You did but that's okay. I had a very real dream . . . about when I first met Ricky. It was so . . . it was like he was really here." She couldn't tell her brother how real every touch had been.

"I take it you haven't seen or talked to him yet."

"No. But I saw Sara and talked with A.J. and he said he'll set something up with Ricky." There was a pause before she softly asked, "What if he won't talk to me, Jake? What will I do then?"

"Don't worry about it, Amber. Wait till you know for sure. Stress isn't good for either you or the baby."

She sucked in her breath. "You're right . . . you're right. What about you? When are you coming down?"

"You have a little while yet, right?"

"Less than a month."

"I'll be down as soon as I can. The weather's been great up here and great for the landscaping business. We have a lot of jobs set up."

"Frank can take care of things. He's been with you a long time."

Jake sighed. "I know but things have been busy."

"Hey, Jake . . . if you can't come down, I'll understand. Don't worry about it."

"I do worry about you. I'm not leaving you there alone to have my niece or nephew."

"I won't be alone. I have Sara and A.J., and Maggie and Matt, if I ever call them."

"You haven't called them after all this time?""

"It took me till today to call Sara."

Another sigh. "Amber . . ."

"I'm hanging in there, Jake. And I know you'll be here when you can."

Jake had been there after the results of the pregnancy test . . . and he held her when she cried. He made sure she ate right, took her vitamins, kept her doctor appointments, walked with her the length of their long driveway, rested, and tried his best to keep her spirits up, which wasn't an easy task at times. They had always been close, being able to talk about most things but did have their disagreements. The best thing was that they adored one another and tried to be there when one of them needed the other.

"Is Lisa coming with you?"

"Probably not. She has plenty to do here." He didn't tell her that Lisa had already told him that she refused to go.

"What do you see in her, Jake? I mean, at first I thought we'd be friends but for some reason, she doesn't seem to like me. What did I do to her?"

"She likes you."

Amber's response was an un-ladylike snort.

"Amber . . ."

"With a body like hers, she must be damn good in bed. Why else would you be with someone who doesn't like your sister?"

"Now you're over-stepping boundaries . . ."

"Sorry." "Well, I have to go. I just wanted to know how you're doing . . . and wondered if you talked to Ricky. Let me know how that goes when you do, okay?"

"I will. Did I tell you that I have a doctor's appointment tomorrow?"

"No. Let me know how that goes, too."

"You know I will. I hope he tells me I'm going to have this baby within days."

"I don't think I can be down there within days." "I've had enough of being pregnant! I'm ready *now*! And how long will it take to get rid of this extra weight I've put on?!"

"By the look of you when you left, it could be a ten pound baby you're carrying."

"Feels like twenty. And the kicking is getting worse . . . my baby is *very* active."

"That's a good thing . . . isn't it? Hey . . . maybe you're having a boy.""

"We'll find out soon!"

Jake laughed. "Okay, talk to you soon . . . like tomorrow night. Love you, sis."

"Love you, too, big brother. I'm glad you called."

"Hey! Just make sure you let me know if you go into labor before I can get there."

"But I want to wait for you to get here so you can be my coach."

"No, I already told you I won't be your coach! That's *one* thing I *cannot* do! You're my sister, Amber! *Why* would I want to watch you give birth?"

She had to laugh. "Sorry, Jake. I have to give it one more try."

"No more tries . . . it won't do you any good."

Still laughing, she replied, "If you say so. 'Bye, Jake."

* * *

Sleep escaped Amber. She felt tired but could not fall asleep. Her mind was filled with many thoughts of Ricky: How soon would A.J. talk to him? Would he see her? When? Where? Will he be happy to hear he's going to be a daddy? She still loved him . . . she never stopped. When she left, she had left her heart with him. Too bad he didn't know that.

Her conversation with Jake came to mind. She was happy he called because he had a way to make her feel better.

Sleep finally arrived.

* * *

The morning couldn't have started out any better. It was a beautiful June day, with blue sky and plenty of sunshine. The weatherman predicted eighty degree weather. Amber dressed in tan shorts and a white maternity top that covered her large stomach but didn't hide it. Looking at herself sideways in the mirror, she told herself that *nothing* could hide her pregnant belly. But she then lovingly rubbed her stomach. "I'm ready, little one. How about you? Well, let's go see what the doctor has to say."

She was tempted to walk but decided against it. Maybe on the way back.

Amber called a cab.

* * *

It was her first visit to see Dr. Rolands. He smiled and shook her hand, introducing himself after a nurse had had Amber put on a paper gown and she sat on the end of an examining table. His warm greeting impressed Amber. He looked to be in his mid to late forties, about six foot tall with a lean frame, salt and pepper hair and he wore gold metal framed glasses.

"I see we have all your files, thanks to Dr. James. It looks to me that other than a little morning sickness, you've had an easy pregnancy."

"I'm thankful for that."

"I can imagine!" the doctor laughed. But then he grew serious. "I'm a little concerned that you made such a long move from Lake Placid to here so late in your pregnancy . . . and in this heat."

Amber looked down at her hands for a few moments before returning her gaze back to her doctor. Clearing her throat, she replied, "The baby's father is here."

"Oh . . . I see. Is he . . . ?"

"As far as I know, he doesn't know about the baby yet" Amber interrupted.

"Oh . . . okay. Well, then, Amber, let's see how things are doing . . . lay back, please."

The nurse appeared to help her lay on the table but Amber said to Dr. Rolands, "One more thing . . ." It had to be said before she lost her nerve.

"What's that?"

"I want my tubes ties after I have the baby."

"Are you sure?"

"I'm sure. One baby is enough for me." *Ricky probably won't be around to have any more.*

The doctor looked at her a long moment before saying, "Okay, we'll discuss it when the time comes. Now, let me examine you . . ."

* * *

After the exam, Dr. Rolands looked pleased. "Everything looks fine. You're due . . . let's see . . . next month?"

"July fourteenth."

Smiling, he handed her a picture of the sonogram.

"Does this picture show the sex of the baby?" she asked, not looking at it.

"No. It's just a side view of the head, with a hand against the side of the face. Looks like the baby has long fingers."

Ricky has long fingers.

Amber looked closely at the picture . . . and started to cry. *Ricky . . . call me soon!*

"Exciting, isn't it?" Dr. Rolands asked, handing her a tissue, misunderstanding the tears.

"I'm sorry." Amber wiped her face.

"Don't be. Your emotions are running on high." He walked toward the door. "Okay, Amber. You can get dressed now."

* * *

Amber took a cab but got out a couple of blocks from her apartment. She remembered the street from before. The street was one way with two lanes. On nice days, some of the shops sold many of their goods on the sidewalk in front of the stores. There was always so much to look at . . . and too much to buy! She found it hadn't changed.

For the baby, she bought a hand-made yellow sweater with matching booties and a hat. She also bought a beautiful mint green fleece baby blanket. The baby had plenty . . . Amber knew it wouldn't wear or use everything she had bought over time, as well as what Jake had bought. The last stop Amber made was at a stand that sold fresh flowers. There weren't any sunflowers so she settled for daisies and carnations. They would brighten up her apartment.

Feeling a little tired, she sat on a bench. She felt good after the doctor's appointment and the weather made it perfect to be outside. Sitting back, she watched people. The walkers either walked fast, as if on a mission, or strolled along, enjoying themselves. There were those on roller blades or bicycles. Traffic was busy, as always. Horns blew, brakes squealed and stereos blasted out of open windows. As she watched, Amber thought about how quiet it was at home upstate, in the country.

There was a shrill whistle that she didn't pay much attention to until it happened twice more. It was when she heard a male voice yell, "Ricky!", that it really had her attention. "Ricky! Wait up! Hold on!" Amber's heart pounded a she looked in the direction the yelling was coming from across the street. She recognized Chris Miller, who worked in the same squad as Ricky. Chris walked quickly, stepping around others. Amber turned her head to see where he was going . . . and her breath caught when she saw *him*.

There he stood.

Her heart felt like it was going to pound out of her chest. Standing, hoping to get a better view, Amber watched as he turned away from a Bronco he had been ready to get in to, wearing the round sunglasses that she had always told him made him look sexier. Ricky grinned as he waited for Chris. Amber stared, trying to soak in every possible detail of him. He had grown a mustache and a goatee. Never would she have thought he could look more handsome.

Then, it was as if he knew she was there. Ricky turned his head and looked straight at her. His head tipped slightly to the side,as if trying to decide who it was. He raised his sunglasses for a better look. In a panic, Amber turned away to grab her bags off the bench. She had to get away . . . but not until she had another look across the busy street.

Amber? "Amber!" Ricky couldn't believe it was her. Even with her wearing sunglasses, he *knew* it was her. That mouth . . . he knew the shape of her mouth . . . the mouth he loved to kiss. He saw her start to move away. "Amber!" He saw her body. She *was* pregnant! A.J. had told him that; he didn't want to believe it. "Amber!" he yelled again. He had to get to her, so he tried to make his way across the street.

Seeing what he was trying to do, Amber walked faster, hoping to get away. She didn't want to talk to him . . . not yet . . . not there on the street. Luck was on her side when she hailed a cab and it pulled to the curb next to her.

"Amber!"

She looked back before getting into the cab. Ricky was in the middle of the street, dodging traffic, as he tried to keep an eye on her. He called her name one last time before she was inside and closing the door. Fighting tears, she gave the driver her address. Leaning back in the seat, she used both hands to wipe away the tears that slid down her cheeks. Ricky . . . she had seen Ricky . . . and she ran away from him . . . again.

Ricky watched the cab merge with the traffic. "*Shit*!" A horn blew behind him. He turned, resisting the urge to slam the palms of his hands on the hood of the car as he glared at the woman driver. Making his way around a few other vehicles, Ricky joined Chris.

"Amber?" Chris asked. "Did I hear you right?"

"You did." Ricky had lost sight of the cab but still looked in the general direction it had gone.

"I didn't know she was back."

"I only found out awhile ago."

Chris suspected Ricky's relationship with Deana. "Do you want to see her?"

Yes, he wanted to see her. He wanted to hold her and tell her that he loved her and missed her. He wanted to say how glad he was that she was back. But he also wanted to grab her and shake her and yell and scream to let her know how he felt about the way she had left him. He wanted to find out *why* she did. Instead, he looked at Chris and said, "Let's get back to the precinct."

* * *

Amber pressed her fingers against her lips to keep from crying out, as the tears flowed down her face. She turned her head to look out the window but saw nothing . . . except Ricky trying to get to her. Did A.J. talk to him? Did he know she was back or did he just find out?

She suddenly realized that the cab wasn't moving. They had stopped at a red light. There were too many lights that stayed red for too long in the City. The baby kicked and Amber rubbed one hand over her stomach while wiping at her face with the other. She couldn't get to her apartment soon enough.

The driver's voice startled her when he spoke: "Are you all right, ma'am? I hope I'm not out of line by saying you look pretty upset."

"I'm fine . . . really . . . thank-you." A few moments later, he spoke to her again: "I'm sure you rode with me not that long ago. I took you to a restaurant."

Looking up to meet his gaze in the mirror, Amber did recognize him. He was the cabbie that gave her back her money when she gave him too much for the fare. "You're right. I'm surprised that you remember after all the different people you have in here."

"Some people I remember . . . for different reasons. I remember you were pregnant . . . and so surprised when I gave you back your fifty dollar bill."

Amber smiled. "You do have a good memory."

Traffic began to move. Amber looked at his I.D. on the dashboard: Warren E. Reed.

"When is your baby due?" Warren asked.

"Next month." "Your first?"

Another smile. "Yes."

"My wife just had our fifth child . . . a girl." He grinned. "After four boys."

"Wow! Congratulations! Now I remember you told me then that she was having another baby."

"See? We both have good memories."

Amber was glad her driver was a talker. He helped to keep her mind off Ricky.

All too soon, Warren announced, "Here we are." He pulled up to the curb and stopped. Amber paid him his fare plus a little extra for a tip. "Are you sure this time?" he asked, with a smile.

"Yes. It was a pleasure riding with you again." She gathered her bags, then looked at the flowers that lay on the seat. She didn't want them now. Handing the bouquet over the seat, she said, "Give these to your wife. Congratulations to you both."

"Thank-you! She will enjoy these!"

* * *

The moment the door was closed behind her in the apartment, all the anguish Amber held back in the cab surfaced again. "Ohgod . . . Ricky!" Deep sobs racked her body. The baby started kicking, as if knowing Mommy was upset. Amber went to her room to lay on the bed, sobbing and also trying to soothe her baby.

Awhile later, she cried herself to sleep.

Thirty minutes later, the phone rang. Not opening her eyes, Amber reached for the phone on the nightstand. "Hello?" she croaked.

"Amber? Did I wake you?"

Her eyes opened at the sound of A.J.'s voice. She struggled to sit up. "That's okay."

"I'm sorry. Anyway, I'm calling because . . . I don't know what happened earlier but Ricky told me a short while ago that he wants to see you . . . tonight, if possible."

* * *

Chapter 6

"*Tonight*?" Had she heard him right?

"That's what he said."

"I saw him this afternoon . . . and he saw me." Her fingers worked the middle of her forehead. And her tears returned.

"I wondered why he changed his mind . . . after I talked to him this morning, he was in no hurry to see you. Where did you see him?"

After explaining, Amber's voice was almost a whisper when she said, "I couldn't face him just yet, A.J . . . I wasn't ready. So, I . . . I ran away from him . . . again." She reached for a tissue from a box on the nightstand, wiping away her tears.

"Huh . . . I'm surprised he didn't tell me that he saw you." He was quiet for a moment before telling her, "Sara and I talked last night about when the time came for you two to face each other and we thought it would be better if you met at our place . . . kind of a neutral zone. What do you think?"

Silence.

"Amber? Are you all right? Are you going to be able to do this?"

Her sigh sounded shaky. "I have to. I have to face him."

"Okay . . . if you're sure. How about around seven?"

"The sooner the better." She drew a deep breath. "I'll be there at seven."

"I'll come get you."

"No, you don't have to. I'll take a cab. You're doing more than enough all ready."

"I will pick you up. It will give us time to talk. Now, what's your address?"

Amber had to smile. "You were always bossy."
He chuckled. "That's because I love you."

* * *

Too nervous to eat, Amber paced the floor between the kitchen and living room. She knew she should eat, for the baby, anyway. But she was afraid if she did, she would be sick to her stomach. A little afer 6:30, the intercom buzzed. "A.J.?"

"It's me!"

"Come on up."

Amber paced some more till she heard the knock on the door. "A.J.?" she double-checked.

"Sure is."

After turning the lock on the doorknob,sliding back the slide-bolt and then unhooking the chain lock, she opened the door. Tears appeared in her eyes because she was so happy to see him.

"Hey, you" A.J. greeted. "I'm a little early."

"I don't care! Get in here!"

He stepped inside, closing the door behind him. "Will you look at you?" A.J. hugged her. "I think that baby is due real soon! Look at the size of you!"

"Well, I'm glad you came to cheer me up." She returned his hug. "How are you?"

"Good for an old man. How about you?" Stepping back, he looked at her. "How are you holding up?" he quietly asked.

"Sometimes I feel like I'm going to fall apart . . . but I know I can't because of the baby."

"Do you know what the baby is?"

Shaking her head, Amber told him," I don't want to know ahead of time. I want to be surprised about the sex . . . I'm prepared for either."

"How soon will we find out?"

"Another month . . . give or take." She watched him closely, aching to know. Finally, she blurted out: "I *have* to know . . . what did he say when you told him I was back . . . and pregnant?"

A.J. took a deep breath, expelling it slowly as he rubbed the back of his head. "Well . . . he was a variety of things . . . surprised, angry, inquiring, and upset." He didn't tell her that Ricky claimed the baby wasn't his.

Her lips pressed together as she tried not to cry . . . but it didn't work. Her eyes filled with tears that escaped and slid down her face, while her bottom lip started to quiver.

"Oh, darlin', *don't* do that" A.J. softly requested.

Knowing how he didn't like tears, she wiped at her face before attempting a smile. "Sorry."

Looking at her for a long moment, he then asked, "Are you ready to go?"

Hesitating, she then replied, "As ready as I'm going to be."

* * *

"Amber, are you sure you're up to this?" Sara asked.

"I have to be. It's six months over due."

With a sigh, Sara looked at her husband. "It's almost seven. We should get out of here for awhile."

Amber looked at the both of them in panic. "You're leaving me?"

"We thought it would be better for you two to talk with nobody else around" Sara explained.

Taking a deep, shaky breath, Amber said, "Okay. Wish me luck."

"You'll do fine" A.J. told her, with a hug.

"How long do you want us to be gone for?" Sara asked.

"Knowing how Ricky can be, about twenty minutes."

"Now, Amber . . . have faith. We'll be back in an hour."

As they walked toward the elevator, they heard it rising and stop. When the doors opened, out stepped Ricky. "Hey, guys" he greeted. Looking down the hall in the direction of their apartment, he said, "Amber must be waiting."

"She is" A.J. replied.

"All right. Let's get this over." Ricky started down the hall.

"Be careful with her, Ricky" Sara told him. "She's fragile."

He stopped, turning his head to look back at them. "The Amber I knew wasn't fragile."

"She wasn't eight months pregnant then."

He didn't reply. He just walked toward the apartment door.

* * *

Amber looked the living room window onto the street below. She wondered if he still drove the Subaru or if the Bronco she saw him getting into earlier was now his. She gently rubbed her stomach. "I saw your daddy today. He's more handsome than he used to be . . . and I never thought that was possible."

"Amber."

The sound of his voice startled her, causing her to gasp before turning to see him standing in the living room doorway.

"I'm sorry . . . I din't mean to startle you" Ricky said.

"I didn't hear you come in."

"I knocked but you didn't answer so I just came in."

There he stood, dressed in denim jeans and a short-sleeve blue cotton shirt that made his eyes seem darker. With the mustache and well-trimmed goatee, her heart swelled with love as she looked at him. Feeling nervous, Amber didn't know where to start but Ricky spoke first.

His voice sounded so different, like he was forcing himself to talk to her. His next words were to the point: "You ran from me again today . . . why? Why did you run from me in the first place?" There was no disguising the pain in his eyes.

Wanting to hold him, comfort him, make things better, she started with, "I'm sorry, Ricco . . ."

"*No*!" he exploded. "You have no right to call me that any more!" *She always seemed to purr his nickname when she spoke it. When they were in bed and she whispered to him while in his arms, telling him how much she loved* him . . . "I was so sure we had a good thing together. *Why* did you up and leave like you did? Like a thief in the night, while I was out working. You have no idea how I felt when I realized you were gone . . . that you just packed up *and left me*! *Why*?" His voice broke, his hurt opened again. *She had left him in November . . . and he had planned to ask her to marry him at Christmas.* "Damn!" he muttered, disgusted with himself.

Tears filled her eyes as she witnessed how much she had hurt him. "What can I say? Would anything make it better?"

"Probably not . . . but tell me anyway why you left me, Amber."

Swallowing hard, she replied, "Your job, Ricky . . . I couldn't deal with your job any more."

He looked at her in disbelief. "*What*? You knew what my job was before we got too involved."

"I know . . . I know! But every time you went out, I was worried sick . . . especially at night. Every time the phone rang or your beeper went off . . . I wanted to tell you to ignore it . . . but I *knew* you couldn't. Ever since that time that guy had a gun on you and you didn't see him but A.J. did . . . do you have any idea how many times I thanked God for A.J.? And that last night . . . two cops were killed . . . *why* did you have to be there? The guy who did the shooting wasn't caught till the next day . . . he could have still been around when you and A.J. were there, wanting to knock off a few more cops. That was it . . . I couldn't take any more!" She angrily wiped away the tears that were on her cheeks. "I'm sorry . . . I shouldn't have up and left like I did . . . I thought only of me that night . . . *spoiled rotten* Jake called me more than once. I've regretted leaving you every day for eight months. I always wished there was a way that I could change things back to the way they were."

Ricky's jaw was set as he stared at her. Clearing his throat, he asked, "Why didn't you talk to me about all that? We never had problems talking things out before."

"I don't know. I guess I was afraid you wouldn't want me any more if I complained . . . Oh! How stupid that sounds now." *Please tell me you still want me!*

His clenched jaws worked as he looked at her. "You ran again today, Amber. Are you going to make that a habit?"

Her temper flared. "I didn't want to have this confrontation on the street!"

He shrugged his shoulders. "You were the one who took off. If you hadn't left, we wouldn't need to have *this confrontation*. You left me, Amber . . . without a word, not telling me *why* or *where* you were going."

"I was at my dad's."

"I know."

"*You know*? And you never called me, never tried to get me to come back?"

"Oh, I called." She looked at him, stunned. "You called? When?"

Ricky looked surprised. "About three months ago. I talked to your father."

"What? He . . . he never told me . . . you called? Why? Why did you call?"

"To find out if you were there. We talked for about forty-five minutes. He said he was going to talk to you and you would call me . . . which you never did."

"I didn't know . . . why didn't he tell me?" She was speaking more to herself.

"I have no idea. And he never said a word about you being pregnant. Why don't you ask him?"

Tears filled her eyes, overflowing. Her eyes met his. "I wish I could" she whispered.

"What do you mean by that?"

"My dad died last month." Her hand quickly covered her mouth but it didn't stop the sob that escaped.

Ricky's arrogant attitude disappeared for the moment. "*What*? I'm sorry . . . I didn't know. What happened?" He automatically moved forward a couple of feet to comfort her before stopping himself.

"Prostate cancer." She looked up at him, tears running down her face. "I don't know why he didn't tell me you called."

"He said he was going to talk to you."

"He was sick then but he got worse later." *He did tell me to call and tell you about the baby but I was too stubborn. But why didn't he tell me you called the house?*

"I am so sorry, Amber. I liked your dad."

After blowing her nose, she replied, "He liked you, too." Wiping away her tears, Amber said, "He kept after me to call you about the baby but I wouldn't."

"Why not?"

"I never told him that I called you once . . . the one time I call and a woman answered. She said you were in the shower. She said to call back but I couldn't." Her eyes met his. "It wasn't long after that I found out I was pregnant." Her chin raised a little higher when she asked, "What would you have said? Would you have told me to go to hell?"

"Probably." He saw her flinch at his answer. It would get worse because he couldn't stop himself: "You come back pregnant." He gestured toward her large stomach. "How do I know it's mine?"

Amber inhaled sharply. "How *dare* you ask that? I haven't been with anyone else . . . I haven't *wanted* to be with anyone else!"

"I don't know that."

"You . . ." She stopped. He was right.

The baby decided then to be in motion. Amber couldn't tell if it was feet or elbows. Maybe both because she winced and rubbed the area.

"What's wrong? Are you all right?" Ricky sounded concerned.

"The baby's moving." When a sudden idea popped in her head, she decided to try it. "Want to feel your baby?"

Ricky hesitated before saying a non-convincing, "No."

She stepped forward, and surprisingly he allowed her to take his hand to lay on her belly.

She wanted his hand on her bare skin.

He wanted to raise her shirt to touch her bare skin.

His dark eyes met hers but when the baby kicked beneath his hand, his expression changed to awe as his gaze turned to where his hand lay. "Is it a boy?"

"I don't know."

His face showed his pleasure as the baby kicked a few more times. After the baby stopped it's movement, Ricky's hand remained on her stomach. His gaze met hers again. He knew he should remove his hand but didn't want to.

Being as close as she was, Amber couldn't stop herself from reaching up to touch his cheek. "I love you, Ricco." It came out so easily, surprising herself.

He held her gaze but didn't speak. Amber watched his eyes suddenly turn cold. "*Don't*!" He pulled back, as if burned by her touch. "Don't *even* go there, Amber! *Don't* tell me you love me! *If* you loved me, you wouldn't have run off like you did! I love you more than life itself and was so sure you felt the same! But no . . . you walk out, with no explanation . . ."

"I was afraid!"

"Of what? Why didn't you talk to me about it?"

"I don't know why! *I don't know!*" She turned and walked to the other side of the room, keeping her back to him. She was crying and didn't want to be. When she was able to control herself, Amber turned to face Ricky. Clearing her throat, she said, "I was wondering if you would . . ."

Not letting her finish, he growled, "Give you another chance?" He snorted. "I doubt it, Amber . . . I doubt it very much. Do you think saying you're sorry and that you still love me will make all the hurt go away?"

Fighting more tears, she raised her chin to him. "Why did you say you would see me?"

He looked at her for what seemed minutes before he answered, "I really don't know . . . So, I guess I'll be going . . ." Turning toward the door, he stopped but didn't look back. "Do you need anything for the baby?"

"No, I don't. Besides, what do you care if the baby's not your's?"

She watched his back stiffen. When he reached for the doorknob, Amber quietly asked, "Do you honestly think I would tell you this baby was your's if it wasn't?"

He didn't answer right away. Amber expected him not to and just leave. But he finally said, "The Amber I thought I knew wouldn't."

She wanted him to leave right then . . . *she wanted him to hold her.* She didn't want to argue any more . . . *she wanted him to tell her that he still loved her*. She didn't need any help from him for the baby . . . *she wanted them to be a family.*

With his hand on the doorknob, Ricky's last words to her were, "I want a paternity test done." He then let himself out the door.

Watching the door close, tears slid down her face as she quietly said, "You won't need a test done . . . the baby *is* yours."

* * *

It took a lot of restraint not to slam the door shut behind him. Ricky stood in the hall, clenching and unclenching his hands. *Damn it*! *Damn you, Amber*! *Why did you go away*? *Why did* you *come back*? Balling his right hand into a fist, he walked quickly across the hall, zeroing in on the wall. Throwing a punch, Ricky stopped it inches from making a conection. *Damn . . . damn*! He still loved her . . . so why did he hurt her with his words? To get back at her for walking out of his life? The baby *was* his . . . he knew she wouldn't lie about something like that. There was no denying the pain in her eyes at his words. How he wanted to hold her and tell her how glad he was she was back . . . and how much he loved her. He wanted to dry her tears and kiss away the hurt. When she touched his face, he almost gave in. He didn't want to think about how she let him touch her stomach . . . how he felt his baby move inside her . . . and how much he wanted to feel her bare skin. Amber smelled good; she wore the same cologne he had given her when they first met. He looked back at the door but quickly decided against seeing her again that night. In the elevator, he checked his watch. A half hour . . . he had only been with Amber a half hour . . . and they had argued for most of it. Sighing, Ricky leaned back against the wall. For a moment, Deana entered his thoughts. She wanted him to stop over to her place after seeing Amber but by the time the elevator stopped and the doors opened, he knew he had to call Deana to tell her that he wasn't going to make it over.

He needed some time alone.

* * *

"Amber?" Sara called out when she and A.J. entered their apartment.

"In here." She was sitting on a large ottoman in the living room. "Hi" she softly greeted.

"Hi, yourself" A.J. replied. "How are you?"

Her shoulders shrugged. "Okay."

"What happened? Is Ricky still here?" Sara asked, looking around.

Amber shook her head. "No."

"How long has he been gone?" A.J. asked.

She shrugged her shoulders again. "A half hour or so."

"How did it go?" A.J. quietly asked, sitting in the chair beside her.

Tears flooded her eyes. "I didn't realize how much I had hurt him! I know both of you told me but to actually see his hurt . . ." Tears ran down her cheeks. "He seemed so cold . . . so indifferent . . . so unlike Ricky. I tried to explain why I did what I did but it seemed so lame." Amber began to cry. "I tried to ask him that even if we weren't together, would he put his name on the birth certificate but he . . ." She broke down at that point. Sara, standing beside her, put an arm around Amber's shoulders and hugged her against her body, trying to give her some comfort. Looking uncomfortable, A.J. didn't say anything. After a couple of minutes, Amber gathered herself together, fishing in her pockets for a tissue. "I'm sorry" she apologized, after blowing her nose. Clearing her throat, she said, "Ricky doesn't believe the baby is his." But a sob caught on the last word, causing her to clamp a hand over her mouth. Amber didn't want to cry any more in front of her friends. "He wants a paternity test done."

"What an ass! I can't believe him!" A.J. muttered.

"But just think, Amber" Sara said. "The test will prove you right."

"I thought of that."

"I'll have a talk with him" A.J. offered.

"No . . . please don't, A.J.. This is between me and Ricky . . . but thanks for your concern . . . even though I don't deserve it."

"And why not?"

"I walked out on you, too."

"But we forgave you . . . Ricky's situation is different. As tough as it seems, he'll come through. Give him time" Sara told her.

Amber tried to smile, fighting back more tears. "I hope you're right."

"My wife usually is" A.J. remarked, beaming at Sara.

"Um . . . would one of you help me up? I've had to pee and couldn't get up off of this thing! I don't know why I even sat on it!"

Both Sara and A.J. laughed.

"Why didn't you say something sooner?" A.J. asked as he and Sara helped her stand.

"I had other things on my mind. Now, is the bathroom still where I remember?"

"It sure is" he told her.

* * *

The ride back to her apartment was quiet. A few times, A.J. looked at her, to find her gazing out the side window. After he parked near the apartment building, A.J. shut off the motor before reaching for her hand. "Hey, kiddo" he softly said, holding her hand between his.

When she turned her head, he saw the tears. Amber tried to smile but then quickly looked away. "I love him so much, A.J . . . how could I do what I did to him?" Her voice broke and her free hand pressed against her mouth. A.J. waited. When she felt she had it under control, Amber stated, "He hates me."

Rubbing her hand between his, A.J. said, "I don't think he hates you."

Turning back to look at him, she told him, "You didn't see the way he looked at me."

"He's hurting, Amber. I don't know why but I think he's glad you're back."

"Don't get my hopes up, A.J . . . please."

"Just remember what my all-knowing wife told you . . . give him time."

Amber wanted to believe that so much but after what just happened with Ricky . . .

"Come on. I'll walk you up."

"You don't have to."

"I know I don't have to . . . but I want to."

A.J. started to reach for the door handle when Amber said, "Wait a minute, okay?"

"Sure, darlin' . . . what's up?"

"I just wanted to thank you again for helping me. It has to be a tough situation for you, being his friend and work partner." Patting his hand, she continued: "And, I want to apologize again for running off like I did . . .

and not getting in touch with either you or Sara. I don't know what I was thinking . . . I guess I wasn't."

He gently squeezed her fingers. "You've apologized enough . . . apology accepted. You have more important things to think about, like a baby that's due weeks from now. If there's anything you need, let us know, okay? Do you need anything for the baby?"

"No . . . no, thanks. My dad made sure I had everything I could possibly need for his first grandchild." She suddenly gripped A.J.'s hand. "My dad died a month ago . . . he didn't live to get to see or hold the grandbaby he wanted so much." Her voice broke but surprisingly, she didn't cry.

"Oh, darlin' . . . I'm so sorry. It had to be tough, especially at a time like this."

Amber only nodded her head, afraid to try to speak for a few moments. Finally, she was able to tell him, "Financially, I'm set. My dad left Jake and I well off. But emotionally . . . I need to have Ricky's love again. Am I asking too much?" Her throat burned and a large lump settled in the middle of it that was hard to swallow.

"Just give him time and space, Amber . . . he has to heal."

She smiled at him through her tears. "You have the knack of finding the right thing to say."

"Sometimes I say too much." "Well . . . that too!" She attempted a smile.

"Ready to go up now?"

"Yes."

Opening her door and helping her out of the car, A.J. put her arm through his and walked with her up to her apartment door. Before she opened it, he asked, "What do you think about joining Sara and me out to supper some night soon?"

"That sounds good. Let me know."

She kissed his cheek and went into her apartment. A.J. watched the door until it closed and heard the locks click into place before he walked back to the elevator.

* * *

Chapter 7

Amber looked for *the* box. Knowing it was somewhere in the large walk-in closet, she tested the weight of boxes before attempting to move them out of the way. "Why did I keep all this stuff when I don't remember what's in most of the boxes?" she muttered, looking around at the mess before her.

Then, she spotted what she was looking for, near the back of the closet, the box with the top flaps held down with clear packing tape. And luckily, it sat on top of three other boxes, so she didn't have to move any of them. Tears pricked her eyes as she carried the box into her bedroom and placed it on her bed before pulling up the tape. Opening the box, she found a scrapbook. It brought a smile to her face as she opened it, looking briefly at memories from high school. There was page after page of newspaper clippings from chorus and drama club, and of the varsity basketball team, featuring pictures of the star of the team, Jim Holland, who was her main man during their junior and senior years. She found a dried flower pressed in among the pictures, a small sunflower that Jim had given her after he found out it was her favorite flower. "I can't believe I kept this." she muttered.

Also in the box were birthday cards that she had saved, including the last one from her mother, who had died two months after Amber's fifteenth birthday. It was the middle of March and her mother had gone into town to buy groceries. It started to snow before she came back. A pick-up truck turned off a side road too fast, fish-tailed and slid into the driver's side of her mother's car. Amber wiped away the tears that fell as she remembered. "Mom, I miss you . . . especially now." Rubbing her stomach, Amber read the words her mom had signed the card with, "*I love you, my baby girl . . . Happy Birthday, Mom*". "I wish you could be here for your grandbaby . . . and I wish you were here to talk with." Smiling through her tears, Amber added, "I need some motherly advice on men, Mom." Setting the card aside, she pulled out a couple of notebooks that she had used as journals during high school, where she had written her deepest thoughts and secrets, for nobody but herself to read. Amber set them aside, too, not in the mood to read them just then. At the bottom of the box, she found what she was looking for. Her tears started again as she reached into the box and gripped what she wanted, then slowly brought it up out of the box. It was a frame for a five by seven inch picture, face-down. Turning it over, she looked at the picture through tear-filled eyes. It was a picture of her and a clean-shaven Ricky, taken at her dad's the year before. Ricky was sitting in a lawn chair and Amber stood behind him, with her arms around his neck and her face pressed against his. They were smiling and looked so in love. Jake had taken the picture and had the enlargement made for them. Tears fell on the glass. Amber tried to wipe them off but she began to cry harder.

Sitting on the edge of her bed, Amber clenched the frame against her breasts. She sobbed, letting lose all the pain and frustration that centered around Ricky. After the storm had passed, Amber was exhausted. Not caring, she wiped her arm across her runny nose before looking again at the picture. Her fingers gently touched Ricky's face. "You were always there for me . . . and so what do I do when you need me after a rough case? I walk away from you with no good-bye." Looking at his smiling face, Amber thought about their conversation in A.J. and Sara's living room. Suddenly, she inhaled sharply. He had told her that he still loved her! She swore she heard him right. He said, "I *love* you more than life itself . . ." Had he misspoke? Did he really mean, "I *loved* you more . . . ?" But she wanted to hang on to the hope that he did love her!

The picture was placed on her nighttstand. It had been packed away for eight months. After taking the bus back home up north, Jake had driven her back to NYC to collect her things. It had been a rush packing job, because she wanted to be out of Ricky's apartment before he came home. The picture wasn't unpacked because it would cause too much pain to be in plain sight. Now she deserved to see it, to remind her of what she had foolishly lost.

* * *

Sara called two days later. "I can't talk long but I just wanted to know how you were doing. We haven't talked since the other night."

"I'm sorry . . . I should have called. I just feel . . . out of it. I keep thinking about Ricky."

"He hasn't gotten in touch with you?"

"No . . . I don't think he will." There was a moment of silence before Sara quietly said, "This has been hard on all of us."

"I know . . . and again, I'm sorry."

"Please . . . stop with the *I'm sorry.* The main thing you have to think about is that you have a little one coming soon . . . and you *have to* take care of yourself."

"Sara . . . ?"

"Yes?"

"Has A.J. said anything about Ricky? Has Ricky talked to him about the other night?"

"I guess Ricky doesn't want to talk about it. A.J. has tried to talk about it a couple of times but Ricky changes the subject. And what makes it harder is that Deana is around most of the time."

Deana . . . how could Amber forget she was in the picture? "Well, then . . . okay. I was just wondering . . ."

"Hey! How about we . . ." Sara stopped talking and then another voice was heard in the background. "I will be with you shortly" was Sara's reply. She said to Amber, "Sorry, but I have to go. I'll call you later."

"Okay . . . I'm glad you called me."

"Are you okay?"

"I'll be fine . . . thanks. Please tell A.J. hi from me."

"He'll be happy to hear that. Catch ya later."

Amber did feel somewhat better after her brief conversation with Sara. When the baby started to move, Amber smiled as she rubbed her stomach. "You're going to love your Aunt Sara and Uncle A.J . . . and they're going to love you back."

* * *

Amber had just finished washing what supper dishes she had when the intercom buzzed. Puzzled, she answered it: "Yes?"

There was a slight pause before she heard, "It's Ricky."

Her heart thudded against her chest. "*Here*?"

A sigh. "Yes."

"What do you want?"

"To talk to you, Amber."

She hesitated before telling him, "Come on up".

He was coming to see her! Amber looked down at what she was wearing. The red silk lounge pants and matching sleeveless top would have to do. Looking in the mirror in the entryway, she used her fingers to try to put hairs back into place. Even though she knew he was coming, she still jumped when there was a knock on the door. "Ricky?"

"Yes."

She managed to unlock the locks without too much fumbling. There he stood, as handsome as ever when she opened the door. "Hi."

"Hi. Um, I know I should have called first . . ."

"That's okay."

They stood looking at one another until he asked, "May I come in?"

She stepped back and Ricky entered, closing the door behind him. One look at his face told her that he was there for a reason . . . and not to socialize. But she had to ask: "How did you get my address and phone number?"

"I asked A.J.."

"Because . . . ?"

He gave her a long look before simply saying, "Just because."

She knew she wouldn't get any further on that subject unless she really pressed it . . . and she wasn't up to that. So, Amber offered him coffee.

"No, thanks."

"Would you like to sit down?"

"No." He looked around. "Nice place. It's a step up from the other place you had."

"My other apartment was just fine for one person. But with the baby, I need more room. And, I'll have you know, I actually have three separate bedrooms, a living room *and* a kitchen. Want a tour?"

"No . . . look, Amber, I'm here because A.J. said that I had better get over here to see you before something happens to make the baby come early." He sounded exasperated. "What do you want from me, Amber?"

Why would A.J. tell him that? She answered Ricky with: "I want you to acknowledge your child."

Shaking his head, he said, "I don't know what to think. You leave me . . . and come back pregnant, claiming it's mine."

Her hands slid protectively around her stomach. "It is" she whispered.

He sighed. "Talk to me, Amber."

"What do you think I've been trying to do? What else do you want to hear from me?"

"Did you know you were pregnant when you left?"

"*No*! I already told you that I tried calling you!"

"Well, then . . . how did it happen? I thought you were on the Pill."

"I was! The Pill isn't 100% non-pregnant proof."

There was no comment from Ricky.

Amber had more to say: "We had to have made this baby the night I left. Remember? We made love twice before the call came for you."

He looked at her, remembering. He loved making love to her . . . he could never seem to get enough of her . . . Pushing those thought aside, he quietly said, "Deana thinks we should have the paternity test done."

Amber bristled at the mention of *her* name concerning their baby. "Who the hell is *she* to have any say in this? "

"*She's* the one in my life right now."

That hurt. It also knocked the wind out of her sails. "What do *you* want?"

"To have the test."

Staring at him, Amber couldn't believe he didn't believe her. "Okay . . . *fine*! If that's what you want! But what about when you're proven wrong?"

Staring back, he shrugged his shoulders. He then said, "Deana's afraid I'm going to leave her."

Afraid of what his answer might be, but wanting to know, Amber asked, "Do you love her?"

The only sound for a few moments was Alan Jackson singing and pleading with someone not to rock the jukebox. Amber had forgotten she was listening to the CD while washing dishes.

"Well . . . do you?" she repeated when he didn't answer.

"I care about her."

There might be hope! "Is that all?"

He stepped toward her, stopping only inches from where Amber stood. He reached toward her, using the back of his knuckles to caress her check. "I still love you,Amber. How can I love her?" Her eyes closed at his touch. She gave a little sigh, and her lips parted. Ricky's body reacted as he looked at her lips . . . wanting so much to kiss them . . . wanting to take possession of them like he used to.

He still loves me!

Amber was disappointed when his hand moved from her face. But she opened her eyes in surprise when he boldly slid both hands around her stomach. She could feel the warmth of his hands through the silk material. His fingers caressed and the baby kicked, as if in reply. A smile touched his lips before he raised his eyes to meet hers.

"*If* this baby is mine, I will take care of both of you."

"What about Deana?"

"I don't know."

His eyes held hers as his fingers worked the material up to expose her pregnant belly. Allowing it, Amber held her breath as she watched him. His eyes moved to her stomach and both of his hands slid over her bare skin, his body reacting to the feel of her again. He forced a soft chuckle. "What ever happened to your flat stomach?"

"I seem to have lost it." Her voice sounded strange to her, breathless.

He made sure her top fell back into place before looking at her. "I was hoping for so long that you would come back . . . but that was before I started seeing Deana."

That was a splash of cold water . . . and he wasn't done.

"How can I trust you again, Amber? I don't know if I can ever forgive you."

"Ricky . . ." she whispered,

"How do I know that you won't walk out on me again?"

"I won't."

His dark eyes looked intently at her before he slowly shook his head. "I don't know that." His hand reached toward her . . . his fingers gently pushed back some hair from the side of her face. "I couldn't take it if you ever left me again." And with that said, Ricky turned and walked out of the apartment.

Amber stood staring at the closed door, not believing what just happened. It only took seconds for the tears to start. "Damn you!" she yelled at the door.

* * *

As Ricky waited for the elevator, he cursed himself for the way he had treated Amber. But he couldn't stop himself. Didn't she realize how much she had hurt him by running away? Just before the doors to the elevator opened, he glanced down the hall to her apartment door. When the doors closed and the elevator began it's descent, he knew he needed to go to Deana.

* * *

Chapter 8

In her anger and frustration, Amber made a decision. Since Ricky didn't want her because he had another woman in his life, she would move back home after the baby was born. Manhattan wasn't big enough for both her and Ricky. Going to the phone, she dialed Jake's number.

But it wasn't her brother that answered. "Hello, Lisa."

"Amber."

"Is Jake there?" She wasn't in the mood for the usual small talk.

"He's bringing in groceries. Do you want to wait or he'll call you back?"

"I'll wait."

Luckily, Amber couldn't see Lisa mouth the word, "Figures" and make a face. "Okay, I'll tell him. He's almost done."

Amber pictured Lisa. She was about her height, with long blond hair, blue eyes, and a body that could make her a Victoria Secret model. Lisa was pretty and she knew it. Amber had never dreamed that her brother would go for that type. There had to be something there that Amber couldn't see. She had preached to Jake more than once about it's not what's on the outside, it's what's on the inside that counts. It didn't help that Lisa had problems with Jake and Amber's close relationship. Amber felt Lisa was jealous.

"Hey, sis! What's up? Did you talk to Ricky yet?"

Wrong question to ask! She tried her best not to cry but that meant not speaking, so then Jake knew she was upset.

"Okay . . . you *did* talk to him. Apparently he said all the wrong things."

Amber cleared her throat before saying, "I'm coming home as soon as I can."

His voice took on the soothing tone he used whenever his sister was upset. "What happened?"

She told him about Ricky, Deana and the paternity test.

"Well, Amber, you did throw a lot at him all at once. You show up unexpectedly after being gone for months . . . and then you're *very* pregnant and telling him that he's going to be a daddy. I don't think I would take it very well, either. His head is probably going in six different directions about now, especially if he still loves you and there's another woman." Jake sighed. "Give him time, Amber."

"You're siding with him." "I'm not siding with him. I'm a man and trying to put myself in his place right now. You are my sister and I want you to have what you want, though you can't always get what you want. That's the way life is, Amber. Dad protected and spoiled you too much. *Jesus*! I'm as guilty as he was!"

Through her tears, Amber said, "But he told me he can't love this Deana because he's still in love with me! So, how can he tell me that and then say he can't trust me in the same breath?"

"I don't know, sis."

Amber started to cry and it took a few minutes to pull herself back together.

Jake leaned back against a kitchen counter, waiting patiently. Lisa was putting groceries away and looked at him when he became quiet. Jake's expression gave away nothing. Lisa rolled her eyes before returning to the last grocery bag. She missed Jake's eyes turn hard as he watched her.

"I'm sorry, Jake. All I do is cry and you seem to be the one who has to listen to it" Amber said.

"Don't apologize now. I've been wiping your tears for thirty-some-odd years!" he teased.

Knowing he was trying to cheer her up, she muttered, "Brat" before blowing her nose.

"And, I can come down the week of the fourth to stay with you, for two weeks. Do you think the baby will decide to make an appearance during that time?"

"I hope so. It'll be so good to see you! And . . . Lisa can't make it?"

"Nope . . . she can't get away from her job that long." His gaze met Lisa's. "Maybe it will do us some good to get away from each other for awhile." Lisa glared at him and let the cupboard door slam shut before walking out of the kitchen.

"Trouble in paradise?" Amber quietly asked.

"We'll work it out."

With the tone he used, she knew better than to press the subject . . . for the moment. "Okay! I can't wait to see you! When will you be here?"

"This Saturday . . . is that soon enough? And if my niece or nephew arrives while I'm there, you two can come back home with me if that's what you want to do."

Swallowing the lump that formed in her throat, Amber said, "That'll be good."

"Will you be okay till then? Call me if you need to talk."

"Don't I always?"

He sighed. "Oh, yeah . . ." And then he laughed. But the smile disappeared as soon as Lisa entered the room. "I'm gonna let you go, Amber. Talk to you soon."

"Okay . . . 'bye." As soon as Jake shut off his phone, Lisa pounced: "She's coming back *here* after the baby's born? I don't want a screaming brat living here, let alone your sister! You *just* moved her down there!"

Jake watched and listened. He waited a few moments after her outburst before letting her hear from him: "*You* will not tell me who can or cannot live in *my* home! Let me refresh your memory that you have your own place and do not live here . . . you are here only because I asked you stay with me a couple of nights and you decided not to leave. That was how long ago? If you have a problem with my sister and her baby living here, then you are more than welcome to go back to your apartment. Do you understand me?"

"Yes" she quietly answered. Lisa knew that Jake meant what he said and she didn't want him to kick her out of an arrangement she was happy with. She wasn't happy at all about Amber coming back, especially with a newborn. But she would deal with it.

Lisa walked to Jake. "I'm sorry." Her arms slid around him. "Don't be mad." Her lips pressed against his. "Let's not fight" she whispered against his lips when they didn't respond to her kiss. "I am sorry." She pressed her body against his 6'1" frame. Jake didn't have an ounce of fat on him. Amber liked to tease him at times about having a 'construction worker's bod'. Lisa threaded her fingers through his shoulder-length brown hair. "Come on, handsome" she purred.

"I think you had better back off. I'm not in the mood for you."

"Oh, I can get you in the mood." Her hand slid down his hard torso to his groin.

Grabbing her hand away, he growled, "I said *no*." He moved away before turning on her. "Don't you ever mock my sister again! Do you think rolling your eyes is funny? She's almost nine months pregnant! I know how your moods are when you're having your period . . . multiply that with carrying a life around inside you for nine months!" He walked toward the back door.

"Come on, Jake! I said I was sorry!"

"I don't want to hear it." The screen door closed behind him with a bang.

* * *

Taking the steps two at a time up the two flights of stairs to Deana's apartment, Ricky pulled the key to her apartment out of his jeans pocket as he walked quickly toward the door. When he stepped inside, he heard Deana say, "There you are!" She stood naked in the bathroom doorway, towel drying her hair. Locking the door, he walked toward her slim, shapely body, unbuttoning and unzipping his jeans. Deana paid no attention as she dried her hair. "I wondered where you were. Your cell is off . . ." Pulling the towel out of her hands, he dropped it to the floor, and roughly pulled her to him. Deana uttered a cry of protest, which died when his mouth covered hers. Ricky backed her into the bathroom, lowered her to the shag bath rug and shoved his jeans down just enough to be able to enter her, with no foreplay. At first, she tried to push him away but it wasn't long before her hips raised to meet his hard thrusts. Ricky cried out as he came, picturing his hands on Amber's bare pregnant stomach.

He rolled off Deana to lay beside her, breathing fast. The rug beneath them was damp from when Deana had gotten out of the shower. Ricky was disgusted with himself, for treating Deana the way he just did. His arm covered his eyes. "Did I hurt you?"

"No, you didn't." She chuckled. "But hey, I like it rough. Whatever brought that on?"

He raised his hips to pull up his jeans before standing, He held out a hand to her, saying, "You don't want to know."

Grasping his hand to be helped up, Deana thought, "*Amber*".

* * *

Late Friday afternoon, Amber answered the phone to hear Sara's voice. "How are you?"

"I'm doing fine . . . ready to have this baby any time soon . . . but doing fine."

"Didn't you have a doctor's appointment today?" Sara asked.

"Sure did." "Well, by the sound of that, it must have been a good visit. You can tell us about it at supper tonight if you're up to joining us."

"How could I pass up a free meal and good company? What time? How should I dress?"

Sara laughed. "We'll pick you up around six thirty and dress comfortably . . . nothing fancy."

Amber debated on telling Sara about Ricky's visit. How was she going to tell her and A.J. about her decision to move again? It was something she had to think about. "Okay. I'll see you later."

* * *

Sal's was a popular Italian restaurant. Amber, Sara and A.J. had to wait fifteen minutes to get a table. Amber was thankful for the bench that was against the wall in the waiting area. When they were finally seated at a table, A.J. had to tease Amber about not being able to sit closer to the table. Giving him a not-too-happy-look, she told him, "Do you have any idea what it's like to be pregnant? Beside the fact of a major weight gain, there's mood swings. I can be so happy and smiling one minute . . . and then, in the blink of an eye, *anything* could make me cry, or the *bitch* in me could make an appearance at any time. *Please* try it sometime, A.J.."

Sara turned her head to hide her smile. A.J. seemed to think about Amber's speech for a moment. Sara tried not to laugh. A.J. looked at Amber and with a serious look on his face, replied, "No thank-you. I'll pass." So much for the serious moment. Amber and Sara started laughing. A.J. innocently asked, "What?", which made them laugh even harder. When the waitress arrived, they quieted their laughter, having to wipe away tears. "Can't take them anywhere" he muttered, then smiled at the waitress.

After ordering their food, Sara said to Amber, "Okay, tell us about your doctor's visit."

"It went great. I thought for sure my blood pressure would be sky high after what I've been through with Ricky but it was fine! And I was given the option of having this new 3-D picture taken of the baby, a new version of a sonagram. The picture will show me exactly what the baby looks like! But I still don't want to know the baby's sex ahead of time! So, we talked and the picture was taken but it went into the baby's file and I'll look at it after I have my baby . . . and keep the picture in the baby book." She smiled, looking radiant. "How about that? A picture of my baby while it's still inside of me!"

"What will technology think of next?" A.J. commented.

"Which would you rather have . . . a boy or a girl?" Sara asked Amber.

"It doesn't matter. Healthy . . . and happy. But if it's a boy, I hope he looks just like his daddy." She then cleared her throat, holding up a hand. "Sorry! I don't mean to go there tonight. I'm out with my friends to have a good time!"

Amber did enjoy herself. When they stood to leave, Amber said she had better use the bathroom first.

"Do you want me to come with you?" Sara asked.

"Women!" A.J. muttered. "You can never go to the bathroom alone when you're out!"

They looked at him and smiled but Amber said to Sara, "No, thanks. I'll be fine."

"I'll get the car and meet you out front" A.J. remarked.

"Where *is* the bathroom?"

"Near the front door" Sara answered.

There were large green plants placed tactfully between the dining area and the bathroom doors. Amber looked at them and asked, "Palm trees? Who puts palm trees in a New York Italian restaurant?"

"Those aren't palm trees" A.J. said. "Those are just . . . large green plants for decoration."

Amber started to giggle. "Well, they're big enough to be palm trees!"

"What was in your water?" he teased.

"Okay . . . okay!" she laughed. "You go get the car and I had better go before . . ." Amber turned abruptly and hurried toward the bathroom.

Someone else entered the bathroom while Amber was in the stall. When she came out, there was a pretty woman at a sink, using the mirror to touch up her lipstick. Their eyes met in the mirror as Amber walked to the next sink. "Hi" Amber greeted as she turned on the faucet. The woman dropped the lipstick in her purse before returning the greeting. She then checked her eyes, watching Amber as she placed her hands on her lower back and bent back. Smiling, the woman asked, "May I ask when you're due?"

"In a couple of weeks but I'm ready any time!"

"Your first?"

"Yes."

"Congratulations."

"Thank-you."

The woman turned her attention back to herself. Her fingers picked at her dark natural curly hair.

"Must be nice" Amber commented. "My hair has a mind of it's own now."

"Oh, this does at times, especially when it's damp outside."

Amber smiled then said, "If you're just getting here, enjoy your meal."

"Thanks. They have good food here."

"Oh . . . so you've been here before."

"Yes. A couple of times with my boyfriend."

Opening the door, Amber told her, "Enjoy yourselves."

"And congratulations again with your baby."

"Thanks." Amber had to get going because Sara and A.J. were waiting.

She didn't notice Ricky, who stood on the other side of the greenery, waiting for Deana to come out of the bathroom so that they could go to a table. What a shock when he heard Amber's voice . . . he never expected her to be at Sal's. Who was she with? She went out the door, without seeing him. How would she and Deana feel if they knew they just had a conversation with each other?

* * *

Amber invited Sara and A.J. up to her apartment. "I want to show it off. When you came to get me the other night, A.J., you didn't get a tour . . . you got a crying, pregnant woman. So, if you two aren't in any hurry to get home . . ."

"I'd love to see your new place" Sara said.

"Let's go" A.J. replied, holding out an arm for each woman. "Now, how lucky can a man get? I mean, how many men get to have two beautiful women on each side of him?"

"Some men have all the luck" Sara teased, smiling at her husband.

Walking through the door into the apartment, they stepped into a large foyer, which had a coat closet to the right of the door and on the far wall to the left, was a large, gold, oval mirror with a small ornate table beneath it with a large bouquet of silk sunflowers in a bowl. The foyer combined with a long hallway that all the rooms were set off of. Opposite the front door was a large entryway that went into a generous size living room. There were two entryways into the kitchen, one from the living room and the other from the hallway.

"Would anybody like some coffee?" Amber asked.

"Would love some" A.J. replied.

As she reached into the cupboard for the coffee can, Amber noticed the red light blinking on the answering machine. *Ricky*? Her heart beat faster at the thought. No, it couldn't be him . . . he didn't want anything to do with her. And why would he call? He had someone else to keep him company. It's probably Jake. She would call him back later.

When the coffee maker was set, she turned on the switch and then continued the apartment tour. But her mind kept returning to the answering machine.

There were three bedrooms, a bathroom and an area with doors for the washer and dryer. Two of the bedrooms were on the left side of the hall, with Amber's being the first.

"Oh! Look how big this is!" Sara gushed.

"I've never had a bedroom this big. I needed room for my queen-size bed and a the TV" Amber said with a laugh. There were also two dressers, a bookcase and doors to a huge walk-in closet.

She had her own bathroom, with a sink, toilet and a shower. The walls were painted yellow, with a border of white with yellow sunflowers.

The bedroom was painted peach . . . and Sara fell in love with the color.

"Yes, it brightens up the room, doesn't it? Did you notice that the lamps go well with the color scheme?" It was then Amber remembered Ricky's picture on her nightstand. She hoped they hadn't noticed.

But they did. She saw the look that passed between them

"Please . . . don't say anything . . ."

"We won't, darlin'" A.J. told her.

The room next door was the nursery. The color scheme was light yellow and mint green. A crib sat to the right of the room, then going to the left was a changing table, a wooden rocking chair, a chest of drawers, and a wooden cradle. A closet was to the left of the door.

"This is beautiful!" Sara exclaimed.

"You're all set for this little one" A.J. commented.

"Between my dad and Jake . . . they both bought too much for the baby."

"A.J. told me about your dad . . . I'm so sorry, Amber."

"Thanks,Sara." Amber drew a deep breath to keep from crying. "The rocking chair was what my mom used to rock Jake and me . . . and the cradle my dad had built when mom was pregnant with Jake."

"You have lots of good memories" Sara softly said.

"I do, don't I?" Amber smiled. "Come on, we're not quite done yet."

The first room on the right was the guest bedroom. It was painted light blue, with a navy blue bedcover on the double bed.There was a closet, two dressers and a TV set on top of one of the dressers.

"A TV in the guest room?" A.J. asked. "Your guests will never leave!"

"Does Jake count? This will be his room while he's here."

"Oh, we'll let him slide . . ." A.J. replied with a grin.

The bathroom was next. It had two sinks and mirrors as well as the toilet and a shower/tub combination. The color scheme was burgandy and Sara sighed when she saw it. "Oh, A.J.! This is the color I want in our bathroom!"

"Thanks, Amber!" he muttered.

"Oops!" She laughed. "Any time, A.J.!"

"You have a very nice place, Amber" Sara commented as they walked back to the kitchen.

"Thank-you. I know it's a little big for me and the baby but . . . I don't know how much longer I'm going to be here."

"What do you mean by that?" A.J. snarled.

"I've been thinking about moving back up with Jake after the baby's born."

"What the hell . . . ? Why? Because of Ricky?"

"Yes! He doesn't want me . . . or the baby. And he has a girlfriend. Why should I stay?"

"New York's a big city" A.J. argued.

"Not big enough. Remember I saw him that day I was out walking."

"We love having you back" Sara put in, taking cups from the cupboard. She turned and added, "And we *just* got you back."

"Oh . . . !" The tears started again. "It's so good being with you two again!" Amber took a deep breath, wiping the tears from her eyes. "But I can't chance . . . I *can't*!" She shrugged her shoulders in frustration.

Everyone was quiet for a few uncomfortable minutes. A.J. then suggested, "How about seeing how things are after the baby is born? Ricky *is* messed up right now . . . between you and the baby . . . and there's Deana he has to consider. Wait till he has the chance to see his child . . . and see how he reacts." He patted Amber's arm. "Sara is right . . . we are happy you're back. So, promise me you'll think about it before taking off . . . okay?"

"Okay" she agreed.

Husband and wife smiled.

Sara poured coffee while Amber took milk out of the refigerator for Sara's coffee. The phone rang. Amber looked at the Caller ID, setting the carton of milk on the counter. "It's Jake."

"Go ahead and talk to him" A.J. said.

"Hey, Jake!" she greeted.

"Where have you been? I've been calling! I thought maybe you went into labor . . ."

"Well, *hello* to you, too!" Amber laughed.

"Are you all right?"

"I'm fine! I went out to eat with Sara and A.J . . . who are here . . ."

"Hi, Jake!" the two chorused.

"*Hi* back to them." He sighed. "Sorry, Amber . . . but I was worried."

"Don't be . . . I'm fine, really. No labor pains as of yet. We're waiting for you to get here."

"Which will be tomorrow afternoon sometime."

"Drive careful . . . watch out for those asses that don't know how to drive."

"Always do. See you tomorrow."

"How long will Jake be staying?" A.J. asked after Amber shut off the phone.

"A couple of weeks, anyway. He can't stay away too long from home because of his work."

"How nice!" Sara said. "Will he be in the delivery room with you?"

Amber started to laugh. "As much as I woud like him to be, he keeps telling me *no*. He was my coach during Lamaze classes but when he realized his job was to help *in the* delivery, he quit . . . cold turkey!" An idea came to her. "Sara, would you like to be there when my baby is born?"

Surprised, Sara exclaimed, "I'd love to!"

"When Jake gets here, he can give you some pointers."

"That would be great!"

Suddenly, Amber's face looked sad. "No offense, Sara . . . but I wish it would be Ricky."

Gripping Amber's hand, Sara sympathized with, "I know, honey."

"He was here the other night."

"Ricky was?" A.J. asked.

"Yes . . . and I asked him how he got my address."

A.J. had the decency to look embarrassed. "He asked where you lived . . . and not even wondering why, I told him." He took a deep breath and expelled it before adding, "He has your phone number, too."

"I know."

"You never told me about this" Sara said, looking at her husband.

"I never gave it another thought." Turning his attention to Amber, he told her, "I'm sorry I did that, darlin'. I should have asked you first."

"That's okay. He's a detective . . . he would have found out somehow, anyway, if he wanted to know bad enough." She looked at Sara then back to A.J. before saying, "He said an odd thing when he first got here the other night."

"What was that?"

"That you told him he had better get over here to see me before something happened to make the baby came early. Did you tell him that?"

A.J. looked puzzled. "Sara had told me that she had talked to you and you sounded depressed. I mentioned that to him . . . told him to get his head out of his ass and start owning up to you and that baby."

"Was this before or after he asked for my address?"

"After." He looked at his hands that were around his coffee cup. "I guess I should keep my mouth shut, huh?"

"No." She reached over to pat his arm. "You don't have to do that."

* * *

Chapter 9

It was going on 9:30 when Sara and A.J. were ready to leave. "Gotta get up in the morning" he said, hugging Amber.

"I understand. Thanks so much for a wonderful evening . . . it was so good to be with you two!" She hugged Sara. "And thanks for agreeing to be in the delivery room with me. We'll leave A.J. and Jake outside the door."

"Ha! You won't hear any argument here! Or from your brother!"

"You two can keep each other company" Sara told him.

"Oh, I imagine we will" A.J. agreed.

Shortly after her company had left, Amber picked up the kitchen. Sara had volunteered to but Amber argued that she needed something to do. She rinsed out the coffee maker and got it ready for her coffee the next morning. Washing and drying the cups took up a little more time. She had just closed the cupboard door when the phone rang. It was almost ten o'clock. Thinking it was Jake, she picked up the phone only to see the Caller ID read only *unlisted number*. "Who the . . . ? Hello?"

"Amber, It's me."

"Ricky?"

"Sorry, I know it's getting late . . . but can I come up?"

"Where are you?"

"Sitting in my car outside your apartment building."

"Um . . . sure. Come on up."

As she waited for him to have her buzz him up, Amber wondered why he was there . . . again. After what he had said to her the other night, she thought he wouldn't be back for awhile.

She jumped when there was a knock on the door.

"Amber . . . open up."

She did as he requested, with her heart pounding at the sight of him. She would always love this man, no matter what happened. Their eyes met and held until Amber stepped back. Ricky stepped inside, closing the door behind him. Standing only five feet from each other, their eyes met again, as if trying to figure out what the other was thinking.

Finally, Amber asked, "How did you get in?"

"Some guy was leaving and after I flashed my badge, he let me in."

"We aren't supposed to let people in like that." "I know . . . but I wanted to see you."

Her heart thudded harder. "But why? You walked out on me the last time you were here." The tip of her tongue wet her suddenly dry lips. "So, *why* are you here?"

He tried to ignore the picture of her tongue and lips . . . and how his body responded. "I don't know why" he told her. "I saw you tonight at Sal's and couldn't stop thinking about you."

"At Sal's? *You* were at Sal's? I didn't see you."

"I was waiting for Deana to come out of the ladies room when you came out. I heard you talking . . . I knew it was you. I was standing on the other side of the greenery so that when you came out, you couldn't see me."

Deana? In the bathroom? "That was Deana I was talking to?" Amber asked, shocked. "She's pretty . . . and seemed nice." *And she told me that she had been at the restaurant before with her boyfriend . . . meaning Ricky*! She looked at him. "Did you tell her it was me?"

"No. I took her back to her place after we ate. I've been driving around, thinking about you . . . thinking about you being pregnant . . . thinking about Deana. I had to stop here. Why? I don't really know, Amber . . ." He wanted to tell her how much he still loved her, how badly he wanted to see her, to talk to her . . . and to touch her. But it wouldn't be fair to either of them . . . or Deana. Ricky took a deep breath and let it out before saying, "I keep thinking we need to talk but we both know it doesn't get us anywhere except more frustrated. And we argue . . . we never used to argue, Amber. What are we going to do?"

"Nothing."

The look on his face was as surprised as she was at herself for saying that one word. Even after what she had promised A.J., Amber couldn't stop talking: "You won't have to worry about me . . . because I'm moving back up with Jake after my baby's born. You don't want me and you won't admit the baby is your's. I don't want . . . I don't need . . . anything from you. My dad left me pretty well off so I don't need or want any support from you even after the paternity test you need to have done proves you wrong. You can go on with your life with your new woman and forget that you ever knew me." Those damn tears started before she finished and the last six words sounded strangled as she spoke them.

Ricky stared at her, not believing what he heard. He wanted to hold her, wipe away her tears and tell her that they could work something out to be a family. Amber stood before him, tears streaming down her face and not looking away.

"I can't do this any more, Ricky . . . I *can't*" she whispered. Turning away from her, he went to the door but stopped, with his hand on the doorknob. He didn't say anything at first but then began with, "Amber, I . . ."

"Don't make it worse, Ricky . . . *please*."

He went out the door, closing it softly behind him.

Amber stared at the closed door for a few moments before walking into the kitchen. Grabbing a hand towel off the back of a chair, she sat in the chair, buried her face in the towel and sobbed.

Ricky didn't wait for the elevator. He ran down the stairs. In his car, he slammed the palm of his hand against the steering wheel again and again. "Damn! Damn! *Jesus*! Dammit!" When he pulled away from the curb, there were tears of frustration in his eyes.

* * *

Jake arrived around four the next afternoon. Amber had never been so glad to see somebody.

"I can't believe you're finally here!" She hugged him against her.

"Look at you! You've gotten as big as a house since I last saw you!"

"You always knew how to cheer me up!"

He laughed, holding her a little tighter. "And I came all this way to tell you that in person!"

"I am so glad you're here" she said seriously, her voice cracking.

"You're not crying, are you?"

"Not yet."

The baby chose that time to kick, which Jake felt against his abdomen. "Wow! That was some kick! How do you stand it?'

"The kicks are easier than the elbows or heels . . . they hurt worse." The kicking continued. "Here, give me your hands." Placing them against her stomach, Amber smiled when she saw Jake's grin.

"That's *so* awesome, sis! Are you sure it's not baby's morse code for *'let me out . . . let me out of here!'* ?"

That made Amber laugh. "It could be! I'm ready, anyway!" Then, with one of his hands in hers, she led him into the living room. "Come on in and sit."

"Sit? I don't know about sitting just yet. That was a long ride in that truck." He looked around the room. "You made it quite cozy in here. It looks great."

"Thanks. I had fun doing it. But hey . . . would you like something to drink?"

"Iced tea? Lemonade?"

"Lemonade."

"That sounds good." He followed her into the kitchen. "I'll let you wait on me this one time but after this, remember, I'm not a visitor . . . I'm your brother."

Amber took two glasses out of the cupboard. "Oh, I'll remember that."

Jake was quiet for a few moments as he watched Amber pour their drinks. Finally, he asked, "Did something happen with Ricky?" He knew the answer when he saw her pause in what she was doing. "Okay . . . tell me" he gently said.

"He was here last night . . . after you called . . . after Sara and A.J. left."

"That was kind of late, wasn't it?"

"Around ten." "What was so important?"

Handing him his glass, Amber told him about her night the night before, starting with meeting Deana in the ladies room but not knowing it was her till Ricky told her. "He says he thinks about me a lot. He sat in front of this building last night in his car for awhile until he called to find out if he could come up."

Jake interrupted. "Called? He has your number? You gave it to him? And your address, too?"

"No . . . he asked A.J. and A.J. gave it to him without checking with me first . . . which he did apologize for."

"How do you feel about Ricky having that info?"

With a shrug, Amber answered, "Okay, I guess . . ."

After taking a long sip of lemonade, Jake said, "Okay . . . you were saying . . ."

"I told him that I was moving back with you after the baby's born and I didn't want or need his help . . . I told him that even though I had promised A.J. I would wait." By that time, she was crying. "It tears me up inside every time I see him, Jake! He stops over here and all I want him to do is hold me and tell me everything will be all right!" She put the lemonade pitcher back in the refrigerator, closing the door harder than it should have been. "*Why* does he come over? He says he can't trust me but yet he comes over and we fight and he leaves . . . he just walks out!" Amber pulled a paper towel off it's roll to blow her nose.

"Do you want my opinion?"

She eyed her brother. "You'd give it to me even if I told you I didn't."

"Well, he told you that he does still love you. I think he does but he's afraid you'll hurt him again if he lets his guard down." Jake held up his hand when Amber started to protest. "I didn't say that you *will* hurt him . . . I'm just saying that *he's* afraid it will happen again. Ricky comes here because he wants to see you . . . even if you do end up arguing." Jake paused, then asked, "Does that make any sense to you?"

Amber thought a few moments before saying, "I think so."

"Not to make you feel any worse but you messed him up bad, sis."

She looked at Jake, tears sliding down her face. She looked so sad. Jake felt terrible, and he opened his arms to her. Stepping into his embrace, Amber clung to him as she cried. Moments later, she whispered, "I messed us both up. Will he ever forgive me? He told me he didn't know if he could."

"I wish I knew." Jake kissed the top of her head. "I think he wants to but . . . give him time."

* * *

The 4th of July fell on a Tuesday. The weather was perfect, with sunny skies and temperatures in the low eighties. Jake asked where there would be fireworks that night.

"All over the place."

"Where would it be less crowded?"

Amber had to laugh. "That one I can't answer!"

"Is there *any place* in Manhattan that's *not* crowded?"

"Do you really need an answer for that?" Amber suddenly had an idea. "Let's go on a picnic! Well, as close to one as we can get around here! We could get subs or sandwiches and whatever else and go to Central Park, sit on a bench and people watch. I know that's something you'd like to do, big brother."

Jake nodded his head. "Sounds like a plan. Do you have food here we can take?"

"No. We'll have to go to the store."

"Okay then . . . let's get going!"

"Where did you park your truck?"

"In the parking garage you told me about."

"Good. Leave it there. We'll take a cab."

"I'm all for that. I don't like all this city traffic."

* * *

Everybody must have had the same idea. The store was busy with shoppers.

"Do we need a cart?" Jake asked.

"I don't think so. I have stuff to drink at the apartment. We could get chips, salads . . . I do have paper plates and napkins at home. We can buy a sub or the makings for a large one."

"Yeah, like meat, cheeses, lettuce, tomatoes, onions . . . you don't have any of that at home?"

"No. So we'll need a shopping cart for all that stuff."

"A basket will be good." Jake grabbed the last one by the door.

The aisles were crowded but Amber and Jake managed to weave their way between people and carts. As they made their way back to the bakery for fresh made rolls, Jake almost collided with a shopping cart that turned a corner at the same time from the opposite direction. He automatically held his arm in front of Amber to keep her from being hurt.

"Oh! I'm sorry!" The man with the cart apologized, stopping quickly.

The voice sounded familiar to Amber.

"Are you okay?" Jake asked her.

"Yes." She looked around Jake to get a better look at the man. "Matt?"

The man did a double-take. "Amber?"

"Ohmygod . . . Matt!" She stepped around Jake to hug the man. Just as she did so, a woman walked up to stand beside Matt.

"A party with my husband and I wasn't invited?"

As Amber and Matt separated, he said, "Look who it is, babe."

The women looked at one another before they each broke into a grin and hugged.

"Maggie!"

"Amber!"

"Where have you been? When did you get back? Just look at you!" Maggie stepped back. "You are *so* pregnant!" Her gaze turned to Jake.

"Oh, no! Don't look at me! I'm her brother!"

"Jake?"

He looked puzzled. "You know me?'

Maggie smiled. "Well, I know *of* you. Amber talked abut you so much that I feel like I do know you."

"You have one up on me. I don't know who *you* are."

Amber laughed. "Sorry, Jake! This is Maggie and Matt Johnson. I worked for them at the T-shirt shop."

"Oh, okay . . . I finally get to meet you. Amber talked about you a lot, too."

"All good things, I bet" Matt replied with a grin, shaking Jake's hand.

"So, what's been going on? How long have you been around here? We haven't heard from you in ages! The last time we saw you was when you told us you were leaving to move back upstate." Maggie stopped to breathe. "There's so much to catch up on!" She looked at her husband, at Amber then back to Matt. "How about . . . ?" She swung back to Amber. "Do you have any plans for today?"

Amber exchanged a look with her brother. "Not really. We're shopping for some picnic things and thinking about people watching in Central Park."

"Why don't you join us? We're getting out of the city! That is, if too much riding isn't too much for you. Please come! We have some much to catch up on!"

"Out of the city? Where?"

"To my parents place, about a forty-five minute drive from here."

"No, Maggie, if you're going to be with family, you don't want us along."

"My parents aren't there. They're in Ohio visiting my sister for most of the week."

Amber suddenly remembered something. "The kids . . . where are Abby and Austin?"

"They're with my parents . . . couldn't wait to get away from mom and dad!"

"Oh, I would have loved to see them! How old are they now?"

"Austin's five and Abby's six."

Amber looked at Jake. "What do you think?"

He shrugged. "It's up to you. Can you handle a long drive?"

"Forty-five minutes? That's not long." She looked back at Maggie. "Your parents' place, huh?"

"Yes. My dad knows we like to get away from city life even for a little while at times so he told us we're still welcome to use the grill and go swimming . . ."

"Swimming?" Jake asked. "I didn't bring a suit with me."

"You look about my size. I'll bring extra" Matt told him.

"I won't swim but you guys can go in . . . Yes! It sounds like fun!" Amber said. "What do you want us to bring?" She looked into Matt's full shopping cart.

"Only what you'd like to drink. And, if you'd like something besides burgers and hot dogs on the grill."

"What tastes better than both of those on the grill?"

"A good steak but that takes too long" Matt commented.

"When are you leaving?" Amber asked, trying to make room for another shopping cart to go around her.

"I don't know . . . an hour?" Matt looked questionably at his wife.

She nodded

"Are you still living by the shop?" Amber asked.

"Yep."

"We'll meet you there. Are you sure you don't want us to bring anything?"

"Nope, just yourselves. And don't worry about chairs or anything. It's all there."

"Okay, we'll see you in an hour." Amber hugged her friends.

Jake shook hands with Matt before they went separate ways.

"What do you want to do with this stuff?" Jake asked Amber, looking in the basket he still carried. Turkey, roast beef and provelone cheese, rolls,a head of lettuce, tomatoes, a large onion and a pound of mustard potato salad were inside it, with a bag of potato chips on top.

"We might as well get it" Amber answered. "We still have to eat during week."

* * *

Chapter 10

Exactly an hour later they were in Matt and Maggie's mini-van. The ride didn't seem long at all with all the talking they did.Jake was even in on the conversations because Matt and Maggie were the type of people that could make someone they just met feel like they have been friends forever.

The driveway was long . . . the house couldn't be seen from the road. The lawn was huge and well kept, as well as the trees, bushes and flowers. The house was a blue one-story ranch, with a large screened-in porch. A two-car garage stood away from the house, and a large shed behind that. To the right of the shed was a large pond with a wooden deck and a floating platform in the middle. Under a canopy nearby was a picnic table and grill.

"This is beautiful, Maggie!" Amber gushed as Jake helped her out of the van.

Maggie beamed. "Thanks. My dad loves to keep everything in shape around here."

"It looks it" Jake replied. "It kind of reminds me of my place . . . except I have a built-in pool instead of the pond. This is great."

"Let's get the van unpacked and get this party started!" Matt suggested.

Amber wasn't allowed to help carry anything but the box that contained hamburg and hot dog rolls and three bags of chips She slowly lowered her body to sit at the picnic table and watched the other three.

Matt was a little shorter than Jake and not quite as built but he still looked good. His brown hair was cut short but not short enough so that he didn't have his curls. His green eyes were kind and his smile was as charming as Jake's.

Maggie's long blond hair was pulled back into a ponytail that hung to the middle of her back. Her brown eyes never seemed to need any make-up because her lashes were long and dark. Her slender body had all the right curves and the sorts she wore were short enough to show off her shapely never-ending legs. Maggie stood two inches shorter than Amber and Amber always felt that Maggie had a far better shape than she did . . . even when she wasn't pregnant. Amber smiled to herself when she noticed Jake checking out Maggie's backside as she bent over to pull bags out of the back of the van.

It wasn't long before Matt had the grill going. He and Jake manned the grill while the women set up everything else for their cook-out. Matt found a battery-operated radio in the garage so they had songs from the 60's and 70's for background music. He sent Jake to the shed for lawn chairs. Conversation flowed easily, not matter what the subject. Amber talked about Ricky when Matt asked but told Maggie more details whenever the friends had a few minutes alone.

Matt wore swimming trunks under his shorts but Jake went into the garage to change for swimming. "Towels are in the van!" Maggie yelled to him when he stepped out, wearing blue and red trunks.

"Okay!" he yelled back, changing directions.

"Whoa! Nice legs!" Amber yelled before whistling at her brother. Maggie and Matt laughed, clapping their hands. Jake stopped, took a deep bow and then continued toward the van.

"Your brother's okay" Matt commented, as they watched Jake walk toward them with towels for the three of them.

"I'm glad you like each other. You'll have to visit us sometime."

Maggie looked at Amber. "I wish you weren't going so far away again. Are you sure you can't work things out with Ricky?" she quietly asked.

For the first time that day, Amber's eyes filled with tears. "I don't think so."

"Hey, don't cry" Matt said, reaching for her. Once in his arms, the tears flowed faster.

"Uh-oh, who made her cry?" Jake asked when he stepped under the canopy to join them.

"I did. I'm sorry, Amber" Maggie spoke, sounding sad.

It took a couple of minutes but Amber finally said, "No, it's not you, Maggie. *I'm* the one who is sorry, putting a damper on a fantastic day. Ask Jake, it doesn't take much to make me cry . . . especially since I've been pregnant." She wiped at her eyes. "Why don't you guys go get wet?"

"I already am!" Matt laughed, wiping at his chest where Amber had cried her tears.

"I'm going!" Jake yelled, dropping two towels onto the picnic table.

Matt grabbed a towel and ran toward the pond. "Hey!" Jake yelled, following Matt.

Amber and Maggie laughed as they watched the guys, laughing even harder as they ran along the deck and both performed a cannonball into the pond. Water splashed high into the air.

"There won't be any water left by the time those two are done!" Amber laughed.

"It's a good thing the pond is spring-fed."

After a few minutes of watching the guys in the water, Maggie stood. "I can't take it any longer! I have to join them!" She quickly peeled off her clothes to reveal a two-piece red bathing suit. "Oh, wow!" Amber sighed, looking at her friend. "I don't think I'll ever be able to wear one of those again!" She rubbed her large stomach.

Maggie posed. "Yes, you will! This is me after two kids! You can do it!"

"You give me hope, Maggie. Now, go have fun!"

"You don't mind sitting here by yourself?"

"No! Now go on!"

Grabbing the last towel, Maggie let out a yell as she ran toward the pond. Both guys waited for her as she dove in, then ganged up on her.

They entertained Amber, who laughed more than she had in a long time. She did feel slightly disappointed that she couldn't join them. While she was laughing when Maggie clung to Matt from behind, trying to dunk him, a sharp pain stabbed her lower back. Amber winced, reaching back to rub the area. The pain reached around to her stomach. She looked toward the pond, ready to yell to Jake, if he heard her over the noise they were making. But then the pain was gone. Sitting up straight, Amber waited for another pain. When it didn't happen again after a couple of minutes, she sat back in her chair. Looking up, she saw Jake drying himself off as he walked toward her.

"You've had enough?"

"Not really . . . but it was time for me to make an exit."

"What . . . ?" Amber looked toward the pond to see Maggie and Matt in a passionate embrace in the water. "Oh! Wow! What brought that on?"

"I don't know." Jake pulled a chair over next to Amber. "Your friend is hot. No wonder her husband can't keep his hands off her."

"Yeah, well . . . I saw you looking at her earlier" Amber teased.

He flashed his sister a sheepish grin. "You caught me, huh?"

"Oh, I sure did!"

"How long have they been married?"

"Six years . . . they got married right after their daughter was born."

"Lucky stiff" Jake muttered.

"What's up with you and Lisa?"

He held up a hand. "Not now. I want to enjoy my time away."

"It's been that bad? You've got to . . . Oh!" Amber grunted.

"Amber?"

She rubbed where the pain had been. "I've been having pains."

"The baby's coming?"

With a smile, she exhaled a breath. "Maybe."

"We should tell those two and get you to a hospital." Jake stood.

"Oh, sit down. I'm okay now. The doctor told me that there could be quite awhile between the first pains and the actual birth."

"Key words, Amber . . . *could be*."

"Please, Jake, don't say anything yet. I want to be sure it's not false labor."

He looked at his sister, wanting to disagree. But Maggie and Matt were suddenly there.

"Sorry, Jake. We didn't mean to chase you out of the water" Matt apologized, looking embarrassed.

"Yes, we are sorry. We were having fun with the three of us" Maggie added.

"Don't worry about it . . . it was time for me to get out anyway. My sister needed me."

"Why? What happened?" Maggie asked.

Amber threw a look at Jake before turning to Maggie. "I had a few pains."

"How are they now?" Maggie wondered.

"Nothing in the last few minutes."

"It could be time . . . we'll wait and see. Even with the pains, it took all day for Abby to be born but with Austin, he wasn't waiting around.

My pains with him were hard and not stopping. I went into labor and had him only two hours later."

"And Austin still doesn't like to be kept waiting" his father commented.

"We have to have patience, big brother" Amber told him.

"Easier said than done."

"Let's enjoy the day. We still have awhile to go. I hope you're not in labor, Amber, 'cause we want you and Jake to join us to watch the fireworks tonight" Matt said.

"Fireworks? I love fireworks!" Amber exclaimed.

"Amber . . ."

"Oh, Jake! Okay, let's see how I'm doing as night gets closer . . . all right?"

"Just as long as we don't have to deliver that baby."

"Can you tell how much he adores me?" Amber asked her friends.

They laughed and Jake's response was a noisy, wet kiss on her cheek.

The four enjoyed the rest of the day. Matt grabbed a Frisbee out of the back of the van and tossed it to Maggie, who threw it to Jake. It was high and off to his right but he chased after it, leaped into the air and caught it. He grinned as he faked a pass in Amber's direction. She laughed and said to him, "I *cannot* do what you just did!"

"Oh, you chicken!" he teased before gently tossing it her way. She caught it with no problem.

She played for awhile, then sat down to let the others run the lawn. There was a little pain nagging at her lower back but she didn't say anything to anyone.

Later, they had a meal of leftovers. Matt reheated cooked hot dogs on the grill. As they ate at the table, converation never lagged. Amber couldn't remember the last time she had had so much fun.

"I'm so glad we saw you at the store" she said to Maggie and Matt. "What luck that Matt almost ran into Jake!"

"It was fate" Maggie replied.

"Whatever it was, I'm glad it happened" Matt said. "It was good to be around you again, Amber . . . and Jake, we finally got to meet the brother we heard so much about."

"Hey, the same here. Thanks, man." Jake held his hand out over the table to Matt and they firmly shook hands.

The subject of the fireworks came up again and Amber declared she still wanted to go. "I'm fine!" she protested.

"You had better be" Jake declared.

"Yeah, don't go into labor during the fireworks. It would be tough getting you through the crowd" Matt added.

After everything had been returned to the shed and the van was loaded, they all walked around to make sure nothing had been forgotten. It was a slow walk back to the van. Nobody really wanted to leave.

"I hate the thought of having to put my sandals back on" Amber groaned. "The grass feels so good under my feet!"

"When she's home she's hardly seen wearing anything on her feet" Jake said. "Even in the winter I have to remind her to wear boots when she goes outside!"

"Yeah . . . right!" Amber playfully pushed at his arm.

* * *

By the time they made it back to Manhattan, dusk had fallen. Matt drove straight to where the fireworks were to be set off, hoping to find a decent parking spot. Everyone else must have had the same idea but Matt was lucky to find a spot not too far away.

"How are you doing?" Jake asked Amber. She had dozed off at times on the ride back.

She yawned then smiled. "Good . . . but a little tired."

"It was a long day for you with no rest" Maggie said.

"Oh but I had so much fun. Thanks, you two!"

"Any more pain?" Jake asked. "My lower back aches but that could be from sitting so much."

"See? There's those two words again . . . *could be*."

Matt threw an arm across Jake's shoulders. "Come on, Jake. Between the three of us, we can take care of her. I've been through it twice and it gets easier each time."

"Yeah but she's my sister . . . not my wife" Jake muttered as he slung the straps of two chair bags over his shoulders.

Amber heard him and stepped close to him to say, "But I still love you, Jake."

He felt a little guilty saying what he had. "That's good . . . sorry, Amber."

They walked around others that were either standing, sitting in chairs or on blankets on the ground. Matt finally stopped. "Is this okay?"

"We'll find out when the fireworks start" Maggie replied.

Amber was glad to get off her feet. Maggie and Jake sat on each side of her, with Matt next to Maggie. More people pushed on ahead of them. Minutes later, the first of the fireworks went up and exploded into the sky, splashing bright colors of red, white and blue.

Single fireworks lit up the sky, as well as muliple displays that lit up the whole area. Oohs and aahs were heard from all directions, including Amber and Maggie.

At times, Amber was uncomfortable and shifted in her chair to find a better position. Jake leaned toward her at one point. "Are you okay?"

"Yeah . . . I guess." She patted his arm then left her hand rested there. It was good that he cared for her but sometimes it seemed too much. The next firework exploded with a loud *bang*! Amber squeezed Jake's arm in reaction. "Whoa!" She looked at him and smiled, patting his arm where she had squeezed. Another went up, a large missle that went way up before exploding, showering the whole area with bright, lighted colors. "That was beautiful!" She looked at Jake again with a smile, noticing a couple standing to his right. The man looked like Ricky. The light faded before she could tell.

She forced herself to look at the fireworks but when another large one lit everything up, she *had* to look at that couple. That time Ricky's eyes met hers. "Ohmygod!" she cried, digging her fingers into Jake's arm.

"Ow!" He yanked his arm away. "What the hell?" He looked closer at Amber. "What's wrong? Is it the baby?"

"Look to your right."

"*What?*"

"Look to your right."

Just as he did, another explosion lit up the area. Ricky turned his head in their direction but when he saw Jake looking at him, he turned away.

"I'll be damned" Jake muttered. "What are the odds . . . ?" He looked at Amber. "Are you okay, sis?"

"Yes . . . I think so . . ." She watched as Ricky placed his hands on Deana's shoulders and leaned his head down to say something in her ear. The next thing she knew, they walked away, hand in hand. But for some reason, Ricky looked back at Amber before they disappeared into the darkness.

Jake had watched it all, too. He shook his head, not believing Ricky would do that to Amber. "*Shit*" he whispered before turning back to his sister. "Do you want to leave?"

"Yes."

But a pain rippled across her abdomen. Amber gasped, looking at Jake. "Take a deep breath" he told her. Moving his chair closer, he put his arms around her. With her forehead against his shoulder, she did as she was told, throwing in a couple more for good measure.

"Better?" he asked her.

"Yes." She sat up. "You remembered your coaching lessons."

"How could I forget?"

"Amber? Are you in labor?" Maggie asked.

"I don't think so . . ."

"We had better get her out of here just in case" Matt said.

Amber looked up as another explosion of noise and colors lit up the sky. Even though it was beautiful, she had lost interest in it. "Yeah, let's go."

The ride back to Amber's was very quiet. Maggie and Matt tried to keep conversation going but gave up after awhile.

When Matt pulled in front of the apartment building, Maggie asked, "How are you doing, Amber? Any more pains?"

"Some but not as strong as that one at the fireworks."

"Jake, please call us to let us know when the baby's here" Maggie said.

"I will do that. Thanks so much for today. It's been awhile since either of us has had that much fun."

"We had a good time, too" Matt replied.

"Okay, 'bye for now." Jake slid open the van side door. "Come on, sis. Let's take the stairs up to the apartment."

"Ha-ha. See what I have to deal with?"

"It could be worse" Maggie said with a laugh. "I know you'll take good care of her, Jake" Matt said.

"I have to. She's the only sister I have. G' night, you two. Thanks again."

"I'll talk to you later, Maggie" Amber told her before the door slid closed.

Matt drove away after Jake and Amber reached the front door. Jake had his arm around Amber as they went inside the building. On the ride up on the elevator, she leaned against her brother. "I am so tired, Jake. I think I'm going straight to bed."

* * *

As tired as she was, Amber didn't sleep much. Her back and legs ached. The baby was active, kicking and poking. When it seemed to rest, Amber swore her bladder was being used as a pillow because she got up to pee more times than she cared to count. She was having mild contractions but didn't want to wake Jake until she needed to. And, when she closed her eyes, she saw Ricky with Deana at the fireworks.

As morning drew closer, Amber finally slept. When she woke, the sun was shining into her bedroom and the clock read 8:22. She figured she had slept almost two hours straight. Her lower back still ached as she got up and went into the bathroom. Deciding to stay up, she walked down the hall toward the kitchen. The door to Jake's room was slightly open and she heard his snores as she walked by. With a smile, she thought he must have worn himself out the day before if he was sleeping at that hour. He was usually an early riser. "The smell of coffee will wake him up" she said to herself.

As she reached for the coffee canister on the second shelf in the cupboard, she felt a stronger contraction, almost dropping the canister. After she sat it on the counter, her hands went to her stomach. "Are you getting ready to come out, little one?" As if to answer, another pain hit her. Gasping, Amber tried to remember her breathing. After it passed, she decided it was time to get Jake up and started toward the doorway. The next pain doubled her over. "Jake!" she gasped, but knowing he couldn't hear her. When she was able to stand, Amber took another three steps before there was another pain . . . and her water broke.

"*Jake*!" she cried out.

* * *

Chapter 11

A.J., Deana and Ricky had just gotten back to the precinct after an early morning investigation and arrest of a 46 year old man having sex with a 17 year old girl. The parents reported her missing after she didn't come home for two nights. She didn't agree with them that she had been a victim of rape; she argued she wasn't a minor at seventeen.

Before they entered the squadroom, A.J.'s cell phone rang. When he saw who it was, he said, "I have to take this." As he walked away, he answered the phone: "Hi! What's up?"

Ricky and Deana stood in the hall, quietly and quickly talking about their plans for that night. Minutes later, A.J. appeared. "Hey, Ricky . . . Can I talk to you a minute?"

Ricky looked from his partner to Deana. She said, "I have paperwork to do" and stepped into the squadroom. The two men watched as she walked to her desk and sat down. After she was seated, Ricky looked at A.J.. "Yeah?" He had a good idea what it was. The way his nerves were strung, he hoped he looked calmer than he felt.

"Sara just called. Amber's on her way to the hospital."

Ricky's heart pounded. His child was about to be born! He looked down at the floor for a few moments before saying, "I hope all goes well for her."

"*I don't believe you*!" A.J. sputtered in a loud whisper. Gripping Ricky's arm, he moved him away from the doorway. "When are you going to wake up and admit that baby is your's? And you should remember that baby's mother is the one you love!" He turned and walked off.

As the next few hours passed by, A.J. noticed how often Ricky looked at his watch or glanced at the wall clock. A couple of times he stared off into space, as his fingers drummed his desk top. Whenever Deana got up from her desk, Ricky asked A.J. if Sara had called back. When they went out on a case, Ricky drove so that A.J. would be free to use his phone.

But Deana took in everything as she watched Ricky from her desk. Knowing something was up, she didn't say anything but had a good idea what was going on.

Their work day was almost over when A.J.'s cell phone rang. He checked who was calling, then got up from his desk and went out of the room. Not long after, Ricky appeared, to hear the end of the call: "Thanks for letting me know, Sara. How long are you staying? . . . I'll be over after work . . . give her my love. "Bye." He shut off the phone and looked at his partner. "Do you care to hear this?"

Ricky sighed. "How is she?"

"Tired after seven hours of labor but happy now that she has an eight pound, nine ounce baby, that, according to my wife, is the spitting image of you."

Closing his eyes, Ricky swallowed hard. "Boy or girl?"

"Girl. She has lots of dark hair . . . and she's twenty-three inches long. Wonder where she gets her length from?"

"So, Amber and the baby are okay?"

"Yes."

Ricky paced the hall for a few minutes before asking, "Did she name the baby?"

"Yes."

He stopped pacing and impatiently asked, "Well . . . ?"

"Rebecca Lynn."

A.J. was stunned to see Ricky smile.

"Rebecca was my mother's name and Lynn was Amber's" Ricky explained. But the smile faded and he didn't look at A.J. when he asked, "What last name did she give her?"

"Wilson. She gave the baby *her* last name." A.J. turned and went into the squad room.

"*Shit*!" Ricky muttered, raking his fingers through his dark hair. His daughter *didn't* have *his* last name. "*Shit*!"

"What's wrong?" Deana asked from behind him.

She had the right to know. "Amber had the baby."

"Oh . . . What now?"

Two officers walked through. Ricky nodded at them, stepping back to let them go by. He then said to Deana, "We'll talk about this later."

* * *

"How are you doing, sis?" Jake asked, as he stepped into her room. He had joined Sara for a cup of coffee when Amber was taken to recovery but when Sara called her husband, Jake wanted to check on Amber.

"Did you see her?" Amber asked, sounding tired.

"Of course I did! I was with you when you had her, remember?"

"How did I get you in the delivery room?"

"You had a death grip on my hand when they wheeled you in . . . it's a wonder no bones were broken!"

With a tired smile, she said, "Well, at least you were in the right place if you needed medical attention . . ."

"I never knew that you could swear like that."

"What?"

"Oh, the words my baby sister yelled!"

"I didn't swear."

"Oh, yeah . . . well, Sara will tell you that you did."

Amber laughed a tired laugh. "I can't believe you stayed with me."

Jake smiled broadly. "It was well worth it. I got to see my niece come into the world. It took awhile but all of the sudden, there she was! It was a good thing Sara practiced your breathing with us."

"What happened to your expertise with the breathing?"

"I forgot all about it those last few minutes before Rebecca made her entrance."

"And after all you put me through when I asked you to be there with me in the first place!"

With a shrug, Jake asked, "What can I say?

Baby noises sounded from the other side of the bed. Amber turned her head to look at her sleeping baby. *Her* baby. Tears filled her eyes but she smiled. Looking back at Jake, she asked, "Do you like her name? Both names are her grandmothers from each side."

"Mom and dad would be happy." He hesitated a moment before asking, "What about Ricky?"

"I don't care what he thinks."

"He can't deny she's his."

Amber shrugged.

Okay, time to change the subject. "How is Becky doing? She has five fingers and five toes, right?"

Amber's face lit up. "She's perfect."

"I knew she would be."

"And I'm going to breast-feed her."

"Breast-feed, huh? Well, I did my part with the delivery . . . I want *nothing* to do with the breastfeeding."

Amber smiled sleepily.

"Is she staying in here with you?" Jake asked.

"Yes she is. I hope diaper changing comes back to me . . . it's been years since I've changed a diaper while babysitting."

"I'll help *if* needed when you two get out of here."

"Have you ever changed a diaper?"

"Never. I'll need lessons."

"Okay . . . that I can do." Amber then yawned.

"Why don't I let you get some sleep while my niece is sleeping?"

Amber's eyes closed, then opened partially. "Okay. See you later."

* * *

Going back to Amber's apartment, Jake showered and put on clean clothes. He had had an abrupt awakening that morning when Amber called out his name. He had quickly put on the clothes that he had worn the day before, grabbing them off the floor near the bed. Not fully awake, he ran to her room to find it empty. "Amber?" Back into the hallway. "Amber!" He could hear her breathing hard and ran toward the sound. She was in the kitchen, standing in a puddle. Amber?"

"The baby's coming."

"I see that." Putting an arm around her, he said, "Let's get you to the hospital. But first I'll call your doctor, a cab, then Sara." His hold on her tightened as another pain racked her body. "And do not have this baby before we get to the hospital."

Amber laughed. "Tell that to the baby!"

The time between that and the hospital was a blur to Jake. When he called Sara, he got her voice mail so he rattled off a quick message.

He remembered Amber's cries of pain . . . and the language she used! He was frustrated because he couldn't help her. But watching Rebecca Lynn's entrance to the world was worth it. Hearing her first cries made him feel proud. Watching her placed in Amber's arms and seeing the look of love on Amber's face . . . Jake would never forget that.

He was glad he was there.

* * *

Walking toward Amber's hospital room, Jake saw Sara coming toward him. They grinned at one another and Sara gave him a hug.

"How are you doing, Uncle Jake?"

"Better after a shower and clean clothes. How about you, Aunt Sara?"

She laughed. "I had a wonderful day!"

"Me, too. But hey, why aren't you with Amber now?"

"A nurse is with her to try breast-feeding again. I'm on my way to the cafeteria for more coffee and something to eat. Want to join me?"

"Sure. I've seen more of my sister today than I ever cared to. I don't think I want to sit in on the breast-feeding lessons."

Walking back to the elevator, Sara said, "I have to call A.J., to tell him to meet me in the cafeteria instead of Amber's room."

"Have you been home at all today?"

"No. I'll go home with A.J. since I took a cab to get here."

Jake happened to turn his head to look through the window in the door to the nursery as they walked past it. His pace slowed and he said, "Um . . . Sara . . . I'll meet you in the cafeteria shortly, okay?"

She looked puzzled but replied, "Yes . . . all right" and kept walking.

Looking through the window again before opening the door, Jake saw Ricky. He was looking at the babies through the nursery window.

"Hey, stranger." His voice startled Ricky, who then smiled at Jake. He held out his hand. "Hey, Jake."

Shaking his hand, he said, "If you're looking for the baby, she's in Amber's room. She's staying in there instead of in there." Jake motioned toward the nursery with his head.

"Oh." There were five babies in the nursery and Ricky looked at them. He finally asked, "Is Amber going to have a paternity test done?"

"Not that I know of. She wants you to see the baby before you decide to have one done."

"I heard the baby looks like me."

"*Just* like you . . . well, except maybe the nose . . . I think that looks like Amber's . . ."

"So . . . Rebecca is in Amber's room?"

Jake was impressed that Ricky used his daughter's name. "Yes, she is. You can go see her."

"No . . . not yet." He turned to Jake. "It was good to see you." Shaking his hand again, he added, "It's been awhile. Take care." He started toward the door but stopped short when Jake spoke:

"She missed you, Ricky . . . every day. You were all she talked about . . . and how much having a baby would make you happy. But the damn fool *would not* call you! No matter how much dad and I kept at her . . . she was afraid you would hang up on her or not believe anything she told you about why she left. Amber loves you, Ricky . . . with all she has to give. And you know that's a lot. I probably shouldn't be telling you all this . . . she would kick me in the ass if she knew . . . but I just wanted you to know how she cried when she found out she was pregnant . . . and she wouldn't be able to share it with you."

"She should have called me then . . . when she found out. But the longer she stayed away . . ." He reached for the doorknob. "I . . ." he began but opened the door and walked out.

Jake didn't mention seeing Ricky when he joined Sara and A.J. in the cafeteria.

"Oh! So, you found each other!"

"Sara called just as I parked in the parking garage. Perfect timing! Now she's eating a hospital-made sandwich . . ."

"Which isn't bad!" Sara put in.

". . . But I'll wait till I get home to find something to eat."

"Is everything okay?" Sara asked Jake. "You disappeared on me."

"Sorry. I had something to take care of."

"So, when do you think it'll be safe to go to Amber's room?" A.J. asked his wife.

"I'm not sure. We can go when I finish this sandwich."

"I hope she's done feeding Rebecca. I can't deal with any more of her body parts" Jake moaned.

"And what are you going to do when she feeds her daughter when she's home?" Sara asked, not hiding the smile she couldn't stop.

"What? I didn't think of that!" He sighed, loudly. "I guess I'll deal with it whenever! This is too much for me in one day!"

All three of them laughed.

* * *

A.J. couldn't get over how much the new arrival looked like her father. "Just wait till he sees you! He will fall in love with you at first sight!" he cooed as he held Rebecca.

It wasn't long before Sara claimed she had to go home. Having been at the hospital since just before nine that morning, it was now after seven. "Thanks so much for letting me be a part of this!"

"I did remember you being there, holding my hand. It's a wonder I didn't break it."

"Tell me about it" Jake moaned, rubbing his hand.

"Oh . . . shush!" Amber blew him a raspberry.

"And did you know that Amber knew such colorful language?" Jake asked Sara.

She laughed. "Now, *that* was a surprise!"

Amber looked embarrassed. "Hey,now . . . come on. I was under extreme pressure of things that were totally out of my control."

Sara chuckled as she leaned to kiss Amber's cheek. "And now you have a beautiful baby girl. Congratulations, *mommy.*"

A.J. kissed Amber, too, before turning to Jake. "If you need any help with her, be sure to call. She's worth it."

"Yeah, I think so, too." Jake shook A.J.'s hand. But as A.J. pulled his hand away, Jake said, "I . . . um . . . I want to thank you two for being there for my sister. I feel so much better knowing she's not alone here. I know that good friends are hard to come by."

"He hates giving speeches" Amber said, her eyes filled with tears.

Giving Jake a big hug, Sara told him, "We're glad that she has a brother that takes good care of her." She brought his head down to hers so that she could kiss his cheek. Turning away, she grasped A.J.'s hand in hers and walked to the door. "See you tomorrow" she tossed back to Amber before going out of the room.

Amber watched as Jake walked around her bed to look in his niece's bassinet as she slept. His hand looked huge as his finger gently touched her cheek.

"Thanks for saying what you did to them" Amber said to him.

Not looking up, he replied, "Well, they are good friends to you . . . and I like them." Rebecca made a noise in her sleep and Jake smiled. "Dad would have loved her."

"I know." Her voice caught as her eyes filled with tears again.

"I bet he's smiling down on her . . . you . . . us right now."

"Oh, Jake! I miss him *so* much! And I wish mom was here!" The tears spilled over and slid down her face.

"Yeah . . . me, too." Jake was silent for a few moments before he said, "Dad worried about you so much after finding out you were pregnant with this one." He turned his head to look at his sister. "He wanted you to work things out with Ricky . . . and be happy."

Amber cried. Jake sat beside her on the bed and held her till she became quiet. "Okay now?"

"I need a tissue."

Pulling one out of the box on the nightstand, he handed it to her. As she blew her nose, he said, "I didn't mean to make you cry."

"I know." She looked at him. "Tell me why you were quiet when Sara and A.J. were here. You seemed lost in thought at times."

He went straight to the point: "Ricky was here."

"*Here*? At the hospital?"

Jake nodded. "I saw him looking in the nursery window."

"He was here. He was looking for his daughter . . ." Amber found it hard to believe.

"I told him where she was and that he could see her . . . but he said not yet."

"But Ricky was *here*."

Jake sighed. "Yes, he was . . . but . . . I know if I tell you not to get your hopes up that you won't listen to me."

Amber sighed. "I wish I *could* listen to you but my heart won't let me."

He looked at her for what seemed a very long time before changing the subject: "Well, how did Rebecca do with nursing this last time?"

"Better. Hopefully soon we'll have the hang of it. My actual milk won't start for another day or two."

Jake winced. "Too much information for me, Amber."

That time she laughed.

* * *

Chapter 12

It was just about time for lunch when Ricky finished his paperwork for a morning arrest. Placing the papers in a folder, he put the folder into a tray at the corner of his desk. Standing, he took his keys and cell phone out of the top desk drawer.

"Ready for lunch?" Deana asked, looking up from her paperwork.

"Um . . . I can't join you today. I have a couple of things to take care of. I might be a little late getting back." Ricky pocketed his keys and phone. After a nod to A.J., he went out the door.

Deana didn't say anything as she watched him leave the room.

"Want to join me for lunch?" A.J. asked her.

"He's going to the hospital, isn't he?" He didn't sleep well at her place the night before. She found him staring out the living room window at two in the morning.

"I don't know. He doesn't say much to me lately."

But A.J. hoped that Ricky was going to see Amber.

* * *

It took two stops to find what he wanted. Forty minutes later, Ricky stepped off the hospital elevator. As he walked toward the desk at the nurse's station, his thoughts were about Amber. He had decided the night before, when he couldn't sleep, that he had to see her . . . and the baby. After finding out her room number, he walked quickly down the hall. Stopping outside the door, he took a deep breath before lightly knocking. Not hearing anything, he slowly opened the door and stepped inside the room.

Amber was asleep. She lay on her side. Ricky smiled, knowing that was how she slept. He sat the vase of a dozen small sunflowers on her nightstand, hoping she would know who they were from, since he forgot to get a card. Ricky took the liberty to look at her while she slept, taking in every detail of her face . . . the way her mouth was slightly open as she breathed through it, which made him smile a he remembered that's how she always slept . . . with her hand tucked under the side of her face. He missed her . . . there was no denying that any longer. He resisted the impulse to brush back the strands of hair that had fallen across her cheek.

A slight noise caught his attention. Ricky then remembered that Jake had told him that the baby was staying in the room with Amber. Quietly, he walked around the bed to the bassinet, to look down and see his image looking up at him. He had read that a newborn's vision wasn't focused but yet his daughter seemed to look at him. Yes, *his* daughter. She was swaddled in a pink and blue blanket. A white cap covered the top of her head but her long, dark hair showed beneath it. He saw himself in her face . . . Rebecca had inherited his high forehead and the shape and color of his eyes. With a smile he remembered that Jake had said she had her mother's nose. She did. Rebecca made little motions with her mouth. Ricky thought her mouth was shaped like Amber's, too.

Why had he given Amber such a hard time? He had known all along the baby *was* his. Was it payback for the hurt she had caused him? "You're a fool, Enrique" he silently condemned himself.

Amber moved in her sleep, drawing his eyes away from their baby. He saw she had rolled onto her back, with a smile on her lips. Was she dreaming about the baby . . . or him? His attention returned to Rebecca, who's eyes were now almost closed. He smiled, suddenly wanting to hold her but not daring to.

He stopped at the end of Amber's bed for one more look before he left. He knew they needed to talk . . . they had to work things out. Could he trust her again? He wanted to . . . It was time to talk to Deana. It wasn't fair to her with the way he felt about Amber.

Leaving the room, the door closed quietly behind him.

* * *

Amber woke to Rebecca's cries. "Okay . . . Mommy's coming." She slowly got out of bed and lifted her baby out of the bassinet. "Are you hungry . . . or wet? Let's try the diaper first." Which did need changing. The crying stopped but Rebecca's mouth opened like a hungry little bird's. "Shall we try this again?" Amber asked, sitting on the bed. She reached for the button to raise the top of the bed and then sat back. Rebecca nuzzled her mouth against her mother's breast before Amber had her nightgown open. After a few minutes of things not going right and Rebecca getting frustrated . . . and Amber trying not to . . . Amber shifted postion and it seemed to work.

The door to her room opened and in walked Jake. "Oh! *Geesh,* Amber!" He turned around and started back out the door.

"No, Jake! Wait!" Amber pulled a receiving blanket over her and the baby.

"I'll come back when you're done."

"You don't have to do that. And besides, you have to get used to this. If you think I'm hiding away every time she's hungry . . . brother, you are *so* wrong!"

"I've got to learn to knock" he sputtered, making his way to the lone chair in the room. "How did you sleep last night?"

She sighed but then smiled. "No more eight hours a night of sleep for me! Becky was awake twice during the night."

"Becky?" "Sure! Do you like it? It's short for Rebecca."

"Well . . . I figured that!"

"I'll use the full name for times of trouble, like when mom used that tone of voice and we *knew* we were in trouble! *Jacob Alan Wilson! Amber Lynn Wilson! Where are you?*"

Jake laughed. "You sounded just like her! Whoa, Becky, you're in trouble when you get older!"

Amber joined in the laughter. "Hey! Mom wasn't *that* bad!"

"I know . . . she was a good mom . . . who would have been a *wonderful* grandmother."

"Don't make me cry."

"I'm not trying to."

Amber checked on the baby, who had stopped nursing. Becky's eyes were almost closed. Keeping the blanket over herself, Amber placed Becky against her shoulder, gently rubbing and patting her back. "The nurse will probably give her a bottle. She didn't drink much."

"Oh, well, till then . . . let me get a picture of you two" Jake said.

"Picture?"

"Or two or three."

Pulling a throw-away camera out of his shirt pocket, he figured out how to use it and snapped a few pictures, having to wind a knob after each picture. "I should have found out where you hide your digital." He took a couple more before asking, "Hey, where did the sunflowers come from? They weren't there earlier."

"Sunflowers? What . . . ?" She turned her head and saw them. Looking back at Jake, she whispered, "*Ricky . . . it has to be.*"

A young nurse entered the room. "I almost forgot to give you this." She handed Amber a folded piece of paper. "A tall, good looking guy wrote this and asked that it be given to you. But he had already been in here . . . he was the one who brought you those sunflowers. You must have been sleeping." As Amber gripped the paper in her hand, the nurse continued talking: "He has to be the baby's dad . . . she looks a lot like him."" She then reached for Rebecca. "Want me to take her? I'll put her in the bassinet." Amber nodded and the nurse, with the name Patti on her name tag, gently took Becky. "Your momma's lucky. She has good-looking men going in and out of her room." Patti tossed a look at Jake with her last comment.

He smiled, knowing he had to be at least ten years older. But the small brunette was pretty and Jake was flattered that she took notice of him. "Down, boy" he told himself. "Behave."

Amber asked Patti, "How long ago was this given to you?"

"Oh . . . about forty-five minutes. I am so sorry but something came up with another patient and I totally forgot about it till a few minutes ago when I found it in my pocket."

"That's okay. I was just wondering." Amber wished that Patti would leave. She wanted to read the note as soon as possible but not with the nurse in the room.

"You have a beautiful daughter, Ms. Wilson." Patti placed the sleeping Becky in the bassinet before turning to Amber. "Anything else I can do for you?"

"No, thank-you. But thanks for bringing this to me."

"No problem. Call if you need me." After another look at Jake, Patti went out the door.

"I don't know just what's going on with you and Lisa but it can't be that bad for you to think about going out on her, is it?"

Jake shook his head. "No, don't worry about that. The nurse is a cute little thing but I'm too old for her, anyway."

With a grin, Amber said, "It doesn't seem to bother her!"

"Read your note!"

Taking a deep breath, Amber slowly unfolded the note. She recognized Ricky's handwriting as she read: "*She's beautiful . . . and so are you. Ricco.*" Her hand flew to her mouth but not in time to cover the gasp that Jake heard.

"What? What did he say?"

Shaking her head, Amber refolded the paper. "I can't say. It's something between me and Ricky." And she smiled.

"Well . . . must be something good. I haven't seen you smile like that in a long while."

"He remembered how much I like sunflowers" she said, looking at her bouquet.

There was no comment from Jake. He then asked, "When can you get out of here?"

"Dr. Rolands said tomorrow."

"Good! City traffic is driving me nuts!" He grinned. "Pardon the pun."

"You've been driving over here?"

"Sometimes I take a cab."

"So, today you . . ." "Drove. Speaking of which . . . I have to leave for awhile. I'll be back later."

"Jake . . ."

He stopped his trek toward the door.

"Have you talked to Lisa?"

"That's on my to-do list for today."

"You never called her after Becky was born? She doesn't know you were there?"

"Not yet."

"Why not? Doesn't she want to know?"

"Don't, Amber. Don't go where you don't know what's going on."

"Well, how am I supposed to know what's going on if you don't tell me?"

Jake took his time in answering. He didn't know how to say it so he told her, "I'll tell you about it when we get back to your place."

Amber knew better than to press the issue. "Okay . . . see you when you get back."

* * *

Sara and A.J. arrived just as Amber's supper tray was being taken away.

"So, how soon are they springing you from this place?" A.J. asked.

"Tomorrow! I'll be glad to get home, though I'll miss being waited on."

"Won't Jake do that?" Sara teased.

"Won't Jake do what?" He stepped into the room.

"Wait on me hand and foot after I get home" Amber told him.

"For a few days . . . just don't get used to it."

"I can feel the love, can't you?" A.J. asked Sara, laughing.

"Is it that obvious?" Jake asked with a grin as he shook A.J.'s hand.

Walking to the bassinet, Sara looked inside. "Oh, she's sleeping. I wanted to hold her."

"That's okay . . . go ahead" Amber said.

"She's going to be so spoiled" Jake commented, as Sara picked Becky up out of the bassinet.

"Look who's talking!" Amber exclaimed. "Let's talk about who's spoiling her, Uncle Jake!"

"Hey! I want her to know who her uncle is!" he defended himself.

"I think that's wonderful" Sara told him.

"Hey, you got more flowers! Who found sunflowers in Manhattan?" A.J. commented.

"Ricky."

Sara and A.J. looked at each other before Sara said to Amber, "Really."

"He was here at lunch time but I was sleeping and missed him . . . but he left me a note . . . he saw the baby."

A.J. was happy to hear that. He thought Ricky had seemed happier when he came back to work from lunch.There hadn't been a chance to talk to him because Deana seemed to be around them all afternoon. She had to know something was up and A.J. felt sorry for her. He wondered how much Ricky had told her about Amber . . . and the baby. From what Ricky had told him, her feelings for him were more than he felt for her. The whole situation was bad for Deana.

They all chatted for awhile, with each taking turns holding Becky, who slept through most of it. Just as they were getting ready to go, A.J. asked, "Do you need a ride tomorrow to go home?"

After a quick look at Jake, Amber replied, "I'll get a cab. His truck isn't set up for a baby seat and everything else that's going with me . . . like all those flowers."

"Nobody's taking a cab. Let me know when you can leave and I'll come get you" A.J. said.

"You don't have to do that! What if you're out on a case when it's time for me to leave?"

"I'll just make sure that I don't go out. Ricky and Deana can handle whatever."

Ricky and Deana . . . alone in the car to a crime scene. No, A.J., I don't like the fact that she can have him to herself. "No, I can't ask . . ."

"You're not asking . . . I'm volunteering. No more argument . . . it's settled."

With a shrug of her shoulders, Sara said, "Now, Amber . . . you know better than to argue with him."

"How could I forget? Okay, you win, A.J.. I'll call you when it's time."

"I knew you would see my way, darlin'." He grinned.

And Amber had to smile back.

Jake sat on the end of the bed after Sara and A.J. left to go home. "Well, sis, you get to go home tomorrow . . . with a baby."

"I know . . . isn't that wonderful?"

"I'll say . . . it's about time one of us became a parent."

Tears filled her eyes as she looked down at Becky, asleep in her bassinet, which was next to the bed. "I wish Ricky was going home with us."

"So, the note he gave you didn't say he wanted to be with you?" Jake softly asked.

"No." Amber wiped at a lone tear that slid down her face.

Gently squeezing one of her feet under the blanket, Jake looked at his sister. "But it must have been something good with the way you smiled after you read it."

"It was . . . it just raised more questions."

"Oh?"

She shook her head. "Maybe when we get home . . . it'll give us something more to talk about besides Lisa."

"Okay. Well, I almost forgot to tell you . . . there was a message from Maggie and Matt when I went home, wondering if you had the baby. I called them back and gave them the news. I was told to tell you congratulations and how happy they are for you. They're going to try to get over to see you . . . if Maggie can find a sitter."

"Oh, it'll be good to see them!"

"I like them . . . and I'm happy knowing that you have more friends like Sara and A.J. here for you." He paused before asking, "Unless . . . are you coming back home with me?"

"I don't know, Jake. I still haven't made up my mind."

When he got ready to leave shortly afterwards, he asked, "Do you want me here tomorrow or wait for you at the apartment?"

"You might as well wait."

"Okay." He moved to the bassinet. "I have to hold her before I leave."

With a smile, Amber said, "Go ahead."

"Uncle Jake will see you tomorrow after you break free of this place." He gently kissed her forehead before placing her in Amber's arms. "'Night, sis." He kissed Amber's cheek. "Get some sleep."

"I hope so. You, too."

The room was quiet after Jake left. Amber held her sleeping daughter a little closer. "I love you, my baby girl. Mommy and Uncle Jake will always be there for you." She glanced at the sunflowers and sighed deeply. "Your daddy will love you, too, once he gets to hold you."

* * *

Chapter 13

Glad to be home, Amber walked around the apartment with Becky in her arms, talking as she showed her every room. Jake played the host and made coffee for A.J. and Sara, who had said she wasn't going to miss out on the excitement of taking the baby home.

Becky fell asleep before the tour of her new home was over and was put to bed in the bassinet in her room. Amber watched her as she slept, hearing the voices of her brother and friends from the kitchen. Thinking about Ricky, she wondered why he had brought her the vase of sunflowers . . . and written what he had in the note, as brief as it was. He didn't try to contact her after that and she wondered why. After a few minutes, she joined everyone at the kitchen table.

"Where's my niece?" Jake asked.

"Sleeping in her room."

"I bet it's good to be home" Sara commented.

"You are so right." Amber pulled a bottle of cold green tea out of the refrigerator.

"No coffee?" Jake asked.

"I don't want to drink too much while I'm nursing."

After she was seated, A.J. said, "I told Ricky you and the baby were coming home today."

"Oh?" was all she said, when she really wanted to blurt out, "What did he say?"

"He called Ricky at work to let him know that he wasn't coming in, figuring that way he could tell him without Deana hearing." Sara explained.

"Is this how things will have to be concerning Deana?"

After a heavy sigh, A.J. answered, "For the time being."

"Oh." Amber opened her tea bottle and took a long drink.

"He doesn't want to hurt her any more than necessary" A.J. tried to explain.

Sara lay a hand on his arm. "Let her have this conversation with Ricky" she said quietly.

"Oh, I'm sorry, A.J.. You're in the middle of this . . . again . . . and you go out of your way to help me . . . and I'm not being very nice."

"I'd probably be the same way . . . except grumpier. Don't worry about it, Amber" he told her.

"You've been so good to me . . . both of you. How will I ever repay you?"

"Me? Well, darlin', I have the rest of the day off . . . with pay" A.J. said with a grin.

"How about you don't move back up north?" Sara asked.

Amber and Jake looked at each other. "I can't make any promises about that one, Sara" Amber quietly replied.

That evening, Amber and Jake watched TV while Becky slept. During a commercial, Amber finally asked, "Are you going to tell me what's up with you and Lisa?"

There was no answer. Amber looked at him, waiting, but he kept his eyes on the TV.

"Well?"

After a few moments, Jake took a deep breath and then exhaled it as he pointed the remote and turned off the TV. He did not look happy when he turned his head to look at Amber. "Do you really want to know?"

"Yes . . . that's why I asked."

Going straight to the point, he said, "She a bitch, Amber . . . a real *bitch*."

"So, then . . . why do you stay with her?"

Jake pushed his fingers through his long hair. "I don't know. I find myself asking the same question. She doesn't understand my relationship with you . . . or I should say that she doesn't *want* to understand. She feels we're too close for a brother and sister . . . '*It's not normal*' is her favorite phrase to use. We talk too much on the phone . . . we tell each other things we shouldn't be telling . . ."

"And when did she become an expert on how close a brother and sister should be and what they should and shouldn't be telling each other?"

He held up a hand to silence Amber. "She's jealous . . . that's all I can figure. It started when you were at the house and found out you were pregnant . . . Lisa thought we spent too much time together *alone* . . . and that I put up with too much of your crying." Jake shook his head. "I know she wants the attention that I give you."

"Oh, tell her to grow up!" Amber muttered.

"I have."

"Don't you two talk . . . I mean, *really* talk . . . talk things over?"

"We used to but not so much any more. We argue more than anything." His head fell against the back of the couch and his eyes closed. "I needed this time away from her."

Amber felt bad for her brother. He was a good person. It surprised her that he hadn't already settled down and married and had a few kids. Lisa never struck her as that type. "Do you love her enough to want to stay with her?"

"I don't know . . . there have been times lately that she can really piss me off . . . and she seems to enjoy doing it."

"Doesn't she want to stay with you?"

"I used to think so . . . but I've told her that I will only put up with her shit just so long . . ."

"It's time for a heart to heart with her . . . make Lisa realize what her attitude can cost her."

Jake looked away, from Amber to the blank TV screen.

"Or . . . unless . . ." Amber stammered.

That brought Jake's attention back to his sister. "Unless what?"

"Unless I become less dependent on you." Her voice caught and her eyes filled with tears.

"After all these years? I've always looked out for you, Amber, even back when I tormented you from age ten to sixteen . . . and then again when you married what's-his-face . . . and when you started hanging out in town at the bars . . . picking up men . . ."

"*They* picked me up."

"Same difference."

"Yeah, you gave me grief then."

"Only because I cared . . . and love you. Lisa can't get it through her head . . . But you're right, I do have to talk with her, hopefully straighten things out for the better . . . Are you coming home with me? Lisa would love to meet Becky."

"I'm not so sure about that one but . . . as for going back home, I don't think so. After getting the sunflowers and note from Ricky, I want to wait if he decides to get in touch."

"How long will you wait?"

She exhaled a long breath. "That's a tough question, Jake. I know he has to deal with Deana . . . and if she has any sense, she won't give him up willingly. But I know now that I can't run home every time things don't go my way."

Jake gave her a long look. "Who are you and what have you done with my sister?"

Amber smiled. "I now have a little person who depends on me . . . my life isn't all about me any more. I have to make decisions to make a good life for Becky."

"I swear I left my sister at the hospital" Jake muttered, then said, "I know you'll do what's best for her."

"Hopefully without too many mistakes."

* * *

Maggie and Matt arrived for a visit Saturday afternoon, with a gift, which was a soft fleece, peach colored blanket. "I had no idea what you needed but when I saw this, I *had* to buy it! As you can see, it's big enough for a single bed, so she will get a few years use out of it" Maggie explained.

"It's beautiful! I love the color!"

"And this is from all of us at the shop" Matt said, handing Amber an envelope.

She couldn't open it fast enough. The card was signed by everyone at the T-shirt shop and it contained a check for $250.00! Amber gasped. "This is too much!"

"It's for not knowing what she needs and if there isn't anything, put it into a savings account for her" Maggie told Amber.

"Okay, that I can do. It'll go into the account my dad set up for his grandchild."

"College" Jake added.

"How long are you staying, Jake?" Matt asked.

"As long as Amber needs me to."

"You'll *never* go home, Jake!" Maggie teased.

Sara and A.J. visited again the same weekend. While Sara and Jake were deep in conversation about a plant she had recently bought (Jake had a green thumb), A.J. followed Amber into the kitchen while she made coffee.

"So, how do you like being a mommy?"

"I love it!" she exclaimed, with a wide grin. "Even without getting a full night's sleep!"

"Does she wake up often?"

"At least twice. Sometimes she'll go right back to sleep but then other times . . ."

"She wants to stay up and party?"

Amber laughed. "Yeah, something like that!"

A.J. chuckled but it died when she asked him, "Has Ricky talked to you about . . . me and the baby?"

He hesitated a long moment before replying, "Yes, Amber . . . he has."

"And . . . ?"

He wiped his hand over his face. "Oh, Amber! I'd rather not get involved any more than I have been! Please, let him get in touch with you."

"He's planning on doing that?"

A.J. looked like he was in pain when he answered, "Yes."

Her heart beat faster. "When?"

"He . . . Oh, come on, Amber! I really don't know for sure!"

As badly as she wanted to know, she knew she had to stop with the questions. It was plain to see that this wasn't easy for A.J.. Amber crossed the room to where he stood and hugged him. "No more questions . . . I promise." She kissed his cheek. "Thank-you for all that you and Sara have done for me."

Giving her a gentle squeeze, A.J. said, "It's now between you and Ricky, Amber. Hang in there."

* * *

By the time Becky was a week old, Uncle Jake had learned how to change her diaper without making gagging noises when the diaper was soiled. Amber smiled as she watched from the nursery doorway. "You're going to make a great daddy some day" she commented, as Jake picked his niece up off the changing table.

"I'm going to miss her. Are you sure you're not coming home with me? I mean, since I'm already here . . ."

Amber shook her head. "No, we're staying here . . . But we'll come visit!"

"Often, I hope . . . like once a month!"

At that remark, Amber laughed out loud.

Jake grinned, and remarked, "It's good hearing you laugh. You haven't done much of that lately."

"You're holding the main reason I'm so happy."

Becky fussed a little but Jake held her, cooing. But when she turned her head and nuzzled his chest, he said, "Whoa! Sorry, little girl but that's one thing I cannot help you with! Here's your mother."

With Becky in her arms, Amber crossed the room to the rocking chair. Jake said, "I'll clean up around the kitchen while you're busy in here."

"Thanks. Supper dishes are off the table but I left them on the counter beside the sink."

"Say no more." He turned toward the door.

"You can stay and talk to me!" Amber called after him, with a smile.

"I'll pass . . . thanks!" he called back.

The phone rang a few minutes later. "Got it!" Jake called to Amber as he dried his hands.

"Hello? Wilson residence."

There was a slight pause, then, "Jake? It's Ricky."

"Hey, man! What's up?"

"Um . . . is Amber there?"

"She is but she's feeding Becky at the moment."

"Becky?"

"Um . . . your daughter?"

"I know." It suddenly came to him how his father used to call his mother, *Becca*. "I was checking to see if it was okay to come over."

"*Yes*!" Jake thought but out loud, said, "Let me check . . . hold on . . ." As he walked toward the nursery, he called out, "I'm on my way! Are you decent?"

Amber had heard the phone, wondering who it was. Making sure the receiving blanket covered where it should, she replied, "Decent!"

Jake leaned against the door frame, with the phone against his chest. "It's Ricky." He grinned. "He wants to come over to see you."

"When?"

"Now."

"Now? Um . . ." The thought of him coming up rattled her. "Um . . . yes! Of course . . . yes!"

Jake kept his smile, watching Amber as he spoke into the phone, "Come on over."

"I'll be there in a few minutes."

"See ya then." Shutting off the phone, he asked Amber, "Will you be ready?"

"I don't think so. You two can talk till I can get out there."

"I have to finish my dishes before he gets here." Jake started back up the hall. "A man's work is never done!"

Amber smiled at her brother's words.

* * *

Chapter 14

Ricky buzzed to go up and Jake unlocked the door to let him in. "It's like Fort Knox" Jake muttered as he opened the door. "Hey! Come on in!"

The two men shook hands. "Amber will be out soon. Becky should be about done eating."

"Oh."

"Amber is breast-feeding."

"Oh . . . I didn't know that."

"Come on in and have a seat." Jake led the way into the living room.

"How long are you staying down here, Jake?" Ricky asked, once seated on the couch.

"I'm leaving Saturday morning . . . I have to get back to work. I thought maybe Amber and the baby were coming with me but nope, they're staying here."

"They are?" Ricky cleared his throat. "I heard you were in the delivery room."

Jake grinned. "Yes, I was! It was awesome . . . even if she was my sister! I wasn't going in but she had a death-grip on my hand and dragged me in with her, cussing all the way . . ."

"Oh, quit your story-telling, Jake" Amber quietly rebuked, standing in the doorway. Her eyes rested on Ricky, watching him as he stood and met her eyes. "Hi."

"Hey, Amber" he softly responded.

"Okay . . . I will leave you two alone . . . you need time alone. I'll be in my room."

"You don't have to go to your room" Amber told him but didn't look away from Ricky.

"Yes I do . . . you two need to talk some things over. I'll see you before you go, man."

"Yeah . . . okay" Ricky replied, not looking at Jake, either.

Jake backed into the foyer, then turned to go to his room. The door closed quietly behind him.

Amber wondered if she and Ricky would end up arguing and he would walk out. She was tired of the arguing. But something felt different. It was a surprise to her that he was in her living room and had been seated on her couch. He always had turned down her requests for him to stay.

"This apartment is nice. You always had good taste."

"Thank-you." What was up? Why was he being so nice? Because Jake was there? No . . . something *was* different.

"Would you like something to drink? I have lemonade, coffee and iced tea. I just made the tea for supper."

"Iced tea mix with lemon and sugar . . . that's the way you like it." Ricky smiled. "See? I remembered." Then the smile vanished. "But I didn't come here for a drink. I want to talk to you."

"About what?" Her insides twisted and her heart pounded as she looked at him.

He turned away to find himself standing in front of an assortment of pictures in frames of all sizes on a wooden table. "This is some collection" he commented, looking at each one.

"Jake liked to take pictures of the pregnant me." Amber stood beside Ricky. Reaching for a 5"x7" frame, she held it in her hands. "This is my favorite." The picture was of Amber and her father. He had an arm around her shoulders and in his free hand he held an hand-made sign that read: MY GRANDBABY IS IN THERE, with an arrow pointing at Amber's round stomach. As she looked at it, she laughed but sadness could be heard. "He was so happy to finally become a grandpa." It took a few tries to swallow the lump in her throat. "The damn cancer wouldn't let him live just a little longer to see and hold his granddaughter." She smiled through her tears. "He wanted so much to be able to tell his grandbaby stories about how spoiled I was!" Wiping at the tears on her cheeks, she laughed. "How he would have enjoyed doing that!" Looking up, she found Ricky watching her. Once upon a time, she would have been able to read the look on his face but this time she had no clue what he was thinking. He turned back to the pictures.

"I really am sorry about your loss" he quietly said.

"Thank-you, Ricky. That means a lot."

"Those were taken at the hospital." He pointed at a frame with three pictures: one of Becky in her bassinet, one with Jake and the last with Amber. "I was in your room. I knew the moment I saw her that she was mine. She was awake, looking up at me like she knew I was her dad. You were sleeping and as much as I wanted to wake you and let you know I was there, I knew you needed what sleep you could get."

"I wouldn't have cared. The sunflowers are beautiful . . . what a surprise to find them!"

His eyes met hers. "I wanted to get you something and that was the first thing that popped into my head . . . even though it took me a couple of flower shops to find them." His eyes searched her face and then he said, "I want to give Rebecca my last name on her birth certificate. Sara said she would take care of the paperwork . . . if that's okay with you."

It was then that Amber realized how close they stood to one another. Stepping back, she said, "But you didn't believe me when I told you the baby was yours." *Stop, Amber! Don't start an argument*!

"I knew you were telling me the truth. But I wanted to hurt you back after . . ." He stopped, shaking his head. "When I first saw you at Sara and A.J.'s, I was so happy to see you . . . but I was also so pissed off with the way you left. After that, I couldn't stop thinking about you . . . and I couldn't stay away. It was hell but I had to see you, even if we did argue." He gently grasped her upper arms but quickly let go and turned back to the table. "I keep looking at these pictures of the different stages of your pregnancy. I should have gone through it with you. Did you have any morning sickness?"

Amber looked at his profile, startled by the change of conversation. "At first. That was one of the first clues that I was pregnant."

"Was it bad? Did it last long? Did you have it only in the morning or during any part of the day?" Ricky walked to the other side of the room. He didn't seem to expect answers; he was only talking, letting out all that had been pent up inside. "I missed the chance of hearing about her first kick . . . I have thought about it so much since I felt her kicks that day at A.J.'s and again here." He began to pace. "I missed doctor appointments, what the doctor said, how you felt at times, I missed watching your stomach get bigger as she grew . . . I missed *everything*!"

There was no mistaking the catch in his voice at times. Amber didn't know what to say . . . where to start . . . so she only watched as Ricky paced . . . and listened . . .

"Jake was in the room with you when Rebecca was born . . . it should have been *me*! Not Sara and Jake . . . it should have been *me*!" He stopped pacing and looked at Amber. Tears were on his face. "Oh,*shit*!" Ricky muttered, wiping them away. But then his face crumbled. "Dammit! I should have been the one there for you! I thought about you all the time . . . even when I shouldn't have been! You didn't come back to me . . . you were pregnant . . . you didn't call!" His voice broke and he covered his face with his hands, bowing his head as he cried.

Amber rushed over to him. "*I'm sorry*! *I'm sorry*!" she whispered, stroking his hair. "I am *so* sorry!" As her tears fell, she placed her hands on each side of his head. "I should have called you. I *know* I should have." She kissed the top of his head. "I did want you with me! I did!" Raising his head slightly, she pressed her lips against his forehead. "*I am so, so sorry*!" Amber didn't know if she raised his head up higher or if Ricky did. Kissing his cheek, she tasted his tears. "*Ricco . . .*" she whispered, before her lips moved down to his jaw line, over his chin and up to his mouth. "*Ricco . . .*" His name was breathed against his lips.

With a groan, his mouth covered Amber's and his arms wrapped around her, holding her body against his . . . something he had wanted to do since her return. His kiss was demanding but she was as eager, claiming his mouth as he had hers. Their tongues met, dueling at first until their movements slowed and they tenderly stroked one another.

Ricky pulled away, his eyes meeting Amber's. Their breathing was hard and fast as their eyes searched each other's face. Amber hadn't been touched by a man since that last night with Ricky, nine months earlier. The times her father and brother had held and hugged her over that time period didn't count. Ricky noticed how swollen her lips were . . . but he didn't want to stop kissing them. And he didn't.

After their mouths parted the next time, he buried his face in her hair. "I missed you . . . I missed you *so* much." Ricky's arms tightened a notch around her. "I missed *us*."

"So did I." She then quietly said, "Tell me something."

"What's that?"

"*Is* there going to be an *us* again? What about Deana?"

His body stiffened at the mention of her name and he slowly backed away from Amber. "I'll deal with her." Ricky looked at her for a long moment, then said, "And what if there is an *us*? I still have the same job . . . the job you left me over. Can you handle it?"

There was a slight hesitation before she replied, "Yes."

"Are you sure, Amber? You have to be sure because I couldn't take it if you left me again."

Tears filled her eyes. "I don't ever want to leave you again."

His phone rang. Ricky let it ring four times before pulling it out of his pocket and checking the caller. Letting it go to voice mail, he put the phone back into his pocket.

"Was it Deana?" Amber asked, looking at him.

"Yes."

She seemed lost in her own thoughts for a few moments before shaking her head. "I can't do it, Ricky. I can't be the 'other woman'."

"Oh, Amber . . . you've always been the other woman . . . for the last nine months. And she knows it. You've always been there . . . in my mind . . . and my heart. I love you."

The tears spilled over.

"Deana has known about you from the start. And she knows about Rebecca. She's pushing for that paternity test but I told her it's not necessary, that I know that baby is *mine*. She argues that you'll leave me again . . . and take the baby with you." The catch in his voice was noticeable.

"I can't leave you again. My heart couldn't take it" Amber whispered.

"Mine, either." His voice cracked before he cleared his throat. "Deana doesn't want me to leave her."

"I can't blame her . . . but do you want to?"

"I love *you*, Amber." Smiling through her tears, she hurried into his open arms. "We can make this work" she said before kissing him.

Returning her kisses, Ricky held her tightly, as if afraid to let go. His kisses deepened and his body responded. Amber felt it and her body ached for his. But it was too soon.

He pulled away, knowing what he wanted but couldn't have just yet. Breathing hard, he looked down at her. "I hope I'm doing the right thing . . . I want to trust you . . . I need to trust you . . . but can I?"

It hurt her to hear it but he was right. Amber knew she had betrayed his trust . . . and having trust destroyed like that took time to rebuild. She looked away, biting her bottom lip to keep from crying. Her eyes were filled with unshed tears when she met his gaze. "I want to prove that you can trust me." She swallowed, then quietly asked, "How long will you give me?"

The tips of his fingers caressed her cheek. "As long as it takes. I have to confess that you're an addiction, Amber . . . you're a hard habit to break." Ricky's eyes met hers. "Even after all this time, I never got over you." His mouth took hers once more as his hands held each side of her face. Tender at first, his kisses turned passionate . . . possessive . . . then close to brutal. He needed her, wanted her, back in his life . . . and his bed. Abruptly, he pulled away, breathing hard as he looked at her . . . saw the want in her eyes . . . saw her bruised, swollen lips . . . heard her breathing hard through those lips. "I think I had better stop" Ricky softly said.

"Me, too" she replied, just as quietly, not moving her gaze from his.

"Can I see the baby?"

"Sure." Amber was surprised when she felt shy about reaching for his hand but felt better when his fingers wrapped warmly around hers. "You can see the apartment, too, if you want."

He nodded his head.

Walking into the kitchen, Ricky looked around. "I think the size of this room and the living-room combined was the size of your whole apartment in the other place!"

"I think you're right!" she laughed.

Going up the hall, they paused outside a closed door with the sounds of the TV volume turned up louder than normal on the other side. "Jake's room . . . A.K.A. the guest room."

Ricky grinned. "I guess he didn't want to hear anything going on out here between us." Amber chuckled then proceeded to point out the bathroom and paused briefly in front of her partially open bedroom door. "My room" she stated before walking away.

But Ricky didn't follow her. "Can I see your room?"

Stopping, surprised, Amber turned back and pushed open the door. Ricky stepped inside, looking at everything in the large room. "Your own bathroom? Nice." His gaze stopped at her queen-size bed. "I'll never forget the pull-out couch in the other place."

"That's up at Jake's."

"You kept it?"

"*I couldn't part with it, with it's memories of you*" she wanted to tell him but only replied, "Yes." Suddenly, she remembered the picture on her nightstand, and hoped he didn't see it. She put her hand on his arm, trying to draw him away. "Let's go see Becky."

Too late. "Nice picture" he commented, his eyes looking straight at it. He then looked at her. "I remember the day Jake took that, up at . . . well, it was your dad's at the time." Wanting to touch her again but not daring, Ricky said, "Let's go see the baby."

Becky was asleep on her back.

"She sleeps better that way" Amber quietly said. "I know they say not to put them on their stomach to sleep but I have, checking on her way too often when I do. So why do I do that? I remember my mom saying she always put us to sleep on our bellies . . . and my mom was right with a lot of things. But now that I know she sleeps better on her back, that's how I put her in at bedtime and I don't worry so much. I learned that much in a week. And as for sleeping well on her back, I know she gets that from you 'cause I don't!" She sighed deeply. "Shut me up . . . I'm rambling."

Ricky couldn't help but chuckle. "You're not nervous around me, are you?"

"Lord help me . . . I am!"

Putting an arm across her shoulders, Ricky pulled her to him. "Don't be." He kissed the top of her head. Turning toward him, Amber slid her arms around his middle and put her head against his chest. They stood like that for a short while, watching Becky sleep. When she moved, making baby noises, he asked, "Is she waking up?"

"She might be. She should be ready to eat any time now. Seems like she eats all the time." With a small laugh, Amber said, "I know she gets that from me!" When Ricky chuckled at that, she heard it in his chest and looked up at him, to find him looking at her. Her lips suddenly felt dry.

He watched a her tongue slid out to moisten them. His head dipped down to gently kiss her now moistened lips. "I so like kissing you again."

"So, do it . . ."

As his mouth moved toward hers, Becky stirred, drawing their attention away from each other to look at her. Amber pulled away from Ricky to straightened the blanket over the baby.

"I heard that you're breast-feeding her."

Who told him? "I am . . . and I love it." His gaze slid down to her breasts and lingered as he remembered how well they fit in in his hands . . . and how much he enjoyed fondling them . . . licking and sucking her nipples . . . and hearing her moans as he did. Ricky became aroused at his thoughts. When his eyes returned to Amber's face, he found she was watching him. His face grew warm. "I was being bad" he softly admitted.

While she watched him look at her, she became aroused, somehow knowing what he was thinking . . . and remembering herself how well his mouth and tongue worked wonders with her breasts as they made love . . . "That's okay" she told him. "I was, too." Swallowing, hoping her instincts were right and she wasn't pushing too far, she told him, "The doctor recommends six weeks before having sex . . ."

His eyes suddenly grew darker but Amber recognized it as desire, not anger. His voice sounded husky as he commented, "Becky is a week old, so that's another five weeks of waiting."

Desire flared. Nine months without Ricky had been too long. And he still wanted her. Amber dared to touch the hair over his lip and around his mouth. "I like this. It makes you sexier than ever, *Ricco*."

His body reacted to her touch, no matter how small it was. "You think so?"

"I know so."

Suddenly grabbing her hand, he kissed the palm. "Don't make me regret wanting you back."

"When are you telling Deana?"

"Soon." But he knew Deana suspected.

Amber looked into the bassinet to find her daughter's eyes open. "Well, hello there, baby girl. Your daddy is here to see you."

"Can I hold her?" Ricky asked.

"Let me change her first." She gently lifted Becky up and carried her to the changing table.

"I was surprised you named her after my mother" he commented.

"Why? *I* knew she was your's . . . and after you knew for sure, I knew you wouldn't mind."

He smiled down at their daughter. "My mom would be happy that she has a granddaughter . . . and to have her named after her would be an added bonus."

"Okay . . . are you ready?" Amber picked Becky up and turned to Ricky. "Put your hand under her head so it won't flop around . . . that's it." She stepped back and watched him, feeling so in love with him . . . seeing the family she wanted with him.

"She doesn't weigh a thing" he commented, not looking away from Becky.

"Yeah, that's true. But to hold her and give birth to her are two totally different things. It felt like she was shaped like a ton of bricks!"

The look Ricky gave her when he looked up from Becky told her again how he should have been there. Her hand reached out to caress his cheek. Offering a small smile, he turned his attention back to their daughter. Amber watched for a few minutes, enjoying the 'family' time. Then, she remembered her camera, which was still in the living room after she had taken pictures of the baby and Jake earlier. "I'll be right back."

She snapped a half a dozen pictures before suggesting that he hold Becky with her head in the crook of his arm. Another half a dozen pictures were taken.

"Hey! Why wasn't I invited to the party?" Jake leaned against the door frame. "It looks like all are having fun."

"Of course you can join us!" Amber grinned at him.

Jake reached for the camera. "Here . . . let me get some pictures of the three of you."

And he did just that. He took lots of pictures, including those of just Amber and Ricky. All of the adults had fun taking turns with the camera.

But the fun ended abruptly when Ricky's cell phone rang. His eyes met Amber's, who hoped it was only Deana calling again. The look on Ricky's face when he checked the caller told her different. He noticed the flicker of panic in her eyes before she blinked it away. Keeping his gaze on her, he answered his call: "Yeah . . . Where? . . . I'll be right there." Closing the phone, he said unnecessarily, "I have to go."

Trying to sound calm, Amber said, "I figured as much."

"I'll be fine, Amber. I'll call when I get back, whatever time that will be."

"Okay."

She held Becky but he gave her a hug and kiss before tenderly kissing the top of Becky's head. Turning to Jake, who had stepped back from them, he extended his hand. "I hope to see you before you leave but just in case I don't, have a safe trip home. It was good to see you again."

"Same here. Take care of my sister, man."

Becky started to cry, turning her head toward her mother. Amber tried to comfort her as she tried to keep an eye on Ricky. He looked her way before going out the bedroom door, flashing her his smile. And then, he was gone.

"Are you okay?" Jake asked.

She put on a brave smile. "Yes, I have to be . . . if I want to stay in his life."

"Hey, this is your brother you're talking to. You don't have to pretend with me."

"I'm not pretending, Jake." But a single tear down her cheek said different. "I have to be okay for Becky."

He looked at Amber, not convinced.

Becky continued to cry. "She's hungry" Amber said.

"I kind of gathered that. I'm out of here." But he stopped at the door and looked back. "Want to talk about it later?"

With a nod, she said, "Probably."

Setting in the rocking chair, Amber opened her bra for Becky, who suckled hungrily. Watching her, images of Ricky with Becky swirled through her head. A few tears fell before they were wiped away. Amber knew she had to stop the fears every time his phone rang and he had to leave. *It's his job*! Gently touching Becky's hair, Amber spoke softly to her: "He's your daddy. You deserve to have your mommy *and* daddy in your life. Your grandpa loved me and took good care of me for a long time. He was there when I needed him . . . he listened and gave honest opinions. Oh, he could be strict when he wanted to be but I think that made me a better person, especially after your grandma died. I want you to know that kind of love . . . and cherish it. Your daddy will be a good father . . . we'll be good parents . . . but not without mistakes." Amber was determined to keep Ricky in her life. She could tell that he wasn't convinced that she could handle the risks of his job . . . but she would prove it to him.

Jake was on his bed, watching TV. Amber knocked and opened the partially open door after he called, "Come in!" He grinned and reached for Becky. "There she is! Is your belly full now?"

"She has a full belly and a clean diaper. She's good for a couple of hours."

Jake held Becky against his shoulder and gently rubbed her back. He said to Amber, "So, I take it things went well between you and Ricky."

"At first it wasn't so good . . . I really hurt him, Jake."

"And the hurt hasn't gone away."

"I think he feels a little better now . . . after we talked . . . but we still have things to work out."

"You two sure looked happy while pictures were being taken."

Amber couldn't stop the smile that appeared. "Things are much better between us . . . we didn't argue this time." But her body warmed as she thought about his kisses . . . being in his arms . . . the body heat . . . the want . . . and the ache.

"You two kissed, didn't you? More than just that good-bye kiss."

The blush on her face answered his question.

"And you liked it, didn't you?" Jake teased.

"Duh!" She threw a burp rag at him.

Laughing, Jake said, "Hey! Be careful! I'm holding an innocent child here!"

Turning serious, Amber sat at the end of the bed. "Oh, Jake . . . there's still Deana."

His eyes narrowed. "He's still with *her* . . . and talking about being with you?"

"I said we had things to work out."

"You'd think he'd get rid of the girlfriend first."

"Jake . . ."

"Well, don't you think so?" He then sighed. "I just don't want you to be hurt any more."

"Thanks, big brother, but I don't think anybody is hurt-proof." She was touched by his concern and gave him a small smile.

"When will you see him again?"

"I don't know. He said he'll call me later, so if you hear the phone ring late, don't panic."

After giving her a long look, Jake asked, "Are you sure you don't want to come back home with me, Amber? Give him time to decide who he really wants?"

"Jake!"

"I'm only thinking of you . . . I want you to be okay."

Her tone softened. "Thanks . . . but I am okay."

Jake looked at her for a long moment before sighing. "But I'm not gonna be."

Looking puzzled, she asked, "Why not?"

"I'm going to miss Becky and everything that goes with her . . . holding her, talking to her . . . I'll even miss the diaper changes!"

"Are you sure you're my brother?"

"Make sure you keep me updated on her . . . everything new thing she does . . ."

"You need a baby of your own, Jake."

He took awhile to answer but he only said, "Maybe . . ."

It was after midnight by the time Becky was asleep in her cradle and Amber was in her night-gown, getting into bed. As she reached for the book on her nightstand, the clock read 12:14. Wasn't Ricky going to call?

Propping her pillow against the headboard, Amber leaned back to read. Opening the book, she found where she had left off. It was the kind of book she enjoyed, a suspense with some romance but she couldn't stay focused. After having to read sentences more than once, she closed the the book with a sigh. Glancing at the clock, she saw it was 12:30. Was he going to call? Putting the book back on the nightstand, Amber shut off the light and tried to go to sleep. But her mind was filled with Ricky. Where was he? He had left shortly after 8 o'clock. Was he okay? *No, Amber . . . don't go there.*

After tossing and turning for awhile, Amber decided to go into the living room. But just as she pushed off the covers, the phone rang. Snatching the phone off the nightstand, she turned on the phone as the second ring started. "*Ricky.*" Relief could be heard in her voice.

"Hi. Sorry it's so late."

"Don't worry about it. Are you okay?"

"I needed to hear your voice."

Her heart warmed at those words. "I'm here."

There was a slight pause before he quietly asked, "Will you always be?"

That question was definitely not expected. "Of course! What brought that up?"

"I need to know . . . I wish I knew for sure. Now that I've held our daughter, I want the two of you in my life. But, Amber . . . I noticed the hesitation when I asked you about my job . . . and I saw your eyes when my phone rang tonight." After a deep sigh, he said, "I can't have you leaving me again . . . and this time with my baby."

Instead of feeling the usual sadness and being upset, Amber felt anger: "*Jesus*, Ricky! What can I do to make you understand that I won't leave? I made a huge mistake before and I won't do it again!" Tears slid down her cheeks. "*I love you*! If I get another chance to be with you, I *won't* screw it up again!" Biting on her bottom lip, Amber tried to keep from losing it. *Don't change your mind, Ricco! What happened since we talked only hours ago?* The answer clicked: *Deana.*

The other end of the line was quiet.

Amber was afraid to speak.

But Ricky broke the silence: "Oh, Amber . . . this wasn't how this call was supposed to turn out. I'm sorry." He sounded tired.

"But it must have been on your mind."

He sighed. "It was. I've been doing a lot of thinking since I left your place. But, hey . . . I'll be over to see you."

"Okay." Amber stopped herself from asking *when.*

"I'll talk to you soon."

"Okay."

"'Night."

Shutting off the phone, Amber placed it on the other pillow on her bed before curling into a ball and crying herself to sleep.

* * *

Ricky tossed his phone onto the couch, not happy with himself. Why did he say those things to Amber? Yes, those thought were in his head but did he have to tell her about them at almost one in the morning? He braced a hand against the window frame as he looked out at the city lights. He loved her . . . why did he continue to hurt her? Was his hurt so deep that he couldn't let it go? It had felt so good to hold his daughter. There was no way to describe the feelings that had raced through him when he took Becky into his arms and she looked up at him. She *was* his! And he was tired of Deana's constant argument about a paternity test.

To break down in front of Amber like he did was a relief, a relief to let his feelings all out. And he held her . . . and kissed her . . . kissed those lips that he never tired of kissing. Amber had told him when she would be able to have sex again . . . he knew she wanted it as much as he did. Sex with Deana had been good . . . she liked things done differently . . . but it wasn't like what he had with Amber. It had taken a long time to get her out of his head when he was in bed with Deana . . . it was good that she couldn't read his mind. But Amber . . . the way she moved . . . the way she touched him . . . the way she whispered in the dark . . . she was who he wanted. Oh, he cared for Deana. She was a good person who had stuck with him to help him out of his funk after Amber left. But Deana wanted more than he could give her. And with Amber always in his head . . . and heart . . . it was impossible to do.

Ricky sighed deeply, raking his hands through his hair, wishing he had never called and said those things to Amber. He had to hear her voice . . . and there was that part of him that needed to know she hadn't gone anywhere. He should have gone to her apartment. Something he had said to her earlier popped into his head: she *was* an addiction . . . one he had never been able to get out of his system.

Now she was back and he desperately craved her.

Ricky knew he would never get over her.

Their daughter would hopefully bind them together.

* * *

Chapter 15

The alarm clock read 7: 42. Amber closed her eyes, wanting to sleep awhile longer. Suddenly, they opened again for another look at the clock. She never heard Becky! Sitting up, Amber checked the baby monitor on her nightstand. The small blue light was lit to show it was on. Tossing back the covers, she ran to the baby's room . . . to find the cradle empty.

Where was she?

It took a moment to realize that Jake had her.

After a trip to the bathroom and then sliding on her bathrobe, Amber walked to Jake's room. The door was wide open and the bed unmade but there was no baby or her uncle in sight. Smelling coffee, Amber went to the kitchen, only to find that room empty, also. But as she poured herself a half a cup of coffee, Jake's voice could be heard from the living room . . .

"You would never believe today that your mommy grew up very spoiled . . . what she wanted she most always got . . . but I'm as guilty of that happening as your grandpa and grandma were. I had a swing made of a rope and an old tire . . . don't get me wrong, I had more fun on that . . . so did my friends . . . but your mommy *had* to have a brand new swing set, you know, the kind with two swings, a slide and a teeter-totter . . ."

Amber leaned against the door frame into the living room, listening. Jake was in the recliner, with his feet up and Becky in his arms

"And your mommy also had to have a playhouse . . . a *big* playhouse! So, your grandpa built her a one-room playhouse, with a ceiling so high that I can still stand up inside it. Yep, little girl, that playhouse is still standing . . . and it's yours to play in when you get old enough." Taking a short pause, Jake then asked, "Hey sis, would you refill my coffee cup?"

"After what I just heard you tell my daughter?"

"I was just stating facts." He looked up to grin at Amber.

"How long has she been up?" Amber reached for his coffee cup on the end table. "We were up a little before four."

"It was around quarter to seven when I heard her. I changed her and then we came in here to rock and talk a little bit. She fussed some but I've kept her entertained with my stories of you."

"I hope she doesn't believe any of them" Amber teased, setting his filled cup back on the end table.

Becky chose that moment to let out a wail.

"She heard your voice . . . now she wants you."

"Will it bother you too much if we sit in here with you?"

"Since I'm leaving tomorrow morning, I'd like to spend as much time as I can with the two of you, so yes, sit here with me just as long as you're covered."

Amber had to remove her nightgown, knowing that she couldn't just pull it up like she did when she fed Becky earlier that morning. And Becky wasn't happy with the short delay as she waited for her mother to put on her bathrobe. Becky ate hungrily as they walked toward the living room with a receiving blanket covering her head.

As she got comfortable in the recliner, Jake came in with two coffee cups. "I didn't know if you wanted any more."

"No, I better not. Thanks anyway."

As he sat the extra cup on the coffee table, Jake said, "You look like you had a rough night. Did you and Ricky talk into the wee hours of the morning?"

Watching Jake sit on the couch, Amber replied, "I wish."

"What happened? Didn't he call?"

"Oh, yes . . . he called." She then gave him a brief synopsis of her conversation with Ricky.

"Sounds like he still has doubts."

"I know . . . and I don't know what else I can do to convince him that I'll be with him forever if he'll let me."

"You can't rush him, Amber. You know that regaining somebody's trust is harder than getting their trust. I think he wants to believe you, especially now with Becky but . . ."

"I know . . . I know . . ."

"Hang in there, sis. It'll take time but won't it be worth it in the long run?"

Her eyes met Jake's. "You know how much I want this."

"Give him time."

"He told me that he'll give me as much time as I need."

"See? There you go."

"I wish there was a solution for you and Lisa."

Jake's eyes narrowed. "You work on you and Ricky. I'll worry about me and Lisa."

*   *   *

"Are you sure you're in for a day on the town?" Jake asked.

"I hope so . . . I want to."

"Well, then, sis . . . let's go."

Amber and Jake spent most of the day touring New York City: Times Square, Macy's, The Empire State Building, and museums. They took breaks to eat, rest, use bathrooms, and to feed and change Becky, who slept most of the time in her baby 'sling', resting against her mother's chest and at times, her uncle's. They returned to Amber's apartment that evening, tired but happy after a wonderful day.

"Wait till Lisa sees all the pictures we took! She'll wish she did come with me!"

Amber laughed. "We did take a lot of pictures, didn't we?"

"We went all over! We needed to take a lot! I don't know about you but I'm beat!"

A yawn hit Amber as she smiled. "Me, too!" she then said.

Jake helped remove Becky from the 'sling' on her mother. "This one slept through most of today. Good thing we took pictures so that she can see what she missed" Jake teased, as he cuddled his half-awake niece.

"She was a good girl, though."

"That she was." He gently kissed her forehead before handing her to Amber. "I'm going to shower. I'm going to get to bed earlier tonight so I can get an early start in the morning."

"I'm going to put her to bed. She'll probably be hungry in a couple of hours."

"Oh, let me put her to bed, then, I'll shower."

Amber had to smile. "Okay, Uncle Jake. She's all your's."

It was 7:30 and quiet. Amber relaxed on the couch. The only sound she heard was the water from Jake's shower. It had been a good day . . . Becky's first real outing. And Jake had finally gotten out after being cooped up for a couple of weeks. It was a wonder he hadn't gone stir crazy when he was used to being outside every day. Well, maybe having to go to the store every couple of days helped.

The phone rang. Amber sighed, not wanting to get up but doing so anyway. Hurrying into the kitchen, she grabbed the phone, not looking at the Caller ID. "Hello?"

"Hey, Amber."

"Ricky." Her heart started to beat faster.

"You're home. I tried calling a couple of other times today."

"I didn't think to check the answering machine after we got home."

There was a slight pause before he asked, "Can I come up?"

"You're outside?"

"Yeah."

After last night's phone call, Amber didn't expect to see him so soon. "Come on up." Waiting for him to call on the intercom, she was surprised when the phone rang again. "I'm on my way up. Would you meet me in the hallway?"

"You didn't use your badge again to get let in, did you?"

"No . . . two women were going out and they held the door open for me. Now, are you out in the hall?"

It was a strange request but one worth doing. "I'm unlocking the door . . ."

"I'm almost to your floor . . ."

"I'm opening the door . . ."

"The elevator is stopped . . ."

Amber stepped out of her apartment and looked down the hall toward the elevator. She heard the door sliding open . . . and smiled when she saw him. His phone was still against his ear. "Hi" she softly greeted.

His dark eyes met hers. "Hi, yourself." His long legs moved his body toward her. "I had to see you but I can't stay long." His phone snapped shut and went into his pants pocket just before he reached her.

Shutting off her phone, Amber watched as he moved close to where she stood. Before she realized it, his arms moved around her as his mouth covered hers. Taking only a moment to get her thoughts together, Amber's lips parted as an invitation for his tongue. Things became heated instantly, not caring that they were in the middle of the hall. Reluctantly, she pulled away, trying to catch her breath. "Let's get into my apartment." Taking his hand in hers, Amber led Ricky out of the hall and he closed the door behind them before drawing her back into his arms.

The kiss deepened. Ricky then held her face between his hands and pulled back, his breathing fast and hard. Seeing the glazed look he had seen so often in her eyes, he knew Amber was ready for him . . . but he wisely knew it was too soon. Her mouth moved toward his but he jerked back. "Listen to me" he told her, his breathing still not close to normal. "I am *so* sorry for the phone call late last night."

"No . . . don't. Not now." Her mouth reached for his again . . . and that time he let her.

They were lost in the moment, not thinking of anything but themselves . . . until Jake's voice quickly brought them back to earth: "Hey, Amber! Do you know where I . . . *Oh, shit*! *Shit*! I'm sorry! Ricky! . . . I didn't know you were here!"

The two quickly separated.

"What do you need, Jake?" Amber asked, keeping her eyes on Ricky since she was too embarrassed to look at her brother at the moment.

"Nothing right now. I'll see you later."

"That's okay, Jake. What is it?" By then, she could look in his direction.

"I was packing and can't find . . . oh, never mind. It can wait." Jake turned to leave them alone.

"That's right . . . you head out tomorrow, don't you?" Ricky called after him.

Turning back, Jake replied, "Yeah and I'm hoping to be on the road by six . . . to miss some of the weekend traffic."

"Well, look . . . I've got to go. I have something to take care of. And this is your last night to be with your sister and niece" Ricky told him.

"Over two weeks together has been plenty." Jake then laughed at the face Amber made at him.

"But I do have to go." Ricky looked at Amber. "I had to see you . . . and apologize."

Jake cleared his throat. "Take care, Ricky. It was good to see you. I'll get back to my packing."

Holding out his hand to Jake, Ricky said, "Drive safe. I'm glad you were here for Amber."

Jake clasped Ricky's hand in his. "I'm glad, too. Catch ya later." He then disappeared into the hall and the quiet sound of his bedroom door closing could be heard.

Not wanting Ricky to leave just yet, Amber asked, "Don't you want to see Becky?"

"Is she awake?"

"The last I knew she wasn't but you can still go in to look at her."

Hesitating only a moment, he agreed and followed Amber to Becky's room.

He gazed down at his sleeping daughter, taking in every detail. The long fingers of one hand lay extended on her chest while her other hand lay beside her head. For the first time he noticed that she had his long, dark eyelashes. He couldn't get over how beautiful she was and was still in awe that she was his. "Isn't she something?" he whispered.

"She sure is . . . we made her."

Ricky felt a tenderness he hadn't experienced for a long time. Looking at Amber, he caressed her cheek. She smiled, then closed her eyes, feeling pure bliss in each touch he gave her. Watching her lips part, Ricky, knowing he had to go, had to taste her mouth one more time. Cupping her face again, his lips grazed hers once . . . then again . . . and again . . . before using his tongue to stroke her bottom lip. With a low moan, her lips opened more . . . and his tongue slid inside. The kiss deepened . . . his hands slid down her back and pressed her body against his. She felt his erection and with a moan, pushed her hips even tighter against him. Uttering a groan, Ricky suddenly backed away from her.

"This has to stop, Amber. You're driving me crazy."

"What do you think you're doing to me?"

He looked at her, listening to her breathing, watching her breasts rise and fall with each breath. Meeting her eyes again, he quietly told her, "One day at a time, Amber. I have to take care of things with Deana before we can get things going between us . . . so now I have to talk to Deana."

Her body tensed. "You're going to see Deana *now*?"

Nodding, he said, "I'll talk to you later." Ricky gently kissed her mouth before reaching down to gently touch his daughter's head.

They walked to the door side by side but didn't touch. Ricky opened the door but then looked back at Amber. "Don't look so sad" he softly told her. "You should be happy about what I'm going to do."

Just come back to me. Amber gave him a smile. "Call me."

"I will." After another gentle kiss, he was gone.

"Ricky's gone?"

Amber looked up from the couch at Jake. "Yeah . . . about ten minutes ago."

"What's wrong?" He walked over to sit on the couch.

Shrugging her shoulders, she replied, "I don't know. I can't shake the feeling that something will go wrong when he sees Deana."

"That's what he had to take care of?"

"That's what he told me."

"Well, that's a good thing, isn't it?"

"Well . . . yeah . . ."

"So, why the glum face?"

Suddenly, Amber stood. "Okay . . . no more glum face . . . for now. I'll have that when you leave in the morning. So, anyway . . . let's make sure that you haven't forgot to pack anything. Lisa will not be happy if you have to drive back down here for something you forgot."

"She'd tell me to buy another one." Jake stood beside Amber.

Putting her arms around him, she rested her head against his shoulder. "I'm going to miss you being around."

He hugged Amber. "You can always come back with me."

"No, I can't. I have to stay and make it work with Ricky."

Giving her a quick squeeze, Jake said, "You'll do it."

"I hope so."

* * *

Ricky kept his keys in his pocket as he walked toward the door to Deana's apartment. He had taken the key to her place off his key ring, planning to give it back to her. Standing outside the door, he took a deep breath and slowly let it out as he knocked.

She must have looked through the peephole because he heard her unlock the door before opening it. "Hi!" she greeted with a smile. "What happened? Did you lose your key?"

"No."

Looking puzzled, Deana echoed, "No?"

Not waiting to be asked, he stepped inside. "We have to talk."

"About what?" Deana closed the door.

His eyes met hers. "You and me . . . us . . . Amber . . ."

Her eyes narrowed. "Three's a crowd."

"I never lied to you about her . . . I was always upfront about my feelings for her."

"You told me you would never go back to her, no matter how much she begged."

"I did say that . . . but that was in anger. We all say things we don't mean when we're angry."

Deana stared at Ricky, knowing what was coming but not believing it would really happen. He cared for her, she knew he did. Amber was somebody that he loved and *she* left him . . . only to return pregnant. Deana knew she would never leave him . . . and she wouldn't get pregnant unless he wanted her to. "So . . . what are you trying to tell me?"

He sighed. "Do I have to spell it out for you, Deana?"

"*Yes*!" she exploded. "Spell it out for me . . . letter by letter!"

"I want my life back with Amber. I want my baby in my life every day! I'm sorry, Deana but I love Amber . . . I always have. You've been great . . . you've put up with a lot but I can't ask you to do that that any more . . . it wasn't fair of me in the first place. I never meant to hurt you. Find someone who will love and treat you like you should be . . ."

"I *don't want anybody else*!" Deana walked toward Ricky. "You are the best guy I have ever met. Amber must have finally figured that out and came back for you." Stopping about a foot away, Deana asked him, "If she had never come back, would you ever have loved *me*?"

"I don't know" he answered honestly. "I probably could if I ever got her out of my head." *And my heart*, he almost added.

"Well, you still have the same job she left you for in the first place. Will she deal with it now? *I* doubt it."

"I'm hoping she does *deal with it now*, Deana. I want her to stay with me."

"Do you want to marry her?"

He shrugged. "Someday . . ."

"It won't ever happen, Ricky! She'll be gone the first time there's shooting with a case you're involved with . . . or something will scare her off! And she'll go, taking that precious baby of yours with her!"

Why did he ever tell Deana the facts of Amber leaving? He became angry when he had started telling her about it . . . and he couldn't stop. But he had been silent about it for too long . . . not even talking to A.J. about it much. When Deana asked questions, Ricky felt the need to answer them but had regretted it more than once ever since. And now Deana had his feelings for his daughter to use for more ammo. "She told me she won't ever leave again."

"And you *believe* her?"

"Yes."

"That's only because you want to. You'll be sorry, Ricky."

The conversation was getting to be too much for him. "I didn't set out to hurt you, Deana."

She shrugged her shoulders. "You'll be back."

He clamped his mouth shut, not wanting to grab at any of the bait Deana threw at him about Amber. Instead, he started toward the bathroom.

"Where are you going?" she asked.

"To collect my things."

Standing in the doorway, Deana watched as Ricky put together in a pile on the sink: a comb, an electric razor, after-shave, deodorant and toothbrush. Gathering everything up, he walked past her to the bedroom, where he set them on the bed and then slid open the closet door. Pulling out a brown leather bag off the floor, he tossed in what was on the bed before going to the dresser and opening a drawer for two pairs of boxers and socks. Walking to the bed, he shoved them into the bag before returning to the closet for two dress shirts and a work suit. Carrying the clothes on their hangers, Ricky grabbed the bag off the bed with his other hand and walked to the door, where Deana stood, still watching him. Their eyes met.

"She will leave you, you know."

"Drop it, Deana." Walking around her, he started toward the door.

"What about work?" Stopping, he asked, "What about it?"

"Can we work together? Do you still want to work with me?"

Turning to look at her, he said, "We just keep it professional like we always have. Can you work with me?"

"I need my job . . . I like my job . . . I like working with A.J . . . and *you.*"

He shrugged. "Just keep it professional" he repeated. His eyes met hers again. "Good-bye, Deana." She watched as the door closed behind Ricky. When she heard it click shut, her tears fell. It hurt, knowing he was gone from her life. There had never been another man like him. But when he had told her that Amber was back, she knew this day was coming, no matter what he had said about her. He was right, he had always been upfront about his feelings for Amber. Deana knew that she was just somebody in his life that would never have all of him . . . never have his heart. But it didn't hurt to try, did it? Wiping the tears off her face, she walked to the couch to sit. He would be back . . . if she worked it right, Ricky would be hers again.

* * *

Jake quietly knocked on the doorframe to the nursery while Amber nursed Becky. She gave him a smile when she looked up. "You're up early." Not hurrying, she placed a receiving blanket over her and the baby.

It was 4 A.M..

"I didn't plan on getting up for another hour but I heard Becky and decided to get up. I'm all packed. And I stripped the bed and put the sheets in the hamper."

"Thanks."

"Is coffee ready?"

"No . . . I didn't think you'd be up this soon."

"I'll take care of it." He started to go into the hall but stopped. "Want any?"

"Maybe a half a cup. I'll join you shortly."

They talked for an hour. Jake held his sleeping niece while sitting at the kitchen table. At 5:30, he got up off the chair. "Do you want her back in her room or the living room?" he asked Amber.

"The living room."

After placing Becky on her back in the bassinet, he whispered, "I'm sure gonna miss you, little girl."

Amber stood back as she watched, and tears filled her eyes. When Jake straightened and turned toward her, she saw the tears in his eyes. Pinching the bridge of his nose, he tightly closed his eyes and inhaled deeply. Amber knew that he didn't want to cry in front of her, so she pretended that the arm covers on the recliner needed to be straightened.

"My bags are packed" Jake said again

"I noticed they were by the door."

Putting an arm across her shoulders, Jake walked Amber into the foyer. "I am sorry Ricky didn't call you last night. Something must have come up."

"Uh-huh" she muttered.

"Hopefully he'll call today."

"Yep."

Jake checked his pockets for his keys and phone. "It's time for me to go, sis."

"I know." The tears she fought to hold back won. Hugging him tightly, she said, "Thanks *so* much for being here."

Returning her hug, he replied, "I wouldn't have missed it for the world."

Amber had to laugh. "But you didn't want to be there in the first place, remember?"

With a grin, Jake said, "I'm glad you dragged me in with you."

Kissing his cheek, she said, "You took time away from work . . . and Lisa . . . to be with me through everything."

He gave her a quick squeeze. "You and Ricky will work things out. Remember . . . give him time."

She sighed. "Yeah, if he decides to call me again."

"Oh, stop! He will . . . I know he will."

"I'm glad you're so sure. But back to you . . . be sure to call when you get home."

"I will." After giving her another hug, Jake picked up his two duffel bags. "'Bye, sis."

"Drive careful."

"I always do."

"Watch out for the idiot drivers."

"Yes, Mom."

Amber opened the door for him.

"Be sure to visit. I need to hold that baby again before she gets too big to hold."

"We will. Love ya, Jake."

"Don't cry." "I won't" she said with a smile as she wiped away the tears on her cheeks.

"Love you, too, Amber." And with that said, Jake was out the door.

Amber watched and waited till he was in the elevator before stepping back and closing the door.

After locking up, the apartment was way too quiet.

* * *

"Hi, Sara! How are you? I haven't been avoiding you . . . honest!"

"Hey, Amber! We're both well. How about you?"

"Coping so far with being a mom."

"How is that little one?"

"Doing well . . . but not walking yet."

Sara laughed. Then, "We have talked about getting over to see you but as you know, we didn't make it over yet. Is Jake still there?"

Amber's voice was soft. "He left early this morning."

"You're so lucky to have a brother like him."

"I know."

"So, how do you like being a mom?"

"Do you have a couple of hours?"

With a laugh, Sara replied, "As a matter of fact, I do!"

Over an hour later, their conversation was still going but Becky woke and demanded attention.

"I'll let you go take care of her "Sara said. "I'm so glad you called."

"Before I forget, do you and A.J. have plans for dinner tomorrow? If you don't, I'd love to have you come over."

"We'd love to see you! But are you up to cooking a meal?" "Jake didn't spoil me *that* much!" Amber laughed.

"Is Ricky joining us?"

The question surprised Amber. "I didn't ask him." "Oh . . . well then . . . what time should we be there?"

"Two . . . if that's good for you."

"That sounds good. What can we bring?"

"Just yourselves."

"We should help with something."

"Why? *I* asked *you* over."

Sara chuckled. "Okay . . . you got me on that one!"

After their good-byes, Amber took Becky out of her cradle, changed her diaper, then sat in the rocking chair to nurse her. Thinking about what Sara had asked her about Ricky and dinner the next day, Amber made up her mind to call Ricky. He never did call her after going to see Deana the night before. Did he end up staying with her? Amber shuddered at the thought. But she would still call him. No . . . wait. She didn't have his number. An over-sight? Or didn't he want her to have it? It came to her that he had called her a couple of times. Hopefully the number would be on the Caller ID. Or did it come up once as an unlisted number? Only one way to find out. And if it was there, she would give him a call. If not, she would find out what it was.

* * *

Chapter 16

A.J. answered when she called. "Hey, darlin'! I hear we're having dinner at your place tomorrow."

"You heard right. But that's not why I'm calling."

"What's up?"

"Would you please give me Ricky's phone number? I found out it's unlisted."

There was silence on the other end of the phone.

"A.J.?"

"Yeah . . . I'm here. Your question took me by surprise for some reason. I don't know why I can't give it to you . . . I gave your's to him."

After writing down the number, she said, "Thanks. I'm going to ask him to join us tomorrow. So, I have to let you go before I get busy and forget."

A.J. chuckled. "Okay . . . !"

Taking a deep breath and slowly letting it out, Amber dialed the number she had gotten from A.J.. Why did she feel so nervous? After listening to his phone ring five times, Amber was ready to hang up when his voice mail came on. Almost hanging up, she decided at the last moment to leave a message: "Hi, Ricco . . . you know who this is. Um . . . Sara and A.J. are joining me for dinner tomorrow . . . would you like to join us? A.J. gave me your number since I didn't have it. Let me know . . . Hope you can make it."

Shutting off the phone, Amber placed it on the coffee table then sat back on the couch. Where was he? Why hadn't he called her? . . . Was he still at Deana's? Grabbing the remote off the coffee table, she put her feet on the edge of the table and turned on the TV to start channel surfing. Nothing caught her eye. Her mind wasn't on the TV . . . it was on Ricky. Minutes later, her phone rang and she grabbed it. "Hello?"

"Amber? Is anything wrong? Is Becky okay?" Ricky sounded out of breath.

"Didn't you listen to my message?"

"No . . . I just got out of the shower. I looked to see if anybody had called . . . and saw your name. Is everything all right?"

"Yes . . . I just wanted to know if you wanted . . ." And she repeated her message.

After a long pause, he replied, "Thanks . . . but no. Sorry, Amber."

"Oh." She was disappointed. She then asked, "Um . . . is there any connection with you not coming here for dinner and with you not calling me last night after seeing Deana?"

There was another long pause before he said, "I'm sorry I didn't call . . . I know I told you that I would. But I just needed some time to think . . ."

"Think? About what? About me and Becky . . . or not being with Deana any more? Does that bother you? Well, I'm sorry but you can't have all three of us any more. Decide who you want and let me know . . . and I hope it doesn't take too long."

It took a moment for Ricky to realize that Amber had hung up on him. Rubbing his hands over his face, he thought about calling her back and accepting her dinner invitation. But he didn't feel like being with her, Sara and A.J. the next day. Deana had called that morning and started in on how Amber wouldn't stick around if he went back to her . . . he got disgusted and shut off his phone. And now he pissed Amber off and he knew he hurt her . . . again She seemed to be so sincere with her vow to never leave him again. He wanted to believe but that small part of him wouldn't let go of her leaving him.

Ricky yanked off the towel that he wore around his waist, opened the hamper and threw the towel inside before slamming the lid down. After pulling on a pair of boxers, he went toward the living room, stopping at the refrigerator. Sitting in his favorite chair, he opened a can of beer and took a long, cold drink before aiming the remote at the television.

* * *

Amber was restless. She couldn't stop thinking about her last conversation with Ricky. She fed and changed Becky then kept her nearby until she fell asleep. Amber then folded laundry and swept the kitchen floor. Glancing at the phone every so often, she thought about calling him to find out what was going on. Did he mean *anything* that he had been telling her? His change in attitude always seem to come after he had seen Deana.

She missed having Jake there to talk to. He had called earlier to let her know that he had made it home safe and sound. Their conversation was short. He was tired after the long drive. Amber felt even more depressed after that call ended.

The apartment seemed too big and too quiet.

* * *

Dinner with Sara and A.J. was a good idea. It took her mind off Ricky . . . he hadn't called her yet. Amber's company arrived a little before the set time and A.J. handed her a bouquet of red and yellow roses when she opened the door. "Hey, darlin' . . . these are for you."

"I told you not to bring anything . . . but these are beautiful." She smiled.

Sara hugged her then asked, "M-m-m-m! What smells *so* good?"

"Lasagna."

"Where's the baby?" A.J. wanted to know

"In the bassinet in the living room."

"Is she awake?"

"She wasn't but could be by now. Even if she isn't, you can pick her up."

Dinner went well. Conversation was good . . . as always. And Ricky's name wasn't mentioned.

Amber asked if anyone wanted dessert. "No more! Take pity on me! That third helping of that delicious lasagna did me in!" A.J. moaned.

"He's right . . . there's no more room. Between salad, bread and the lasagna, there *isn't* any place to add more!" Sara said.

"It was very good, darlin'. Thanks for inviting us over" A.J. added.

"We should get together more often" Amber remarked, standing to start collecting dishes. "Though I shouldn't eat like this too much . . . I'd *never* lose this weight I gained while pregnant!"

"You look good" A.J. told her.

"Thanks but I still want to lose a few more pounds. You saw how big I was with Becky."

"It takes time, Amber. And didn't I read somewhere that the weight comes off faster when breast feeding?"

A.J. stood. "I think it's time for me to leave the room and spend time with my little princess."

"You read right, Sara" Amber replied, watching as A.J. went into the living room. "And I have lost some weight . . . just not fast enough for me, I guess."

"You'll get there." Sara picked the glasses up with her fingers. "You never mentioned Ricky. A.J. told me that you were calling him to invite him to join us today."

"I did." Amber carried the plates and silverware to the dishwasher.

"And he said no." Sara sat the glasses on the counter for Amber.

"How'd you guess?" She put the dishes into the dishwasher.

"I know he's been here to see you. He's told A.J.."

Amber shrugged, fighting her tears. "I don't know what's up with him, Sara. He tells me that he loves me and wants it to work out between us but then he backs off . . . disappears . . . doesn't call when he says he's going to . . ." The tears won, sliding down her face . . . and she wiped them away with both hands. She noticed that Sara looked behind her, and she knew that A.J. was there. He then spoke:

"He wants so much to believe in you, Amber. Ricky loves you . . . he never stopped. And now he's totally in love with this little girl of yours . . ."

Amber turned to find Becky nestled in A.J.'s arms, looking up at him as he talked. She had been fed shortly before their guests arrived and Amber hoped it would be awhile before she was hungry again. Her eyes met A.J.'s. "I did call him . . ." she quietly said. "And I guess you could say that I gave him an ultimatum . . . us or her."

He softly replied: "Deana's not making it easy for him."

Amber's eyes filled with tears.

Sara's hand rested on Amber's shoulder. "Go in and sit with A.J. while I finish up in here." When Amber opened her mouth to protest, Sara said, "Now, git! No argument."

A.J. chuckled. "I'd listen if I were you . . . you won't win, darlin'."

It was shortly after six when Sara and A.J. went home with a container of left-over lasagna.

Amber was sad to have them leave . . . the apartment was quiet again.

* * *

After putting a sleeping baby into her cradle, Amber stopped at her own room to get the paperback book she had been reading. Getting comfortable in her recliner, she then opened the book and was ready to read when there was a hard knock on the door. Frowning, Amber went to the door and looked through the peephole. Ricky stood on the other side of the door. Closing her eyes, she took a deep breath before opening it. "Hi" she quietly greeted.

"Can I come in?"

Stepping back, Amber waited for Ricky to walk in and then closed the door. She wasn't going to ask how he got in this time. But the question that she asked just slipped out without her thinking about it: "You've made up your mind so soon?"

He spun around to face her, his handsome face hard. "No, Amber. I . . ."

But she interrupted. "How long do you need? A week? A month? Two months? Long enough for you to be with your other woman until *I* can have sex? Yeah . . . let's do that. We always had great sex. And when you do decide to come back, we can make a brother or sister for Becky . . ."

"*Stop it*!"

"No! I'm sick of this whole thing! Either you want me or you don't . . . you chance it or you don't . . . it's that simple!"

"*Listen to me*!"

"*No* ! I know I hurt you . . . I can't apologize enough! And I can't seem to make you believe that I won't do it again! Jake told me that I have to earn your trust again . . . but damn it! Why won't you give me a break? You have a beautiful daughter . . . but you did doubt that she was yours when I was pregnant with her. So, if you don't want *us*, say so, because we'll move upstate and you will be able to have Deana free and clear." Amber impatiently wiped at the tears on her face.

"Stop it."

"And you seem to get an *I don't want to see you or talk to you* attitude after you talk to *her*. Please correct me if I'm wrong." Once she started with all that had been on her mind, Amber couldn't stop.

"What's gotten into you?"

"*Oh, no*! Don't go turning this on me! Either you want me or you don't."

"Amber . . . *don't do this.*"

"Come on, Ricky! You told me that I could take all the time I needed to prove to you that I'm here for good but you know what? I'm done trying to convince you! You keep coming to me, making me think that you're here to stay and then *she* speaks and you listen, shutting me out. I can't do it any more!"

Ricky's eyes flashed. "Amber! Will you listen to me?" He sounded angry.

"Okay . . . talk. Explain things to me."

"Explain what? You can't explain to me why you couldn't call or come back to me after you walked out . . . or explain why you couldn't call to let me know that you were pregnant. So, what do you want to hear? There's no words to describe how I felt when I finally realized that you were gone for good . . . that you *weren't* going to call or come back to me. Work was the only thing that held me together. Isn't it ironic that what kept me from falling apart was what drove you away? And then Deana came to work at the squad. At first I wasn't interested in her. It was over a month before I finally accepted an invitation to have coffee with her. I told her about you, not thinking at the time about getting involved with anyone. I talked and she listened. It was different with her . . . she wasn't A.J. and Sara, who knew you so well. Deana hung in there, trying to keep my mind off you. A month or so later, we went out for dinner and then I accepted her offer to go back to her place . . . where I spent the night."

Amber's body stiffened at his words.

"What's wrong? I thought you wanted me to explain things . . . and Deana's part of the explanation. I loved *you*, Amber . . . and I hoped that she could take away the hurt. It took a long time before you weren't in my thoughts *all* the time. Deana knew but *she* didn't leave me. But then, oh!, out of the blue, you come back, messing with my life . . . and Deana's."

More tears fell. "Then stay with her."

"I don't want to." It was Amber he wanted . . . and he was wrong to let Deana's words keep him away from her and their baby. If he was making a mistake, that would be on him, one he had to find out for sure. No more *what if's*.

Amber turned away, walking toward the living room. Ricky followed, stepping into the room just in time to hear her say, "The first time I felt Becky kick, I was so excited! I was in my room, where I spent most of my time. My first thought was of you, how I wanted to call and let you know.

I even picked up the phone before realizing that I couldn't do it. I hurried downstairs to find my dad, who was at his desk in the den.He held me like he used to when I was little and got hurt. I cried while telling him about the baby kicking and he listened as I rambled on about how you should know. And again, he *told* me to call you . . ." She turned her head to look at Ricky as the tears slid down her face. "I couldn't . . . I couldn't make myself call you."

"You should have" he quietly said.

"And said what? 'Oh, hi, Ricco . . . I'm pregnant with your baby and just felt it kick. Just how awesome was that? I wanted to let you know . . .'." Her voice broke and she started to sob.

Quickly crossing the room, Ricky wrapped her in his arms, holding her close as she cried. He shed a few tears of his own when he heard the anguish in her sobs. With her face against his shoulder, Amber tried to speak: "I wanted to . . . I should have called you . . . I love you so much . . . but I couldn't . . . I was afraid . . ."

Amber cried till she couldn't cry any more.

Ricky kissed the top of her head. "Are you all right?"

"Yes" was her muffled reply, as she spoke with her face against his shoulder.

"Let's sit down."

Amber pulled a tissue out of a box on an end table to wipe her face and blow her nose before sitting beside Ricky on the couch. "Sorry" she muttered. "I didn't cry to make you feel sorry for me."

"Don't be sorry. We've both been under a lot of stress lately."

Amber sighed. "I have no more secrets. You just heard everything."

Ricky gently pushed some hair back from her face. "I told Deana that she and I are done."

Her eyes were red and puffy when she looked at him, not quite believing what she had just heard. "And you're *just* telling me this? Why didn't you tell me when you first got here?"

His eyes met hers. "Because you didn't give me the chance. You gave me an *attitude* the moment I walked in."

"But you let me rant and rave . . ."

Ricky's eyes narrowed. "Again, you never gave me a chance . . . I couldn't get a word in edge-wise."

Amber returned his look. "But you had a lot to say when you talked about Deana."

"You asked . . . that was how I met Deana . . . but I *never* loved her."

Opening her mouth to reply, Amber then shut it. She didn't want to argue with him any more. But she *had* to know one more thing . . . "What did she say to keep you away?"

His shoulders shrugged before his eyes met hers. "She said some things that made me think . . . and foolishly kept me away from you."

"She said things? Like what?"

"They're not important now."

"*What* did she say?"

Taking a deep breath then letting it out, Ricky replied, "She said something about how easily you walked out before and what would stop you from doing it again, except the next time you'll be taking Becky with you."

"She knows *nothing* about me or what happened that night."

"She only knows what I told her."

Amber moved back from him and her voice sounded a bit cold when she said, "You talked to *her* about *that* night?"

"I didn't think I would ever see you again."

"And even now that I'm here, you believe what she tells you and you don't call me or come to see me. *How could you*?"

He sighed. "Look . . . I know I was wrong! She doesn't want me to leave her."

"*So*? So you believe what she says about me? *She* doesn't know me!" Standing suddenly, Amber moved away from the couch. "I can't believe you listened to her! Don't we have enough problems?"

Angrily, she walked toward the kitchen doorway. "I need you to talk *to me* . . . to work things out . . . and instead you listen to *her*!" Amber sputtered. She suddenly turned around, saying, "*Why* do you . . ." She stopped in mid-sentence when she found Ricky standing right in front of her. His hands grabbed her by the upper arms and pulled her to him. "Shut-up, Amber" he muttered, before covering her mouth with his. She resisted at first but he held on and then his arms moved around her when her lips parted for him.

When the kiss ended, Amber looked at Ricky. Breathing hard, she asked, "Did you really tell me to shut-up?"

"Yes . . . and I'd do it again." His mouth found hers once more as his body moved closer.

That time Amber didn't resist. Her hands framed his face as they kissed, before they slid down over his body, enjoying the feel of his broad, solid back and his solid chest. Her mouth sucked his tongue as her hands continued on down to his tight abdomen. Ricky groaned into her mouth when her hands slid slowly over his throbbing erection. She moaned as her fingers explored, remembering the size of him. With her fingers fumbling, she tried to unbuckle his belt. It had been too long without Ricky . . . Amber was desperate to touch him without his clothes in the way.

The belt finally opened.

But Ricky's hand stopped hers. "No, Amber." His voice sounded husky.

"Please let me, Ricco" she whispered. She tried to move his hand. "You know I can make you feel better in more ways than one . . . I know you remember."

"Oh, I remember. But this isn't what I wanted for our first time together after all this time . . . Is it what you really want?"

Her eyes looked into his for a long moment before admitting, "No."

"It'll be here sooner than we think." Ricky hugged her. "We just have to stop driving each other crazy."

"I know . . . but that'll be easier said than done." Her body pressed against his. "I want you so much."

"I want you, too" he breathed in her ear.

They stood holding one another, not speaking. But suddenly, Ricky quietly said, "I won't let you move back upstate."

Her heart pounded, extremely happy to hear those words. But she had to ask, "How would you stop me?"

"I don't know . . . but I would."

* * *

Chapter 17

The following Wednesday morning was Becky's first doctor's appointment at 9:45.

Her daddy went, too.

Ricky carried the diaper bag while Amber carried Becky in the baby sling. As he walked beside them, Ricky's hand was pressed lightly against Amber's lower back.

She enjoyed the feel of his touch.

The waiting room was quite full with mothers, grandmothers and children, who ranged in ages from infant to five years. After signing in and filling out paperwork, Amber sat beside Ricky in one of the two chairs he had been lucky to find empty. He placed the diaper bag on the floor next to his feet and looked around the crowded room. "Geez" he muttered.

"What did you tell them at work?"

"That I would be in in a couple of hours. I don't know about that . . ." He looked around the room again.

"You don't have to stay . . ."

"But I am." He wrapped his fingers around her hand and held on.

Amber smiled up at him. Her love for him grew even more at that moment.

They had a twenty-five minute wait in the waiting room and another ten in the examining room before Dr. Marley walked in. Thirty-ish, medium height and slim, with blond hair and wire-framed glasses, he greeted Amber and Ricky with a warm smile. "Sorry about the wait." His smile grew when he spotted Becky in her mother's arms. "And this has to be Rebecca . . ."

Becky was weighed and had lost a pound and a half since her birth. "*Lost*?" Amber found that hard to believe. "With the way she eats, she should have *gained* five pounds!"

"It's normal for a baby to lose weight the first week or so after birth. It's good she eats well. You're nursing?"

"Yes."

"It's good that you have enough milk for her. Your baby is doing well. Keep up the good work."

* * *

Ricky had planned on taking Amber and the baby back to the apartment but Amber had other ideas. "There's a couple of stops I want to make before going home."

"Oh? Okay, I'll give you a ride."

"No, that's okay. You have to get to work."

Even though he wore his 'sexy' sunglasses, Amber felt his stare.

"How do you plan on getting around?"

"Taxi . . . walk . . ."

He wasn't too keen on the walking part. "Where do you want to go first? I'll drop you off on my way to the precinct."

"To the T-shirt shop."

"Want to show off our daughter, huh?" There was no mistaking the pride in his voice.

Amber smiled. "I have to! Jake and I spent the day before Becky was born with Maggie and Matt. I started having labor pains but didn't let them stop the fantastic time we were having! I was having them during the fireworks that night, too."

"I saw you there . . . remember?" Ricky quietly asked.

The image of his arms around Deana that night flashed in her head. "Yes" she whispered.

"You were having pains?"

In my heart, too, seeing you with and leaving with Deana. Amber nodded. "And my water broke the next morning . . . well, you know the rest."

He reached to stroke her cheek with the backs of his fingers. "I love you" he softly told her.

Tears filled her eyes. "I'm glad."

* * *

Not long afterwards, they stopped in front of Amber's former place of work.

"Take a cab back to your place" Ricky told her as she unbuckled her seatbelt.

"I have to stop at the drugstore, too."

"The cab will take you there."

With a noisy sigh, she replied, "Yes,*Dad*." Amber then reached for the door handle.

"Wait." Ricky gently grasped her arm. "Hey, look . . . I don't mean to sound bossy but I just don't like the idea of you wandering around alone . . . just you and the baby." He removed his sunglasses to meet her eyes. "I've seen too much with my job."

Her resentment quickly disappeared. Touching the side of his handsome face, Amber then brought his head forward to kiss his lips. "I'll call a cab" she told him after the kiss but her lips brushed over his as she spoke.

"*Amber* . . ." Ricky groaned her name before his hand slid behind her head to bring her mouth to his to kiss her . . . hard.

The baby moved as if to remind her parents that she was between them. Amber gently touched the top of her head. "Sorry, baby girl" she murmured, then looked up at Ricky. He noticed how puffy her lips were from his kiss . . . and he wanted to kiss her again . . . but said instead, "I'll see you later."

"Okay." She smiled as she opened the door. "Tell A.J. I said 'Hi'."

"I will."

As Amber got out of the car, she tried to push away the thought that Deana still worked with him . . .

* * *

The familiar tinkle of the bells on the door brought a smile to Amber's mouth when she stepped into the shop. She anxiously looked for somebody to be behind the counter but it was empty. "Just a minute!" a voice she recognized called from the door behind the counter. Moments later, he appeared in the doorway, brushing something off the sleeve of his shirt.

"Sorry . . . how may I help you?" Matt then raised his head . . . and his eyes widened while his jaw dropped.

"I'm tempted to ask for my job back" Amber teased, smiling.

"I'm tempted to take you up on that" he replied, making his way around the counter. "Look at you!" Matt exclaimed, reaching to hug Amber when he noticed what she was carrying on the front of her body. "Will you look at her?"

"Where is everybody? Out back?"

"Well, everybody but Hank. He had to drive to Jersey."

"I hope he gets back before I leave

"Me, too. He'll be disappointed if he doesn't get to see you and the baby." He kissed Amber's cheek before taking her hand in his. "Come on . . . let's go surprise some people."

It was a good thing that Becky was used to being held by a lot of people. Maggie was the first to see Amber walk in with Matt. She let out a squeal, then rushed to her for a hug. With a soft, "Oh-h-h-h!", Maggie took Becky out of the sling. "Look at you!" she cooed, looking at Becky. "What a beauty you are!"

Steve, Merrie, Scotty and Nell stopped what they were doing to circle around Amber, greeting her with hugs. She was very happy to see them, having worked with them for over a year. When she left Ricky, these were more people she had left behind. But none of them mentioned how she had just disappeared. They were happy to see her.

Steve and Merrie were in their mid-twenties and both were tall and slim. Scotty was in his early thirties and the jokester of the group. He thrived on making everyone laugh. Amber tugged on his blond hair that was long enough to be in a ponytail. "What's this?"

He grinned. "It's my new look! Don't ya like it?"

Nell was the oldest of the group at fifty-five. She was the 'mother-hen' and treated everyone as if they were her kids. "What a surprise to hear about the baby! We're all so happy for you! But we wondered if we would ever get to see the two of you."

"Sorry I took so long but here we are . . . finally!"

Becky was good as everyone took turns to hold her. She even stayed awake as each of them talked their baby talk. When Steve held her, she smiled, which he gloated about. But Nell felt she had to explain: "I doubt that was a smile at her age. It was most likely gas."

Amber stayed for an hour. Maggie and Matt took turns with customers and hurried back as soon as they could.But then it was time for Amber to leave. "I have another stop to make" she explained during their protests. "And I have to get home. I still tire a little easier than before I was pregnant."

"Come back to see us. Don't be a stranger" Scotty told her.

"You could come back to work . . . and you wouldn't even need a day care" Merrie said. "There are more than enough sitters here!"

"That's true!"

"We wish you luck" Merrie said, hugging Amber. "But we miss you around here."

"I miss you guys, too." After giving everyone a hug, Amber put Becky into the sling.

"What a great invention" Steve commented.

"You aren't kidding." Amber agreed.

Maggie and Matt walked to the door with Amber. "Tell Hank I'm sorry I missed him. Now I'll have to get back here so I *can* get to see him!" Hugging each of them, she felt sad to go.

"Let me call you a cab" Matt offered.

Forgetting Ricky's warning, she replied, "No thanks. I feel like walking for a little while. I don't get out as much as I used to."

"Well, visit any time" Maggie said. "And I hope it'll be soon."

* * *

Amber knew there was a drug store on the way as she walked toward home. There were things she needed for herself and the baby, with disposable diapers at the top of the list. There were many others walking and most of them walked faster than Amber was. While waiting for a light at a busy intersection, Becky started to fuss. "Oh, you're hungry, aren't you?" Amber cooed but angry with herself for not realizing how much time had gone by. She gently bounced the baby to calm her. "We'll be home soon, Becky."

The light changed and the crowd moved, taking Amber and Becky along with them. Becky complained and Amber tried to get her bearings on where she was. She cursed herself for not taking a cab like she told Ricky she would do. Spotting the drugstore sign ahead, Amber knew they were closer to home but still had at least two blocks to go. By the time they reached the door to the store, Becky was letting it be known that she was hungry and upset. Amber had never heard her cry like that . . . had never waited so long to feed her. Not knowing what else to do, Amber started for home. The drugstore would have to wait. She moved to the curb, looking for a cab. Of course, there were none available for her. She started walking again.

"*Amber*!"

Recognizing Ricky's voice, she stopped and turned, looking for him. He was across the street, getting out from behind the wheel of a vehicle she didn't know. "Daddy's here" she said to her crying daughter.

After he finally made his way across to them, Ricky saw the relief in Amber's eyes. "What's wrong?"

"She's hungry. I stayed too long at the shop and then I didn't take a cab from there and now I can't get one."

"Come on. I'll get you home." With his arm around her shoulders, they made their way back across the street. Ricky held out his free hand to slow traffic; a few horns sounded their disapproval.

There was somebody else in the Durango. Amber smiled,thinking it was A.J.. But the smile disappeared when the door on the passenger side opened and out stepped Deana, who looked miserable. "What the hell are you doing?" she asked Ricky.

"You can sit in the back" he told her.

Deana looked at him, clearly not believing what he had just said.

Seeing the look, Amber quickly said, "No, I'll sit in the back. Becky needs to be fed."

Ricky paused briefly to glare at Deana before opening the back door for Amber. He helped the crying Becky out of the sling and held her as Amber got into the car. She grabbed a receiving blanket out of the diaper bag and then opened her shirt before reaching for her daughter. Deana slid into the front seat when Ricky asked Amber, "All set?" Amber nodded and he closed the door. Becky found her mother's breast and the crying stopped. Amber looked up to meet Ricky's eyes in the rearview mirror, before he pulled out into traffic. Deana stared out the front window.

"Did you go to the drugstore?" Ricky asked Amber.

"No . . . she was too upset. I'll go later."

"Make a list . . . I'll go."

Finding a pen and paper in her purse, Amber wrote down what she needed, then reached for her wallet. "Don't worry about that" Ricky said, looking at her in the mirror again.

They stopped for a red light. Ricky offered her a smile in the mirror. After returning it, Amber glanced at Deana. What do you say to your baby's father's ex-lover? So, she tried with, "Hello, Deana. I'm . . ."

"I know who you are, *Amber*" Deana interrupted. Her voice sounded stiff as she talked to the windshield.

Ricky's head snapped sideways to look at her but he didn't say anything.

Minutes later, he pulled into a parking spot near Amber's apartment building. He shut off the engine but left the keys in the ignition. "I'll be back" he told Deana, as he opened his door. "We have to get back to the squad."

"I know" was his short reply before shutting the door hard. Opening the door for Amber, he took her purse and the diaper bag before carefully helping her out, because Becky was still nursing. Making sure the blanket still covered her, Amber walked beside Ricky. The building wasn't too far away but far enough. She felt like the people walking past her knew that she was nursing her baby. When she commented to Ricky about it, he replied, "Remember that you're in Manhattan. Nobody is paying any attention to what you're doing."

Once inside the building, he continued walking toward the elevator with Amber. She told him, "You don't have to go up with us. I know you have to get back to work." *Deana's waiting for you.*

As he pressed the *up* button, Ricky said, "But I want to take you up." He looked at her, then leaned to kiss her lips.

A smile played at her lips when he stepped back. "You can do *that* on company time?"

"I won't tell if you don't."

The elevator arrived and they had to wait for others to get off. Being the only ones to ride up, after the door closed, Amber asked, "Where's A.J.?"

"Back at the squadroom."

"But *why* isn't he with *you*?" Embarrassed, her head dropped forward. "Sorry. I *know* you work with Deana, too."

Placing his fingers under her chin, he gently raised her head to look at him. "You have nothing to worry about." His mouth covered hers and he took his time enjoying her taste.

All too soon, they felt the elevator stop and heard the chime as the door opened. But Ricky and Amber didn't separate, not until Becky moved under the blanket and Amber knew she had had her fill. Pulling her mouth away from Ricky's, she said, "Let's go."

Inside the apartment, Amber turned to Ricky and removed the blanket. He looked at Becky and his eyes took in the sight of Amber's breast. Her body tingled at his gaze but she said, "Here" and handed his child to him. Holding Becky, he watched as Amber pulled her bra over to cover her breast and then hooked the bra together. He almost protested but forced his attention back to the baby, who was looking at him. "It's the first time I've seen her with her eyes fully open" he commented, with a smile.

"Is it like looking in a mirror?"

"Yeah . . . she does have my eyes." He gazed down at Becky for a few moments before looking at Amber. "Why didn't you get a cab like you told me you would?"

She shrugged her shoulders. "I don't know. I wanted to walk . . . to enjoy the outside. I haven't been able to do that for a couple of weeks . . ."

His cell phone rang. Ricky muttered under his breath when he checked the Caller ID before answering: "I'll be there in a minute!" he barked before closing the phone.

There was no question as to who called but Amber didn't comment.

"Give me your list and I'll be back after work" he said to her.

Her purse was in the foyer. Handing him the list, he glanced over it. "Do you need anything right away?"

"Nope. I'm all set for now."

"I'll be back after work."

Taking Becky from him, Amber asked, "Want to have supper with me?" She half expected him to decline.

"What time?"

"What time is best for you?"

"Six-thirty . . . seven?"

"That time hasn't changed" she commented. "Okay, let's plan on seven."

"I'll call if things change."

Please don't let it. "See you later."

He kissed her. "Later." And he kissed her again, a little longer this time. "I have to go . . . but I have something to look forward to." With a smile, he was gone.

* * *

"*Don't* you *ever* call me like that again!" Ricky fumed as he got into the car.

"You were gone long enough" Deana retorted.

"And who are you to keep track of my time?" He started the engine.

"I have every right when I'm sitting around waiting for you."

Finding a break in traffic, Ricky pulled away from the curb. "I was gone ten minutes."

"Fifteen . . . and see your girlfriend on your own time."

Ricky's head turned quickly to glare at her, then turned back in time to avoid hitting the U-Haul truck in front of them that had stopped for a red light.

"We should have been back to the squad by now."

"What's the big rush?" "A.J. is waiting so that the three of us can speak to the Lieutenant about the Bridger's case."

"*Shit*!" He had forgotten all about that after seeing Amber walking with the baby. "Let him know we're on our way."

"I already called to let him know what the hold up was."

"Figures" he muttered.

Deana called A.J. and Ricky only half-listened until he heard her say, ". . . he finally left his girlfriend's . . . Oh, that's right . . . you know Amber, too. Yeah, we're on our way now." She snapped her phone closed.

Ricky's hands gripped the steering wheel tightly. "This was a bad idea. I don't know why I thought it would but . . . this isn't going to work."

"What isn't?"

"You and me . . . working together . . . it's not going to work."

"Why not?"

"Because you're not keeping it very professional. I'm *not* going to deal with your little digs and comments on Amber."

Deana looked out the windshield with a scowl on her face. "Okay . . . and because you have seniority, *I'll* have to be the one to transfer?"

His answer waited till he parked outside the precinct. "Transfer? You don't have to transfer . . . unless you want to. I just meant switching partners."

*   *   *

Chapter 18

Jake called around three that afternoon.

Amber was sleeping, trying to catch a few winks while Becky napped. Getting up at least two times a night to nurse was catching up with Amber. And there were times that Becky was in no hurry to go back to sleep. As much as Amber loved her daughter, she missed her eight hours of sleep!

"I woke you, didn't I?"

It took a few tries to focus enough to look at the digital clock on her nightstand. "That's okay, Jake. I got about forty-five minutes in . . . which is good."

"Go back to sleep. Call me later."

"No . . . I'm awake now." She stretched then asked, "What's up?"

"I was just wondering about Becky's doctor visit. How did it go? Our little girl is healthy, right? She didn't have to have any shots, did she?"

"She's great, Jake . . . and no, she didn't need any shots this time. And, hey! Guess what?"

"Hey! Tell me . . . I have no idea!"

"Ricky went with us."

"No shit! Things must be going better for you."

"We're working on it. Speaking of which . . . how about you and Lisa?"

Jake sighed. "I tell you, Amber . . . some days are great . . . everything is going good. And then . . . Bam! She's back to being an A #1 bitch!"

"But things are better . . ."

"For the most part . . . yes."

"Keep working at it."

"We'll see . . .

Amber changed the subject and told him about her visit to the T-shirt shop. He said to tell Matt and Maggie *hi* whenever she spoke to them again.

Their conversation lasted about a half hour before Jake said, "I've got to go, sis. Have to go check on some cement that was poured shortly before I called. I just wanted to see how things were going with you."

"I'm glad you called."

After replacing the phone in it's cradle, Amber listened to the baby monitor for Becky but didn't hear anything. She rolled onto her side to try to go back to sleep.

No such luck.

She thought about Ricky . . . about how he went to the doctor's with Becky . . . and how he came to their rescue and took them home . . . how he looked at her bare breast . . .

No use . . . might as well get up.

Going to the kitchen, Amber had to find something to feed Ricky. She hadn't cooked for him in a long time . . . she hoped his tastes hadn't changed. Looking in the freezer, she found a package with three boneless skinless chicken breasts. She had at least three hours to plan a meal.

The phone rang while she peeled potatoes. Setting the knife on the counter before wiping her hands on a towel, Amber answered the phone, hoping it wasn't Ricky to cancel. "Hello?"

"Why did you come back, Amber?"

It took a moment to realize who had called. "How did you get my number, Deana?"

"It doesn't matter. What really matters is that you came back and spoiled everything."

"I didn't mean to." And she meant that.

"Bullshit."

"I didn't even know about you, Deana."

"Did you think he wouldn't want anybody after you left him? Did you think he would pine for you, hoping you'd come back?"

"Deana . . ."

"But not only did you come back, you come back *pregnant*! You don't know how much I prayed that the baby *wasn't* his! But there's no denying who her father is. Both Ricky *and* A.J. have a picture of her on their desks at work. And I know you must have made the *perfect little family* going to the doctor this morning. He was so proud when he came to work. It made me sick to see your perfect little family when he *had* to stop and give you a ride home. I don't know what took him so long to get back to the car because I know it's too soon for you to get laid so I know he wasn't fucking you . . ."

"That is *enough.*"

"You took what I've always wanted. Oh, I knew he still thought of you but I knew I could make him forget you after awhile. You left him . . . why do you deserve to get him back? He took you back, even though I tried telling him that you'll do it to him again. *Why* didn't you stay away from him?"

"I don't have to explain anything to you, Deana."

"He's a good man, Amber . . . you *don't* deserve him! You took him from me!"

"If he was your's, Deana, I would never had been able to *take* him from you." Knowing that there was no reasoning with her, Amber ended the so-called conversation with the push of a button.

She thought Deana would call back but she didn't. Where had she been when she called? At work?

The big question was whether to tell Ricky about the call or not.

* * *

Ricky called at 6:15.

"Uh-oh" Amber said when she answered the phone.

"I'm going to be a little later than I thought. I have paperwork to finish. You don't have to wait for me . . . go ahead and eat. We can do this some other time."

"*Hello*! I haven't forgotten how your hours can be! I'll wait . . . or if it gets too late, I'll save you some food and we can reheat it when you get here." Amber softened her voice and tried to sound sexy. "And I've been *so* looking forward to see you tonight."

"Oh, *Amber* . . ."

Mission accomplished!

"How long do you think you'll be?"

"Um . . . give me an hour . . . and I'll stop at the drugstore, too."

"Okay . . . see you in awhile."

* * *

At 7:00, Ricky called to let her know that he was leaving work.

Amber turned on the burner under the potatoes and turned on the oven to preheat for the chicken. When it was ready, she set the timer. The tossed salad was made and in the refrigerator. She turned to Becky, who was strapped in her 'seat' on the table. "Daddy's coming over!" Humming to the oldies on the stereo, Amber set the table, working around Becky. She even took the time to dance to the Jackson 5's song, "ABC".

* * *

She wasn't surprised when there was a knock on the door. "Ricky?"

"Who else?"

After unlocking the door and opening it, there he stood, looking as sexy as ever. The work suit jacket was gone, as well as the tie but the shirt was unbuttoned halfway down and the sleeves were rolled up to his elbows. Ricky held a plastic bag in each hand. "Hi" he greeted with a smile. "Special delivery from the drugstore."

"Whoa . . . the delivery guys have gotten pretty sexy looking "Amber gushed, as her eyes slid down his body then back up to meet his eyes. "You'll have to come inside for your tip."

"No problem."

He stepped inside as Amber stepped back. She took the bags from him, their eyes looking at nothing but each other. Her eyes moved to his mouth, wanting him to kiss her. Her tongue slid out to moisten her suddenly dry lips. She heard a low moan from Ricky and he then said, "Put the bags down, Amber."

"You had better close the door" she replied, as she set the bags by her feet.

He did just that and locked all three locks before turning back to her. Pulling her toward him, Ricky's hands framed her face. "I didn't think I was ever going to get here."

And I was afraid you wouldn't show up. "Did you have problems finding anything?" Amber asked, her gaze alternating between his eyes and his mouth.

"Not really . . . I needed a little help. I've never had to buy diapers and pads before."

Taking a step closer, she asked, "Embarrassing?"

"Not with the diapers . . . and the only person I could find to help with the pads was a teenage boy . . . but he was helpful."

Her lips moved closer to his. "Thank you."

"You're very welcome." Ricky was breathing fast. "What was that about a tip?" His lips skimmed over hers as he spoke.

With a groan, Amber's arms moved around his neck as their mouths connected. Ricky's hands moved around her to hold her firmly against his body as his tongue entered her eagerly waiting mouth. His erection pressed against her, long and solid. She arched her pelvis, wanting to feel as much of him as she could . . . though she wanted more.

He pulled his mouth from hers but didn't let go of her body. "This isn't good, Amber. We're doing it again . . ."

"To wait a month is going to seem like forever" she panted.

He kissed her again . . . and again . . . and again. Then, he pulled away. "I don't know if supper will taste as good as you do . . ." His voice was low and husky as he spoke.

Amber was glad his arms were around her because if they weren't, her knees wouldn't have held her up. The huskiness of his voice and his words made the *want* even stronger. Her hand moved to his mouth . . . her fingers caressed his lips . . .

A noise sounded from the kitchen. The timer!

Her head dropped forward to rest against his chest. "The chicken's done."

"I guess we were saved by the bell." When she looked up at him, Ricky said, "Things were getting a little *too* heated, don't you think?"

"Well, just think how good the sex is going to be."

"You are bad" was his grinned comment.

Amber laughed, feeling very happy. Not being able to resist one more kiss, she took what she wanted before stepping back.

His eyes watched her and Ricky debated on whether or not to kiss her one more time. But he was afraid he wouldn't stop if he started. "Where's Becky?"

"In here" was Amber's reply as she stepped into the kitchen.

The bassinet was beside the doorway into the living room. Ricky went in the direction while Amber walked to the stove. She turned the oven dial to *off* then checked the pot of potatoes on the stove. The water had almost boiled away. "Whoa! Good thing the timer went off when it did! That was too close." She poured out what little water there was.

"Need help?"

"No, thanks." She turned to see Becky in her father's arms. "Enjoy yourself."

There weren't many leftovers. Ricky had eaten like he hadn't eaten in awhile. "That was so good . . . homemade mashed potatoes with fresh sweet corn and chicken . . . I haven't had a home-cooked meal like this in . . . a long time. Thanks for the invite."

Almost asking if Deana cooked, Amber remembered the phone call and decided not to bring up her name. She didn't want to spoil their time together. "You're welcome. It felt good to cook for somebody else."

Pushing back his chair, Ricky said, "Let me help with dishes."

That part of him hadn't changed but Amber shook her head. "I have a dishwasher."

"I can load that." He stacked her plate on his before collecting the silverware and glasses. "I remember our first meal together . . . meeting at the grocery store, the snow, going to your place with a pizza and a coconut cream pie . . . and I can't forget the timer! Do you remember?"

"How could I forget? I'll never forget that night . . . I'm surprised you remember."

"Why?" He looked at her. "It was the start of something good."

Tears filled her eyes. "And I let it get away."

"*No* . . . don't go there." Taking her hand, he helped her get out of her chair. "Let's move forward . . ." His lips gently touched hers but then kissed them again with passion as her lips parted for him. His tongue slid in . . . but he pulled his head back. "We can't . . . this has to stop! But I can't stop kissing your mouth . . . I shouldn't even start!" The backs of his knuckles stroked her cheek before he stepped back from her. "Let me get these dishes put away."

She watched him as he worked with his back to her. Amber had an idea and left the kitchen.

By the time she returned, Ricky had just finished wiping the counter by the sink. "Here" she said, holding out her hand. "If you don't want this, tell me *now*." A puzzled look creased his face but he held out his hand, palm up. Amber dropped a keyring with two keys on it. "These were the set Jake used when he was here. One is for this door and the other is for the front door of the building, though you seem to get in without one."

He grinned. "Other tenants must be getting used to me. There's always somebody there to let me in . . . and that's without using my badge." Suddenly, the smile diappeared. "Are you sure about this?"

"I am. I thought if you're coming over more often . . . you can let yourself in. But I don't want to rush you . . . if you don't want them . . . that's up to you."

He looked at her, seeming to think about the situation. Then, "What about the chain and deadbolt?"

Surprised, Amber replied, "Um . . . I never thought about them! Jake was never gone much so only the door lock was used when he went anywhere. I . . . um . . . there is a key for the deadbolt . . . I won't use the chain."

"But you feel safer with all the locks."

"Yeah but . . ."

"Did something happen to make you want all the locks?"

Shaking her head, she said, "No . . . but I guess when a country girl moves to the big city, she doesn't want to take any chances."

"Good girl." He leaned forward to kiss her. "I lock my doors, too." Laying a hand against her cheek, Ricky said, "I'll keep the keys . . . and I'll let you know when I'll be here if you want to unhook the chain."

Amber smiled. "We'll figure something out." And her heart beat faster knowing he had a key to her apartment. Ricky was going to be back in her life! They would work things out . . . if Deana didn't try to interfere. Again, Amber remembered Deana's phone call. There was no way she was going to spoil her evening with Ricky. Her mouth sought his and the kiss lingered. Pulling back, she murmured, "Your kisses *are* like Lay's potato chips . . . I can't have just one." She then moved in for another.

"Why do we keep doing this to each other?" Ricky pulled her into his arms.

"I know . . . we *have* to stop!" She backed away. "I'll find the deadbolt key."

Ricky had the kitchen back in order by the time Amber returned. "I was beginning to think you went to make the key" he commented with a grin.

"It wasn't where I thought it was. I finally found it in the drawer of my nightstand." She looked around the room. "You are just totally amazing!" Her gaze moved to Ricky and stopped. "I still remember how you helped clean off the table that first time . . . and I didn't even ask you to!" Stepping toward her, he quietly admitted, "It was the least I could do . . . I wanted to get you into bed."

Stepping into his arms, Amber replied, "Oh, yeah? You had a motive, huh?" Her body moved close as her arms slid around his neck. "I wanted you in bed, too . . . just like I do now."

"*Don't, Amber*!" he groaned. "You know we *can't*!"

"I *know*!" she moaned, and tried to step away from him

But he wouldn't let her. "We just have to be good for a month."

"Yeah . . . right! The only way to do that is to stay away from each other."

"And I *can't* picture that happening, now that you've come back" Ricky murmured, before taking a good taste of her mouth.

* * *

Before getting comfortable on the couch with Amber and Becky, Ricky emptied the pockets of his pants. His keys, wallet and cell phone were placed on the coffee table. Sitting next to Amber, he leaned back and sighed. "I missed you . . . I missed being together like this." His head turned to look at her as he added, "Except things are a *little* different." They both looked down at the nursing Becky. "Do you plan on nursing her for long?"

"At least six months."

His eyes watched as the tiny mouth suckled at the nipple . . . and he almost envied his daughter. His body responded at the thought. His hand gently brushed back her dark hair . . . and his fingertips brushed against Amber's breast. He heard her gasp softly. "Sorry" he whispered.

"I'm not" was her quiet reply. But her pulse had gone haywire at his touch.

Pulling back his hand, he put it in his lap. Clearing his throat, to change the subject, he asked about the first thing that popped into his head: "Are you going to try her with a bottle?"

"I plan on it. I'll need a back-up if I happen to not be around when she gets hungry."

"Yeah, most people can't help you there."

Laughing with him, Amber leaned her head against his shoulder. "You're right. I have a breast pump that I have to figure out how to use."

"I'll help."

She chuckled. "I bet you will." Amber raised her head to look at Ricky. "And I'll appreciate the help. You can read the instructions."

He lowered his head to gently kiss her lips. Sitting back, he lay his hand on her knee.

Her free hand wrapped around his.

Ricky had a lesson on burping the baby after she had eaten. Lucky for him, Amber had put a burp rag over his shoulder because a little of Becky's supper came up with the burp. "Welcome to the world of babies" Amber said, as she wiped Becky's mouth and removed the burp rag. "Wait till it happens with nothing to protect you."

"Thanks for the warning but I've had a little experience with my sister's two kids . . . even though I wasn't even burping them!"

They tried to watch a movie but their interest in the baby wouldn't let them concentrate on the story. Ricky held her, talking and cooing to her. Every little facial expression brought ooo's and aah's from both Mommy and Daddy.

After awhile, Ricky said, "Here,Amber . . . you have to take her for a few minutes." As he put Becky in her mother's arms, he asked, "The bathroom is down the hall and to the right?"

"Yep . . . just past the guest room." She called out to him as he left the room, "If you go too far, you'll end up in the laundry room!"

"I found it!" he called back.

Just as she heard the door close, his phone rang. Looking toward the doorway as if expecting him to appear, Amber then picked up the ringing phone. Recognizing the number on the Caller ID, she answered: "A.J.! Hi!"

There was a slight pause before he asked, "Amber? Ricky's with you?"

"Yes! He was here for supper. What's up?"

"Um . . . is he right there?"

"No . . . he's in the bathroom. Can I take a message?"

"No . . . just have him call me as soon as he comes out." A.J. was all business.

Hearing other voices in the background, Amber had a gut feeling that this wasn't good. "If you want to wait . . ."

"No, I can't, Amber. Just have him call me, okay?"

"I will."

"Thanks. 'Bye, Amber."

And before she could reply, A.J. hung up.

Her heart was pounding as she shut off the phone. Something bad must have happened.

A.J. was Ricky's partner and he wanted him there. She gently kissed Becky's forehead, trying not to cry. "I can handle this" she whispered.

Ricky stepped into the room. "Okay, you have to give her back to me . . ."

"You have to call A.J.."

"What?"

"Your phone rang and I saw A.J.'s number and answered it. It sounds serious." She handed the phone to him.

Taking the phone, Ricky punched some numbers. "A.J., it's me . . . Where?" His eyes met Amber's. "I'll be there shortly." Shutting off the phone, he said the dreaded words, "I have to go."

"I know." She was sitting on the couch, with Becky beside her.

He sat on the couch, putting on his socks and shoes. "I'm glad we had tonight. We need more times like this." Turning his head to look at her, Ricky smiled. "Thanks for a delicious supper."

Trying not to show the fear she fought inside, Amber attempted a smile. "You're welcome. We will have more of them."

Standing, Ricky grabbed his keys and wallet off the table and looked again at her as he slid them into his pocket. "Will you be all right?"

Nodding, she answered, "I'll be fine." *Was it her or didn't her voice sound normal?*

"I'll call you later."

"No, you don't have to. It's after nine now . . . I'll talk to you tomorrow."

"Are you sure?" His phone disappeared into his pocket.

"Yes." Placing Becky against the back of the couch, Amber stood and her eyes met Ricky's.

He opened his arms and she stepped into them, sliding her arms around him . . . trying not to cling. Giving her an extra squeeze, Ricky then framed her face with his hands and kissed her. "Talk to you in the morning." Gently touching Becky's hair, he walked out of the room.

"Be safe" Amber whispered as she heard him unlocking the door. She chewed on her bottom lip until she heard the door open and close. Automatically, she reached for the phone on the end table and dialed Jake's area code.After dialing the next three numbers, she abruptly shut off the phone. "I *can't* do that any more! I can't call Jake every time I get upset . . ." She took in a shaky breath before exhaling. "I'm fine . . . he'll be fine . . . nothing's going to happen. I can do this . . . he's doing his job . . . I'll be fine!" After another shaky breath, Amber sat on the couch and gathered her daughter into her arms. "Daddy will be fine . . . he'll come home to us . . ."

* * *

"How did Amber do after my call?" A.J. asked. They stood by one of the two bodies on the floor of the convenience store.

"She tried hard to put on a brave face."

"She wanted to talk but I didn't have time. I hated to do that."

"She understands."

"Does she?"

Ricky's head snapped around and his eyes met his partner's for a moment before turning away. "She's trying, A.J.! Give her a break!"

A.J.'s hand briefly clasped Ricky's shoulder as he walked away.

* * *

Chapter 19

The following morning was sunny and warm. Deciding to go out for a walk, Amber put extra diapers and a change of baby clothes in a fanny pack, along with a pacifier. Yes, she broke down and bought one for Becky, even though the whole time she was pregnant she swore she would never give her baby one of those. But after what happened that day on her way home from seeing Maggie and Matt, Amber decided to have one on hand.

Putting on the fanny pack and then placing Becky in the sling, Amber slid her keys and a few dollars in the front pocket of her shorts before heading out. Just to get out for a little while would do her good.And she wanted Becky to get used to being outside. The time to go was early, before the heat set in.

And because she hadn't heard anything from Ricky yet she had to get out of the apartment. She hoped he had had a late night and overslept. She didn't want to think about any other reasons why he hadn't called.

* * *

The sidewalk was busy. Most people paid no attention to the woman walking with a baby but a few smiled and or nodded their head in acknowledgment. A couple of people in their haste to get wherever bumped against Amber and neither looked back to offer an apology.

Twice Amber sat on a bench and watched those who walked past. Becky was good, and she slept only for a short while. Amber talked softly to her, as if explaining the hows and whys of different things. A young man who looked to be in his early twenties asked if she minded if he sat at the other end of the bench. She told him she didn't, thinking there were too many others around for him to try anything. He talked, telling Amber how he had just recently become engaged to his girl of four years. It wasn't a get-down-on-one-knee proposal . . . he had been thinking of asking her and just the other day when they had been in Central park, playing with his Katy's dog and they were all tired out afterwards and resting under a tree, when he just blurted out *Will you marry me*? And she said *yes*! No date had been set as of yet but they had talked about within six months, because they wanted to start a family in the near future. He smiled at Becky, who's eyes were open and seemed to be watching and listening to the young man. He asked how old she was and congratulated Amber. After a glance at his watch, he stood, saying to Amber that *he hoped he didn't bore her too much with his rambling* and that he had to meet Katy to look at an apartment. Watching him walk off, Amber was happy for the young couple . . . and wondered if Ricky would ever ask her to marry him . . .

Walking back to the apartment, Amber noticed an older couple walking ahead of her . . . and they held hands as they walked at a slower pace than most of the others. Again she wondered if she and Ricky would be still holding hands at that age.

* * *

The light on the answering machine flashed when Amber walked into the kitchen. She had put a sleeping Becky in the bassinet in the living room and then needed something to drink. Amber took a pitcher of lemonade out of the refrigerator before pressing the play button on the machine. There were three messages and each one was from Ricky: "Morning, Amber . . . sorry it took me so long to call. I got in late but was allowed time to sleep. Amber? I'll call back." The next message was fifteen minutes later: "Amber? Are you there? Pick up . . ." The last message was only ten minutes later: "Amber?" He took a breath and let it out. "Where the hell are you?" A pause, then "Call my cell when you hear this, okay?"

Her first thought was *not* to call . . .

He answered on the third ring. "Davis."

"Hi."

"*Where have you been*?" He sounded angry.

"I don't think I like your tone."

"Where did you go with the baby?"

"For a walk. Any other questions?"

Ricky sighed. "Look . . ."

"No . . . *you* look! I will come and go as I please! I wanted to get Becky and me out of this apartment before it got too hot outside . . . I *will not* be cooped up in here! I'm used to being outside and I want Becky to get used to it."

"You're not upstate now, Amber."

"Well, *maybe I should be*!" She stopped and took a deep breath to calm herself. "If I knew this was going to turn into an argument, I wouldn't have called you back."

His voice was cool. "I'll be over later and we can talk about this."

"If you mean you're coming over to argue, I *don't want* you to come over!"

There was a moment of silence before he said, "I don't want to argue with you, Amber."

"All right, then. I'll see you later."

But as she hung up the phone, she was afraid there was going to be an argument or two.

* * *

"Hey, sis, I want to give you my new phone number."

"New number? What happened to the old one?"

"I needed another phone and after having to replace my phone one too many times, I decided to go with another company and get a new number."

"What happened to your phone?"

"Okay . . . don't laugh . . . but somehow I dropped it into a goldfish pond . . ."

"A *what*? You dropped your phone into *what*?"

"A goldfish pond."

"You're kidding, right?"

"I wish I was."

Amber couldn't stop the laugh that bubbled out of her. "*How* did you manage that?"

"It was at a job we're doing at the new housing project over on West Hill."

"Houses are going up there? It won't be the same."

"I know . . . but we've had a lot of work there. Anyway, I leaned over to check out the size of a goldfish in the pond at one of the houses . . . and that fish *is* huge! . . . forgetting that my phone is in the pocket of my shirt . . . need I continue?"

Amber laughed as she pictured this scene. When she finally calmed down, she chuckled, "You have *got* to be kidding!"

"Would I be telling you this if I was?"

"But if you change your phone number, you'll have to change it at a lot of places for your business."

"I know . . . I have Lisa working on it. Okay, here's my number . . ."

"Hold on! I have a pen but no paper! Where did that pad go to that was here by the phone?" She rummaged through a stack of bills then muttered, "I'll use the envelope from the phone bill. Okay, I'm ready, Jake."

The sound she heard over the phone was snoring.

"Okay . . . now you're *not* being funny!" But when Jake started to laugh, Amber joined him.

"Well, you do take your time at times, Amber."

"I wasn't *that* long!" She was still laughing.

"Long enough! Okay, here's the number . . ."

She wrote it down before repeating it back to him to make sure she had it right.

"Time for me to go, sis . . . my break is over."

"I'm so glad you called! I needed a good laugh."

"Uh-oh . . . what happened?"

"I made Ricky mad." And she told him some of the conversation.

"Hmmmm . . . want to know what I think?"

"Okay . . ."

"I think he's still afraid of you leaving him again. When he called and you weren't there, he panicked."

"But I have told him more than once that I *won't* do that again!"

"You have to convince *him* of that . . . not *me*."

Sighing, she asked, "What more can I do?"

"There's where that word *trust* comes in, Amber . . . and I repeat . . . you have to *earn* his trust."

"Yes, that's what you keep telling me."

"Well, listen."

* * *

The sound of his key in the locks was music to her ears. He didn't call to tell her that he was coming but she hoped he would . . . and he did! When he called out, "Amber! It's me!" her heart sang. She lay the spatula on the spoon rest and replaced the lid on the frying peppers and onions. "I'm in the kitchen!" she called to him. When she turned, Ricky was standing in the doorway. "Hi" she greeted.

"Hi, yourself. Supper smells good . . . sausage with peppers?"

"And onions."

"Is there enough for me, too?"

"Yes . . . I made plenty . . . just in case you did show up." Hesitating a moment, Amber said, "I'm glad you came over."

"I had to."

Their eyes met. She wanted to run and throw her arms around him. He wanted to hold her and never let go.

"Are you still mad about this morning?" she asked.

"I could ask you the same question."

"I'm sorry I snapped at you then but there was no reason for your interrogation on the phone."

He rubbed the back of his neck. "I shouldn't have talked to you the way I did. I'm sorry. I got nervous when you didn't answer your phone. When you hadn't answered by the third call . . . I just thought the worst."

"Like what?" *Come on . . . tell me*!

His hand dropped and he looked at her.

Amber wouldn't let the subject drop. "Tell me, Ricky. What did you think? That me or Becky got hurt? What are the odds of that happening?"

"Some days the odds are more than others. You never know . . . Oh, Amber! Anything can happen, especially here! I want you to be safe . . . I want you . . . here." His voice caught. "I can't lose you again."

Tears filled her eyes as she rushed to him. "I'm not going anywhere" Amber told him, as her arms slid around his neck. "I'm *not* going anywhere . . ." Her lips pressed against his and then she looked up at him. "Believe me, Ricco . . ." The tears slid down her cheeks.

There was no reply as his eyes met hers. But he did wipe off her cheeks. "Hopefully there will be no more of these."

Attempting a chuckle, Amber said, "According to Jake, you're talking to the *wrong* person."

"Yeah, I guess he's right about that" Ricky agreed, smiling down at her.

Suddenly, the aroma of well done peppers and onions caught her attention. Reluctantly she stepped back. "I'd better take care of supper." She turned off the burners and moved the frying pans to the cold burners. One side of the Italian sausages was done more than the others but not burned. Returning the lid, she turned to Ricky, not wanting to drop the conversation that were having. "Are we okay?"

"I think so." He grasped her arms and pulled her against him.

Enjoying the comfort of his embrace, Amber rested her head against his chest and closed her eyes. After a few moments, she told him, "I'm here to stay, Ricco. If I go anywhere it will be with you."

His fingers tilted her face up as he looked down at her. "I like hearing those words." He leaned down to kiss her. "I love you" he murmured before his mouth covered hers again. He had been too long without her. To have her again . . . to hold her . . . kiss her . . . he didn't want to stop taking. He couldn't forget the fear he felt earlier . . . the pain in his gut when Amber didn't answer her phone . . . especially by the third time. The thought that she had left him again was there . . . but she didn't . . . and she was there . . . she was back where she belonged . . . with him . . . back in his arms . . . Yes, there had been Deana . . . but she wasn't the woman he loved. He kissed Amber as if he were starving . . . and it didn't help that she returned the passion with each kiss. His body reacted as it always had with her . . . he was hard and throbbing and aching. But that little voice that had started quietly in the back of his head finally found it's strength to be heard . . . *Stop! Stop it now!* He was surprised he listened. Ricky slowed his onslaught of her mouth and finally pulled away, trying to catch his breath. "We can't keep doing this, Amber . . . but damn, *I want you*!" His thumb stroked her swollen lips. "It's going to be a long month."

Amber's eyes were closed and her lips were parted as she took pleasure in the sensation his thumb continued to stir through her body. She wanted him as much as she knew he wanted her. Feeling his large erection against her, she almost threw caution to the wind . . . her breasts ached for him . . . his brief caress the night before started that . . . her body ached for his touch . . . and the ache between her legs was becoming too unbearable . . . but she knew she couldn't. When his thumb moved from her lips, her eyes slowly opened to find him looking at her . . . and her heavy breathing slowed when he whispered, "You are so beautiful, Amber."

Tears filled her eyes and her smile trembled.

His hand gently pushed back a strand of her hair as he softly spoke: "I know this is killing both of us . . . and we should know better because we aren't teenagers . . . but I can't help myself. You're back in my life . . . and that's where I want you to stay."

"I will" she whispered.

His eyes met hers as he stepped back. "Okay, how about we eat? It smells so good and I'm starving . . . not only for you." At that he smiled.

It took a few moments for her thoughts to register the abrupt change of subject. Minutes later, they were at the table.

"I need some more milk. How about you?" Amber got out of her chair.

"Sounds good." Ricky handed her his glass.

Setting the glasses on the counter, she poured milk in one, then the other. Turning to put the container back in the refrigerator, Amber hit one glass with it and it fell against the other glass. It all happened so fast but it also seemed to be in slow motion as the milk spilled over the counter and onto the floor. "*Dammit*!" She quickly put the milk container on the counter to grab the glasses before they fell to the floor with the milk. Grabbing a dish towel, Amber tried to stop any more milk from going over the edge of the counter and running down the front of the cupboard. Ricky helped with the dishcloth and she tossed a hand towel over the mess on the floor. "What a mess!" she sputtered. "It had to happen with two *full* glasses of milk!"

Ricky chuckled as he wiped off the counter, rinsing the dishcloth a couple of times. "Hey, it could have been worse. The only casualty I see up here is this stack of envelopes." He picked up the pile to let them drip into the sink.

"Just toss them" Amber said.

Minutes later, the mess was pretty well cleaned up.

"I'll be mopping tomorrow."

"Rather you than me" Ricky stated, pulling her against him. After a kiss, he suggested, "Now I want to go in and hold my daughter."

Ricky left the apartment a little after 11:00. As Amber locked up after him, she thought about the good night they had together . . . with no phone calls.

*   *   *

Amber told Ricky the night before that if he ever called and she wasn't there, leave a message and she would get back to him . . . or call her cell phone if necessary. Giving her number to him, he put it into his cell phone. And so the next morning, she took Becky out for another walk.

Going into the kitchen after her walk, Amber saw the light flashing on the answering machine again. "Ricky?" she wondered . . . and hoped . . . as she pressed the message button.

But it was Jake.

"I don't know why you don't take your cell with you so I can talk to you on that instead of this stupid thing! Anyway, Lisa and I are planning a party the weekend before Labor Day. We would like it if you and Ricky could join us . . . and spend a couple of days here. I'd get to see my niece! I hope she hasn't forgotten who Uncle Jake is! Oh . . . and it'll be great to see you, too! Anyway, give me a call after you talk to Ricky. Later, sis . . . love ya!"

Checking her cell phone, wondering why it didn't ring if he had called her on it, Amber started to laugh. "I guess it would have rang if it was on!"

Still smiling, Amber pressed the delete button to erase his message. But then her nose wrinkled at the awful odor that she suddenly smelled. "What the . . . ?" With the sling and Becky still attached to the front of her, Amber checked inside the sling. What a mess! "Oh, no! What happened, little girl?"

It took awhile to bathe Becky and dress her in clean clothes. Amber placed her in her crib while she rinsed Becky's clothes and the sling in the bathroom sink before tossing them into the washing machine. While they washed, Becky was moved out of the crib and into her seat on the kitchen table. Amber then looked for Jake's new phone number on the counter. "Where did I put that?" she muttered to herself, looking for the envelope she had written on. "Where is it?" Becky started to cry. "You're hungry, aren't you, sweetie?" Amber asked, as she continued to look under and behind things on the counter. Becky's cries sounded a little louder. Amber straightened, suddenly remembering the milk incident . . . and telling Ricky to throw the wet envelopes into the trash . . .

The garbage went out that morning.

"*Damn*!"

She thought about checking the Caller ID for the number but Becky's cries grew louder. Looking for the number was forgotten. "Come on, little girl . . . let's get you fed." She took Becky out of her seat and carried her to the rocking chair in her room.

Becky fell asleep after eating. After putting her in the crib, Amber put the wash in the dryer. She thought about how much she missed hanging laundry ouside like she did at home up north. Everything smelled so nice, especially sheets.

Feeling hungry, Amber looked in the refrigerator for some lunch. Instead, she got a whiff of something else that smelled bad and finally found a bowl of moldy *something* in the back of the lower shelf. After disposing of bowl and contents in the garbage, she decided to thoroughly clean the inside of the refrigerator. Anything that was at least a week old was tossed. Shelves and drawers were washed down with soap and water.

An hour and a half later, Amber finished the job and grabbed a container of Black Cherry yogurt for a quick lunch. Her thoughts of a nap were forgotten when she heard Becky over the baby monitor. She was put in her seat which now sat on the coffee table while Amber dusted. The stereo played oldies, music from the 50's, 60's and 70's. Amber was in her glory! She sang and danced, even holding Becky at times as she danced around the room. "Your daddy is a great dancer . . . wait till you get to dance with him" Amber told her daughter as she put her back into her seat.

As Becky nursed later on, Amber heard a key in the door . . . then a knock. Ricky! The chain lock was still in place. Glancing at her watch, she saw it was twenty after five. And she didn't know Ricky was coming over. With Becky in her arms, Amber got out of the rocking chair and started up the hall. "Hold on, Ricky!"

Once the door opened, she saw him standing there with a smile. "Hi" she greeted.

"Hi. Sorry . . . I didn't call . . ."

"That's okay . . . I should remember to unlock that earlier just in case."

After closing and locking the door behind him, Ricky turned back to Amber. "You were busy" he commented, looking at Becky.

With a quiet laugh, Amber agreed. "Yeah, I've been busy all day . . . and not with things I planned on doing!"

"Why's that?"

"Um . . . come on . . . let's go back to her room."

Setting again in the rocking chair, Amber got comfortable with Becky, who continued to nurse. She looked up to find Ricky watching them as he loosened his tie. "You're early tonight" she commented.

"Kind of a quiet day."

"That's good. You need one of them more often."

"Amen." He walked over to kiss her. "Was it a bad day for you?"

"No . . . I guess not." After a brief synopsis, Amber finished with, ". . . Becky and I danced some to Jailhouse Rock and La Bamba . . . to name a few."

"Oh . . . I should have been here. Our daughter will be a dancing queen if she takes after her mommy and daddy!" As he talked, he removed his jacket and tie, then pulled his shirt out of his pants and unbuttoned it. Amber watched, her body reacting to what she saw. He was one sexy guy. Her eyes returned to his face when he said, as he unbuttoned his cuffs, "I wish I had thought to have something here to get comfortable in after work."

"Um . . . Jake left a pair of sweatpants that should fit you. They're washed and on the bed in the guest room. Oh! Speaking of Jake! Before I forget . . . would you please check the Caller ID for his new number? He left a message this morning while Becky and I went walking. He wants me to get back to him about going to some party he's having the weekend *before* Labor Day weekend. We're invited to stay a few days . . . do you want to go?"

There was a hesitation before he asked, "It's not the same weekend that . . . um, your six weeks is up, is it?"

It took a few moments for his meaning to come clear . . . when they could make love. "No, the party is the weekend after." She smiled at him as her body suddenly felt *very* warm.

He returned her smile. "Good." He leaned over to kiss her again. Standing, Ricky said, "Okay, I'll change into those sweats and then look for Jake's number."

Becky had finished eating, been burped, changed and was just being put into her cradle when Ricky stepped back into her room. Amber turned to him. "She'll be down for an hour or so . . ." She looked puzzled at the look on his face. He didn't look happy. "What's wrong?" Walking toward him, she asked, "Did work call?"

"Let's go into the other room so we won't bother the baby." He turned and walked off, not waiting for Amber.

"What the . . . ?" she muttered, following him.

Ricky turned on her in the foyer. "When were you going to tell me? Or weren't you planning on it?"

"Tell you *what*?"

"Deana called you . . . I saw her number on the Caller ID. When and why did she call?"

Amber shrugged. "It wasn't anything."

"*When* did she call?"

"That first night you were here for supper."

"And you didn't tell me *because* . . ."

"Because I didn't want to spoil our time together . . . but you ended up having to leave anyway."

"What did she want?

Amber stared at him. "Why all the questions?"

With a sigh, Ricky pushed a hand through his hair. "Amber . . . *please*."

Taking a deep breath, Amber let it out slowly before she answered: "She wanted to know why I came back . . . she said I had no right to do that and to come back pregnant. She was mad because I . . . quote, unquote . . . *took you away from her*."

Ricky was pissed. Amber watched as he buttoned his shirt and tucked it back into his pants. For some reason the thought came to her that he didn't put on the sweatpants. His jaw was set when he looked at her. "I'll be back." Pulling her to him, he gave her a short, hard kiss then unlocked the door and left.

There was no question as to where he was going.

* * *

Chapter 20

Ricky took the stairs two at a time, all four flights. His long strides made short time to Deana's apartment door. Without knocking, he used the key he forgot to give back to open the door. In his rush, the key didn't want to cooperate to come out of the lock.

"Well, I wondered when you would use that key again, since you never gave it back."

His body stiffened at the sound of her voice. Then, the key finally came out and he heaved it across the room before slamming the door shut. Turning on Deana, he demanded, "*Don't* you *ever* call her again!"

After a brief hesitation, she came back with, "I wondered when she would get around to tell you about it."

"She *didn't* tell me! I found your number on her ID when I was looking for another number! What *the hell* were you thinking?"

"I was thinking of you . . . about *us*."

"*Jesus,* Deana! There is no *us*!"

"There was! There was before *she* came back!"

Ricky sighed, exasperated. "Yes, Amber came back and now we have a baby. They are in my life now."

"Oh, yeah . . . and I get tossed aside!"

He sighed again, rubbing his hands over his face before looking at her. "I never meant to hurt you, Deana. But whatever we had between us is *over*! Do *not* call her again, do you hear me?"

"But I thought you cared about me! I thought . . ."

"I did care . . . you were there when I needed someone. You brought me out of the funk I was in . . . and I gave you back the physical part but I couldn't give you any more than that."

"So . . . you just needed somebody to fuck."

Ricky looked stunned at her remark. "You put that so nicely."

She gestured toward herself with both hands. "*I* was just a fuck to you."

Times with her passed quickly through his head: against the wall in the room where they now stood . . . with her against the kitchen counter . . . with her bent over the back of the over-stuffed chair in the living room . . . sex in her bed . . . and his. The times were wild . . . and good.

But she wasn't Amber.

"Call it what you want. I told you from the start it probably wouldn't be anything serious."

"But I love you."

Ricky stared at Deana. "You're kidding, right?"

"No, I'm not. I know it's not what you wanted but . . . it happened."

"But I don't love you, Deana . . . I never did. I love Amber . . . and now our daughter."

She stared at him a few moments and then her eyes filled with tears. "You're right, you did tell me from the start that you weren't looking to be serious. But I had hope. After you told me about Amber taking off, I tried my best to make you change your mind. I just couldn't believe that anybody with any sense could leave a great guy like you. I knew you didn't love me but you kept coming back and I kept *hoping*! Can you blame me for trying?" Deana attempted a smile as the tears ran down her face. "You didn't give me back my key the last time you were here, even though that was one of the reasons you came over. I was hoping you decided to keep it in case things didn't work out with Amber." She wiped the tears away. "You never really gave *us* a chance . . . you *wouldn't* forget *her*."

Ricky's eyes narrowed as he looked at Deana. "I *couldn't* forget her . . . as much as I wanted to at the time. And as for your key . . . we argued when I was last here . . . after getting my clothes and things, I left, remember? But when I found out you called her . . . how could you? Did you honestly think Amber would change her mind about me *just* because *you* didn't think it was fair she came back? That's high school, Deana." He turned to leave but stopped to say, "Your key is over there on the floor."

Suddenly, Deana moved quickly across the room to him and raised herself up on her toes to cover his mouth with hers. Simultaneously, her tongue entered his surprised mouth as her hand grasped the front of his pants. He shoved her away. "What are you . . . ?"

"You can't deny that we've always had great sex. And I know that when you fucked me on the bathroom floor that time not so long ago, it had something to do with Amber. You must be ready for some because *she* can't give it to you yet . . . and *I* know how much you like it and how often. Come on, Ricky . . . for me . . . *and* you . . . *one last time* . . ." She reached for him again.

"Deana . . . *stop it*!" Ricky turned and walked to the door.

"Yeah . . . well . . . *get out*! You're not welcome here any more!"

But when the door closed sharply behind him, Deana gave in to her misery.

* * *

"Hey! I was beginning to wonder if you got my message! I'm glad to hear you're coming up for the party. Things are now good with you and Ricky?"

"Oh, yes . . . things are good! Sorry it took me so long to get back to you . . . but sometimes it's hard to get Ricky to sit still long enough to talk!" Amber playfully cleared her throat. "And then there are the times when talking just doesn't enter our minds . . ."

Jake laughed. "Okay . . . no details needed!"

"Anyway, we'll be up on Friday . . . if that's okay with you . . . and Lisa."

"Ricky's getting the time off? Good for him! And you know you can stay as long as you want. This is still your home."

"It'll be so good to see you! It seems like forever since you were here!"

"It's been a little over a month. Hey . . . our little girl just had a birthday!"

Amber laughed. "You could say that!

"Thanks for the pictures you've been sending on the computer."

"I'm lucky I get on that any more . . . but you are so welcome."

"Okay . . . I know I'll talk to you before then but I'll see you in a week and a half."

"That soon?"

"That soon. You've been cooped up too long, sis. Time to get into the fresh air . . . and let that little girl know what country life is like."

Amber only half-listened to what Jake was saying. Her six weeks will be up next week . . . her baby will be six weeks old . . . and she could make love to Ricky. A warm flash flushed through her body . . . she had heard and read where some women don't wait the recommended length of time . . . and it had been such a long time since the night Becky wa conceived . . .

"Hey . . . Amber! Are you still there?"

"Um . . . yeah!"

"Good . . . I was beginning to think I was talking to myself."

"Tell me something new."

"Ha-ha."

"Oh . . . you know I love you, Jake."

He chuckled. "Right back at ya, sis."

"What do you want us to bring for the party?"

"Nothing. Just yourselves."

"Does Lisa agree with that?"

"Never mind her. Just get up here safely."

"Things aren't any better? Then why is she still there?"

"Sometimes . . ." Jake exhaled loudly. "It's just . . . no, never mind. We can talk while you're here and we can have a long talk. Now, before I hang up and forget to tell you . . . don't bother bringing any big stuff for Becky because I have it here . . . a port-a-crib, a bassinet, a crib, and a changing table."

"Oh, Jake . . . you didn't have to go buy all that! I wasn't bringing all that anyway."

"Chill, Amber! I bought it all second-hand and it's in great shape. Remember Tom Wyle? His twins are almost three now and they aren't planning on having any more kids, so he and Rosie are trying to get rid of all the baby furniture. I got it all for a great price! Now I'm ready for my niece!"

"That's good. Where are you planning to set it all up?"

"In my old room . . . it just became a catch-all after I moved my stuff into mom and dad's bedroom. My old room is now Becky's . . . unless you were planning on keeping her in your room."

"No . . . I hadn't even thought about that. I'll bring the baby monitors with us."

"Nope! You don't have to do that . . . I have those, too."

"Well, you just thought of everything, didn't you, Uncle Jake?"

"I hope so!"

Amber suddenly thought of something. "Hey, Jake . . . now that you have baby furniture, you and Lisa can . . ."

He cut her short. "Don't go there, Amber."

"Sorry. Um . . . see you soon."

"Pray for good weather!"

* * *

"I think she fell asleep before she burped."

Becky was against her mother's shoulder. Amber gently patted her back a couple more times before moving the baby into her arms. Sure enough, Becky's eyes were closed and her breathing was soft and even. "I hope you don't wake up later with an air bubble in your tummy, baby girl" Amber softly told her.

"Here . . . let me take her" Ricky offered, reaching for Becky. Cradling her in his arms, he sat back on the couch. "Does she have air bubbles a lot?"

"No . . . not too often . . . and luckily it hasn't been anything that a few good burps won't take care of." With a chuckle, Amber added, "She wakes me to eat." She started to put her nursing bra back together.

"Not yet . . . please don't."

Surprised, she looked up to meet Ricky's eyes.

"Hold on" he softly said, standing to lay Becky in the bassinet.

Her heart pounded as she watched him, his quiet plea echoing in her head. When he sat beside her again, his next words made her catch her breath:

"I haven't touched you in so long. I can't take it any longer."

Without a word, Amber removed her shirt. She was so sure Ricky could see her heart pounding against her chest as her fingers fumbled to unhook the bra and push the straps over her shoulders. Moments later, her bra lay on the couch. Her breathing was quick and shallow as she watched his hands reach for her.

"You're more beautiful than I remember" he whispered, as his fingertips skimmed over the tips of her nipples, causing them to instantly harden. "I've missed you . . . I've missed us." He watched as his thumbs worked across the raised tips. A low moan from Amber caused him to look at her, to see her eyes closed and her tongue moisten her lips. "Look at me." After her eyes slowly opened, Ricky leaned forward to kiss her . . . gently at first . . . but then his tongue slid into her mouth, wanting more. His hands covered her breasts as his lips and tongue worked her mouth with passion.

Pressing into his hands, Amber captured his tongue with her mouth and sucked it, drawing a deep moan from him . . . and awakening her desire for Ricky. Her moan of protest when he abruptly pulled away turned into a cry of ecstasy when his mouth moved to the breasts he held in his hands. When his tongue licked at her nipples, she inhaled sharply. Her breathing stopped momentarily when he suckled one breast. "I can taste your milk" he whispered, before sampling the other.

She had to stop him . . . she wanted him . . . she had to stop how good he was making her feel. It had been *too* long . . . but they should wait . . . only one more week. They could do it . . . they had waited this long . . . what was one more week? Her mouth parted for his when he raised his head from her breasts . . .

Pulling his mouth from hers, Ricky gathered her into his arms, pulling her close and burying his face into her hair. "I want to stay the night."

"But, Ricky . . ."

"I know . . . I know . . . we have to wait a little longer before I can make love to you but I've wanted to stay, to hold you while you sleep. You don't realize how much I have missed you . . ."

"Why didn't you say something before?"

He shrugged. "I'm saying something now." She sat back to be able to look at his face. "You won't get a full night of sleep. Becky gets me up at least twice a night."

"I don't care. I'm her daddy and it's something I have to get used to."

"This feels like our first time together. But then, I wasn't this nervous our first time" Amber rambled as her arms slid around his neck. "And this time, it's not like anything's going to happen."

"You're right . . . nothing's going to happen." Ricky pulled her closer. "I remember our first night vividly . . ." His mouth closed over hers, slowly seducing her lips before his tongue entered her mouth, continuing the seduction.

Pulling away, her breath coming fast, Amber protested, "This isn't a good idea . . . you're not playing fair!"

"Are you trying to say that you don't trust me?" His eyes twinkled at his question.

"It's not you I'm worried about!"

Chuckling softly, Ricky said, "I won't let you get carried away."

"Thanks." She flashed a nervous smile before saying, "There's an extra toothbrush in the bathroom . . ."

He smiled. "It seems like I remember you telling me that that first night I spent with you."

With a laugh, Amber said, "I think I did!"

He followed her into the bathroom off her bedroom. Amber pointed where to find towels if he wanted to shower . . . which he always used to do before bed. Taking a toothbrush out of a drawer, she told him, "Toothpaste is in the medicine cabinet. I'll be back . . . I want to check on the baby."

"Are you sure you don't want to shower with me?"

"Oh, don't tease!" Images of showers they had taken together filled her head.

"I know . . . sorry. I won't be long."

Amber had to get away from him. This was a bad idea . . . she shouldn't have agreed for him to stay with her. The temptation would be too great . . . because she *was* willing . . . body and soul. There had to be couples that didn't wait the whole time . . .

Going to Becky's room calmed her thoughts. The nightlight gave Amber enough light to see that Becky was asleep . . . on her back, with her left hand fisted up next to her chin. Sometimes she sat in the rocking chair, watching Becky sleep . . . it didn't matter what time it was.

Ricky was already out of the shower when Amber went back to her room. With a towel wrapped around his waist, he stood in front of the steamed mirror, trying to wipe the steam off as he combed his hair. Amber drank in the sight of him, feeling her resistance waning. He turned and smiled at her. "Is Becky all right?"

"Sound to sleep. She'll probably be awake in three to four hours."

He stepped into the bedroom. "How long before she sleeps all night?"

"Now, that's a good question!"

He laughed then asked, "Do you still sleep on the same side you used to?"

"I do." Her body ached for him, seeing him standing before her in only a towel. "I'll be back." Stepping into the bathroom, she partially closed the door, which seemed very strange because she never did before. Undressing, she took her nightshirt off the hook on the back of the bathroom door and slid it over her head. Ricky was in bed when she stepped back into the bedroom, sitting with his back against the headboard, and the sheet covering him up to his waist. His dark eyes watched as she walked toward the bed.

"I wondered what happened to that shirt."

Amber stopped, sliding her hands down the sides of the blue long-sleeved shirt she wore. "I took this the night I left. I knew it was one of your favorites . . . and I wanted it." She swallowed the lump that tried forming and continued: "I've slept in it just about every night since then."

Ricky didn't reply as he looked at her.

Her next question just popped out of her mouth: "You're naked, aren't you?"

"You know that I don't sleep any other way."

"Oh . . . I don't know about this! It's not going to work!"

He flipped back the sheet and blanket on her side. "Come on . . . get in."

She looked at him for what seemed a long time, contemplating whether she should or not. But then with a slight shrug, Amber shut off the light on the nightstand and got into bed with the man she loved . . . better yet, with the *naked* man she loved.

Ricky slid down beside her, sliding an arm beneath her head. Amber turned toward him, sliding an arm across his chest. His arm held her close. "This feels so good" she murmured, closing her eyes as he hand stroked her back. With a sigh of contentment, she whispered, "I've missed this."

"Me, too." *With Deana, it was just sex . . . no romance.*

They talked quietly and whispered softly like they used to. Every so often they heard baby noises over the monitor.

"Is she waking up?" Ricky asked.

"No, not yet. When she's hungry, she gets loud."

With a chuckle, Ricky teased, "Just like her mother."

"Hey!" Amber tried to tickle him in the ribs.But Ricky knew her moves and pulled her tighter against him, pinning her hand between their bodies. "*Now* what are you going to do?" he asked.

With their bodies so close together, their mouths were closer when Amber turned her head to look at him. "Kiss you" she whispered, in reply to his question, her lips brushing against his as she spoke. Releasing her hand, his fingers grazed her cheek as she added, "I love you."

"Say it again."

"I love you, *Ricco*."

Her mouth covered his,with each kiss she gave him as soft as butterfly wings. And then passion took over. When her tongue met his, Ricky took control. Their tongues entertained each other before his pushed into her mouth. His hands slid to her butt, holding her firmly against his erection. That was all it took to shatter her resolve. Amber wasn't going to wait any longer. Tearing her mouth from his, she panted, "Do you have any condoms with you?"

"*Condoms*?"

"Yeah . . . those latex things used to prevent pregnancy."

"I *know* what they are . . . no, I don't have any. But I thought . . . I was told . . . that you had your tubes tied."

"I was going to . . . but changed my mind right after I had Becky. My doctor asked me again about having it done . . . but after I held her, I knew if I ever had the chance to give her a sister or a brother, I wanted to be able to do it."

The conversation doused the fire that had raged between them. Ricky held her for quite a long time before they decided to get some sleep. Amber kissed him and turned onto her side, with her backside to him. His body molded around hers and his arm slipped around her waist.

The want was still there. Amber thought about what had almost happened between them . . . the warmth of his body seeped through the shirt she wore . . . the desire wouldn't go away. The more she thought about it, the more she wanted to turn in his arms and start kissing him . . . Ricky wanted her *now*. He cursed himself for not having condoms with him . . . but how was he to know? His body moved closer to hers . . . she felt so good . . . he wanted more. But it would be soon enough that they could make love like they used to . . . As he thought about how his lips, tongue and hands would touch every possible place on her body, his body responded.

Feeling his erection throb against her backside, she pressed back.

"*Don't*!" he hissed, afraid he would lose control.

But Amber turned to face him, slowly pushing him onto his back.

"Amber . . ." Ricky watched as she straddled his stomach.

"*Sh-h-h-h-h*." She leaned to kiss him on the mouth, then proceeded to kiss everywhere on his hard body as her body slowly slid down over his. "Just lay there and enjoy." By the time she was able to wrap her fingers around the top half of his erection, they were both breathing hard and fast. Amber looked up to see him watching her. Her tongue flicked out to taste his tip . . . and he moaned, low and deep. “If I remember right, I wanted to do this to you not that long ago and you stopped me . . . remember?” As she lowered her head, Amber whispered, “*Not this time* . . .”

* * *

Opening his eyes the next morning, Ricky looked at a dresser that he didn’t recognize. But he quickly remembered who’s bed he was in . . . *Amber’s*. With a smile, he turned to her . . . to find her side of the bed empty. The disappointment he felt at first disappeared when he realized she must be with Becky. Getting out of bed, he made a trip to the bathroom before walking to the door of the baby’s room.

Amber stood with her back to him, changing Becky’s diaper. She had heard him coming up the hall. “Good morning” she greeted, turning her head to offer him a smile. And seeing him dressed only in his boxers sent a rush of warmth and desire through her body. “How are you?” Her attention returned to Becky.

Ricky was suddenly standing right behind her, his arms sliding around her body. “Good morning to you” he returned, pressing his lips in her hair. “I feel wonderful . . . how about you?”

“I wanted to be next to you when you woke up but our daughter had other ideas.” Amber leaned back against him for a moment. “I’m glad you stayed last night” she softly told him.

His arms gave her a small squeeze. “Me, too.” Peeking over her shoulder at Becky, he asked Amber, “How long have you two been up?”

“About forty five minutes. She’s been fed and changed. I was just telling her that we have to wake you up soon so that you can go get ready for work.”

Checking the Winnie-The-Pooh clock on the wall, Ricky said, “I have time to have coffee with you.”

“Yes you do . . . and it’s all ready.” Picking Becky up off the changing table, she said to her, “Daddy can hold you before he has to go.” Amber turned, placing Becky in his arms.

It was then that Ricky noticed that the blue shirt of his that she wore was completely unbuttoned. “And Daddy wants to hold Mommy, too, before he has to go” he added, meeting Amber’s eyes.

She smiled as she turned, leaning to pick the soiled diaper up off the floor and dropping it into the wastebasket. “Let’s go have some coffee.”

Washing her hands in the kitchen sink, she asked Ricky if he wanted any breakfast.

"Don't go to any trouble" he replied from his seat at the table.

"I have some bagels and I think there's an English Muffin or two . . . there's eggs . . ."

"A bagel sounds good."

Amber poured him a cup of coffee after putting two bagels in the toaster, and poured herself a half a cup. Setting his cup in front of him, she said, "Let me take her" and lifted Becky out of his arms to place her in her seat on the table. Buckling her in, Amber gently kissed her forehead. "You can keep an eye on Daddy from there."

"That thing is a great idea. You can keep her with you in that."

"Yeah . . . between this and the bassinet, she stays pretty much with me all day. I very seldom put her in her room when she naps . . . I want her to get used to the noise of the stereo or the TV or just talking so she can sleep through it. I can't see trying to keep really quiet while she sleeps."

"You're a good mom" he commented.

"I try to be." She smiled at him. "This is all new to me . . . I do what I think is best . . . or hope is the best for her." The bagels popped up. "Breakfast is almost ready. Butter and cream cheese?" she asked, on her way to the counter.

"If that's what you're having."

"Oh, you know it!" And she giggled.

He watched from his chair as Amber gathered the margarine tub as well as the cream cheese out of the refrigerator. He watched while she spread margarine on the bagels . . . and watched where the shirt she wore ended and met with her bare shapely legs . . . he watched till he couldn't take it any more. Ricky got out of the chair . . .

Amber wasn't surprised when he stepped behind her. She had hoped he would. Sliding inside the open shirt she wore, each of his hands cupped a breast as his thumbs tormented her nipples, causing them to harden and peak. His mouth found the side of her neck, kissing it tenderly. Finding she could no longer concentrate on breakfast, Amber set down the butter knife and leaned back into his body. "I love you" he whispered, letting his hand slide further down . . . over her not-quite-flat stomach . . . and her body tensed briefly. "Is everything okay?" Ricky asked, in a low voice.

"Yes" she whispered, though it bothered her that she hadn't lost all the extra weight she had gained while pregnant. A lot it had disappeared but she had more to work on, to feel good about herself. Breast-feeding helped . . . but it wasn't going fast enough for her! Turning to face him, her arms slid around Ricky's neck. "It was a good idea for you to stay last night. I'm not sure about you but I enjoyed myself . . ." Amber chuckled softly as her mouth raised to his.

His mouth covered hers and his tongue slid inside. When he pulled back, Ricky met her gaze and said, with a smile, "You *know* how much I enjoyed myself!"

Laughing, Amber realized it had been a long time since she had felt that happy. Holding him as tightly as she could, she whispered, "Don't *ever* let me go again!"

As his embrace tightened, he replied, "I won't."

Another cup of coffee and the bagel was a quick meal. Ricky figured he had just enough time to get home, change and get to the precinct on time. "I'll call you later" he told Amber after a last kiss before going out the door.

* * *

He did call her after he got home from work, tired. It had been a good, long night and a very busy day. "I'm staying home tonight. I'm beat and afraid I wouldn't be much company."

"Oh . . . okay." Amber tried to hide her disappointment.

But Ricky heard it. "Hey . . . tomorrow is Friday . . . and I'll spend all weekend with you if you want me to."

Her spirits rose. "Oh, you know I do. I'll have to get rested up tonight myself."

With a chuckle, he told her, "And we can nap over the weekend when Becky is sleeping."

"Yeah . . . and I bet we'll get a lot of sleep then!"

After talking for another hour, they said their goodnights and hung up their phones. Amber missed him, wishing he was there but took comfort in knowing he would be there at least for the next two nights. Ricky almost thought twice about his decision but figured he did need to get his rest.

Instead of the TV, he turned on the stereo, listening to the oldies. He lay on the couch, with the only light in the apartment coming from the street lights, listening to the songs that he and Amber used to sing and or dance to. Listening to Chuck Berry, The Archies, Herman's Hermits and so many others brought back so many happy times with her. But when the music to a certain song started to play, he wished he was with Amber. Ricky closed his eyes, remembering the night when that song played and Amber got up on his coffee table to dance and took off her clothes, slow and seductively, to *I Want To Kiss You All Over*. As each piece of clothing came off, his lips did as the title stated. His body reacted to his vivid memories and the urge to go to her was strong. But he would wait another night . . .

* * *

Chapter 21

Ricky was in the office of his boss, Lt. Clancy. He had gone in to request a partner change for Deana. There was no working with her any more, especially now knowing how she really felt about him . . . and he clearly wasn't interested in any relationship with her.

A.J. sat at his desk, watching Ricky through the window. He wondered what was going on, since Ricky hadn't said anything about having to talk to the lieutenant.

"What's going on in there?" Deana startled A.J. with her question. She had stepped up beside his chair and he never noticed.

"I have no clue."

She didn't say anything for a few moments but then quietly asked, "Did he tell you it's over between us?"

A.J. glanced around to make sure nobody was close enough to hear. "No . . . I haven't seen much of him lately except here."

"He came over to my place the other night . . ."

Ricky had told A.J. that he had taken all of his things out of her apartment a week or so ago but didn't comment to Deana.

"I miss him. I went by his place last night . . . his car was there but there weren't any lights on in his apartment. I wonder if Amber was there with him. I almost went to his door but decided I had better not. It's hard, A.J., I miss him at night. So many times I have wanted to call him He hasn't said anything to you?"

Glancing up at her, A.J. wondered just how hard she was taking this split with Ricky . . . and with Amber being here with his baby . . . he hoped it wasn't so bad she would crack. "Please don't ask, Deana. I'm really not at liberty to say . . ."

Shrugging her shoulders, she said, "I know you two are best friends . . . and I thought you and I were at least friends. But I believe by your answer that he has talked to you but being his friend, you won't confide in me. I understand . . ."

Seeing Ricky standing at the door, still talking, A.J. suddenly wished he would hurry up and get back to his desk, which was by his . . . and Deana's. There were times like this that he wished he had the skill to talk to people about anything like Sara did. He relaxed a little when he saw Lt. Clancy shake Ricky's hand and then the door opened. The lieutenant stepped outside the door after Ricky left his office. He looked over at their desks and said, "Deana, would you come into my office, please?"

She threw a look at A.J., then Ricky before starting toward the office. Ricky didn't look at her as they passed by one another.

"What was that all about?" A.J. quietly asked Ricky after he was seated at his desk.

"I asked Clancy to put Deana with another partner . . . it will be either Chris or Larry."

"Why?"

"I can't work with her like that any more. It's gotten too personal where she's concerned."

"She doesn't want your relationship to be over."

Ricky looked at him. "You know better."

"I know you and Amber love each other very much . . . I am so glad you *finally* came to your senses. I also know that Deana is having a hard time with it."

Ricky sighed. "That's why she has to be working with anyone but me."

"And me. She was asking questions . . . Ricky, she was by your place looking for you last night."

Frowning, Ricky looked from A.J. to the Lt.'s office. Deana looked upset as Clancy spoke to her. "I was home."

"She wasn't sure, even though your vehicle was there, you didn't have the lights on in your apartment . . . she thinks maybe Amber was with you."

"Now she's stalking me?" Ricky hissed in a loud whisper.

Just then, Deana returned to her desk, very upset. Not looking at either of the men, she started opening drawers and slamming their contents on top of the desk. Suddenly stopping and taking a deep, shaky breath, Deana glared at Ricky. "Thanks to you, I have to change desks and work with Chris and Larry. What did you say to the boss?"

His eyes met hers. "That it was a personal thing and we can't work together any longer. I'm sure the whole squad knew about us . . . it was a hard thing to keep secret . . . even Clancy had his suspicions. You're a good detective, Deana . . . I can't argue about that but we *can't* work together. If circumstances were different, I'd be pleased to continue to work side by side with you."

Leaning over the desk as far as she could, Deana hissed, "Why? Because I told you that I love you?"

A.J.'s eyes widened at that statement but then looked down at some papers on his desk.

Ricky opened his mouth to respond but instead, closed his mouth, got up from his desk and disappeared into the men's bathroom.

"A.J., I . . ."

"*Don't*" he cut in. "No more, Deana. It's between you two."

* * *

Knowing that Ricky would be with her that night, Amber tried to stay busy and clean around the apartment, then soaked in the tub with some Gardenia bath salts in the middle of the afternoon while Becky napped.

But Ricky's work changed those plans. It was after one a.m. when he entered his apartment. He knew it was late but he needed to hear Amber's voice. All of those involved had just spent hours trying to talk a young man in his twenties out of killing again.He had already shot and killed his live-in girlfriend of two years in a drunken, jealous rage, and then he went after the other man, who had been his best friend. Their year old son had been left in his crib near where his mother lay dead on the floor, screaming and sobbing so much that a neighbor called the police. Yes, they had heard a gunshot but after hearing so many of them in the surrounding neighborhood, they had no idea it was only next door. Another call came in about a hostage situation. Hours later, the suspect surrendered and the other man was in bad shape after being pistol-whipped with the gun that had already killed and he had been threatened with.

Ricky started to dial Amber's number, hesitating before pressing the last numeral. She answered on the first ring. "Ricco?"

"I'm glad you're awake."

"Becky just went to sleep. Are you home?"

"Yeah . . . but I wanted to hear your voice."

"Come over" she softly invited.

"It's late."

"I don't care . . . come on over. Crawl into bed like you used to."

He needed no more urging. "Okay. I'll be there soon."

Yawning, Amber got up to unchain the lock. Tired, she crept back into bed. Becky hadn't slept much that night.

Ricky walked into the quiet apartment. After locking the door, and taking off his sneakers, he went to Amber's room. He heard her even breathing when he walked in. Setting his duffel bag on the floor, he stripped off his clothes and slid into bed.

The slight movement of the mattress woke her. She turned slowly toward him, glad he was there. "Hi" she whispered, moving close to him.

"I didn't mean to wake you."

"I know . . . that's okay." Her arm slid across his chest and she snuggled closer. "Talk to me."

Ricky wished he could. But just to hold her took away much of the tension that night had caused. He tried not to bring his work home with him. There was so much he didn't want Amber to know about . . . she didn't need to know what terrible things people could do to one another. It was bad enough she could read about it in the paper. With Deana it had been different because she was there to see what he did . . . they had discussed things. Amber and Deana were two totally different women . . . two different situations.

"Just hold me, okay?" he requested.

"Okay" was Amber's soft reply.

* * *

He must have been tired. Ricky didn't stir when Amber slid out from under his arm when she got up to go to Becky. She shut off the baby monitor and quietly closed the door behind her.

* * *

It was close to nine when Ricky got out of bed. He checked the baby's room, only to find it empty. He entered the kitchen just as Amber put the pitcher of OJ back into the refrigerator. "Hey, you . . . morning" he greeted sleepily.

She smiled as she turned to him. "Morning." Amber noted the sweatpants he wore as she walked to him. He smiled after a big stretch and stepped forward to meet her. As she moved into his arms, she commented, "Nice sweats. I know those aren't Jake's."

"I . . . um . . . brought some things to keep here . . . if that's okay."

"You bet it is" she replied, as she raised her mouth for a kiss.

Ricky pulled her close. "How long have you been up?"

"Since about 7:30."

"You should have gotten me up."

"You needed your sleep."

He gave her a lop-sided smile before asking, "Where's our little girl?"

"In the living room, listening to Sesame Street."

"She's *what*?"

Amber laughed. "While I was pregnant, I watched that show every day . . . and now I leave the TV on for her to listen to for an hour. Becky's going to know all the words to the songs when she starts talking!"

"This I have to see!"

Taking his hand in hers, Amber went into the next room. Sure enough, Ernie was on the TV screen, singing about his rubby ducky. Becky lay in her bassinet a few feet away, with her head slightly cocked toward the TV. "It's the only program I'll let her 'watch'" Amber laughed.

"You're too much!" Ricky pulled her into his arms.

"I hope that's a good thing."

"Oh, it is . . ." Kissing her, Ricky wondered how he made it without her all those months. "Thanks for letting me come over in the wee hours of the morning."

"Any time . . . that's why you have a key."

He pushed back some unbrushed hair from her face. "I love you" he whispered.

"I know." She kissed him. "I know." Another kiss . . . then, she asked, "Did you bring . . . ?"

"Yes" he interrupted, knowing what she wanted to know. "I bought four boxes."

"*Four* boxes?" She laughed.

He grinned sheepishly. "I want to be prepared at all times." After a kiss that made her knees buckle, Ricky told her, "Just let me know when you're ready . . ."

Her heart pounded harder as her body grew warmer at his remark. "I'm ready now" she whispered, but then said in a louder voice, "I figured it will be better to wait until after Becky's next feeding . . . and she'll sleep for at least an hour and a half."

"When will that be?"

"Probably not for another hour. She used to eat like clockwork . . . I always could figure when but now she's eating more and it's a little longer between each feeding."

Ricky's mouth took hers, showing the impatience he felt. Abruptly pulling away, he held Amber tightly against him. "I think I had better stand under a cold shower till then." Then, a strange look crossed his face as he suddenly backed away from her, wiping a hand across his bare chest. "What the . . . ?"

Amber felt it, too. Looking down at the front of the shirt she wore, she saw it was wet at both breasts. "Oops! I leaked!" She couldn't help but laugh. "It must have been that tight squeeze! I'm sorry!"

Ricky started laughing, too. "I do need a shower now!"

While Ricky was in the shower, Amber listened to the water, remembering again their times together under the spray of water. As she pulled off the blue shirt, she caught her reflection in the full-length mirror on the outside of the bathroom door. Looking closer at herself, she saw that her nipples were hard and peaked . . . the result of thinking of their showers together. Her breasts were larger . . . Oh! If they could only stay that way! Her hand slid over her larger stomach . . . would it ever slim down? But she smiled, knowing Ricky still loved and wanted her. Sliding her hands up to cup her breasts, Amber's eyes closed a she remembered how his mouth felt on them just a few days ago . . . and knowing he would be doing it again soon. Opening her eyes to look at her reflection, her fingers skimmed over her peaked nipples before reaching for her short robe on the chair near the door and putting it on. She heard the water shut off in the shower . . .

While in the shower, Ricky thought about what was to come. As he soaped himself, he thought of past showers with Amber and how she soaped him . . . Between the two thoughts, he grew hard. He reached for the water temperature control knob . . . and turned it in the opposite direction from the hot water . . . Minutes later, he turned the knob to off.

Over the baby monitor, Amber heard Becky making her hungry noises. Going to the bathroom, she gently knocked on the door before opening it. Her breath caught when she saw his naked body standing on the bath mat as he towel-dried his hair. Her eyes moved from the towel at his head to his broad shoulders and chest, well-shaped arms, his washboard stomach and narrow waist to his slim hips and long, muscular legs. Looking at her, he was turned on by her reaction.

"Ohmygod!" she uttered, thinking he was more beautiful than he was when she was last with him. Licking her suddenly dry lips, she told him, "I'm going to feed Becky . . . she's hungry."

"She's not the only one" Ricky replied, his voice husky sounding as his gaze swept over her open robe . . . and his erection grew hard quickly. When she didn't move, he said, "You had better leave now or our daughter won't get to eat when she wants to."

The urge to run to him for a kiss was strong but Amber knew if she did, it wouldn't stop there. Her eyes didn't leave him until she closed the door between them. Standing outside the door, she took deep breaths, trying to get back to normal to take care of Becky.

Amber's head was lowered as she softly sang to their nursing daughter. She knew that Ricky stood in the doorway . . . again she had heard him walk toward the nursery. She didn't want to stop rocking the chair . . . she wanted to make sure Becky had her fill and would go to sleep. But when she finally looked up at him, her breath caught once more, seeing him standing there with only a towel wrapped around his waist.

His breath also caught as he watched her eyes move from his face and slowly slide down his body to the towel. When her eyes met his again, he recognized the desire in them . . . and saw the soft smile on her lips. His body reacted again to her.

Returning her attention to Becky, Amber saw that her eyes were almost closed and her mouth was slack at her breast. Putting Becky up to her shoulder to pat her back, Amber's eyes met Ricky's again. He had leaned against the doorway, watching them . . . but he wasn't at ease. The short while it took Becky to burp seemed like an eternity to her parents. Becky then sighed and relaxed against her mother. It took much restraint not to get up and put her to bed just then. Amber rocked a few minutes more to make sure she was asleep, with her eyes on Ricky the whole time. She could tell by his eyes . . . and the front of the towel . . . that he wanted her.

After putting Becky in her cradle and making sure the monitor was on, Amber turned toward Ricky. He stood tall, looking at her, then turned and went out of the room. She followed, shutting off the light and partially closing the door. Ricky was just stepping into her room when she started up the hall, willing herself not to run.

Closing the door behind her, Amber felt Ricky step close. As she turned to him, he made the first move, reaching out to caress her cheek with his fingertips. Then both hands moved to her shoulders and pushed her robe over them. It slid down her arms and pooled at her feet. Her first move was to reach for where his towel came together and pull it apart . . . it landed at his feet. But Amber frowned as he turned away, reaching inside his duffel bag. Her frown disappeared when his hand come out with some condoms. He tossed them toward the nightstand, where one fell to the floor. Not bothering to pick it up, they reached for one another . . .

* * *

Chapter 22

Her lips parted for his tongue as his arms circled around her warm body. Feeling his erection pulsing against her bare skin, Amber's body arched, wanting to feel more. Moaning into her mouth, his hands slid down to cup her bottom and hold her tighter against him. Moments later, Ricky growled, "*Don't move*!" Her eyes met his and he missed the hint of a smile on her lips. It took only seconds for his mouth to take hers again . . . again . . . and again. His mouth lowered to her jaw line, then her neck. Amber's head dropped back to accommodate him, inhaling sharply when his mouth lowered to her breast. His lips, tongue and mouth licked, nipped and suckled at each nipple, taking his time to enjoy.

The ache between her legs was fierce, burning. What he was doing to her breasts made it seem more intense. Grabbing one of his hands, Amber guided it down. "*Touch me*!" she pleaded. He straightened his body to look at her face as his hand slid between her legs. "*You are so wet*!" he groaned, as his finger slid along her damp folds. When his finger slowly entered her, Amber grasped his shoulder to keep herself from falling over. She moaned, low and deep, the pleasure almost unbearable. Realizing the moan wasn't caused by pain, his finger began to move. Her eyes closed and her breathing became short and quick. "*No*!" she protested when his finger pulled out. "*Ohgodyes*!" Two of his fingers slid inside . . . and out . . . inside . . . and out . . . it wasn't long before her body moved in rhythm with his fingers . . . "Okay . . . hold on a sec . . ." Ricky whispered, as he removed his fingers and then his thumb settled on her mound and began to rub gently. It took only a few moments before Amber pressed her pleasure point against his thumb, her body moving back and forth . . .

back and forth . . . and Amber's breathing became faster and shallower. Knowing she was close to her release . . . Ricky hoped he could wait when it happened. He was so hard . . . so ready . . . he throbbed to be inside her. After a loud gasp, Amber cried out as her body started to convulse . . .

She didn't think it was ever going to end. Wave after wave of pleasure coursed through her body. When her cries lessened, Ricky removed his thumb and held her as she tried to catch her breath. Amber's body leaned into his . . . and he wanted to give her time to be ready for him, even though he throbbed, needing his release. With his voice low and husky, Ricky chuckled. "Why didn't I think of doing that to you a month ago?"

She chuckled softly, not able to speak at that moment. But when she was able, Amber slowly said, "Don't let go of me just yet. My legs feel like rubber."

"Here . . ." And in one sweep, he picked her up in his arms and turned to the bed. There was no ceremony after he laid her down. Up on his knees between her legs, Ricky grabbed a condom package and tore it open. "I'm sorry, babe . . . I can't wait. I hope I don't hurt you . . ."

Amber only nodded impatiently, wanting him inside her.

Ricky entered her, forcing himself to go slow. *Damn*! *She felt good*!

Oh! *He felt so good*! She hadn't forgotten how big he was . . . Amber moaned as he filled her. And to help him along, Amber raised her knees and hips for deeper penetration, taking all of him. He thrust into her only twice before he came . . . his moan became louder with his much needed release. Spent, Ricky's body collapsed on Amber's.

But, as much as he wanted to cuddle, first things first. He sat on the edge of the bed. "Is there a waste basket around?"

"On the other side of the nightstand."

Reaching to bring it closer, Ricky tossed the used condom and it's wrapper in it. After using the towel that was on the floor, he lay back next to Amber. "Are you okay? Did I hurt you?"

"No. It hurt a little at first but . . ." She sighed. "I feel so good right now."

Reaching over to push her hair back from the side of her face, he told her, "I've missed you . . . it's been too long. I needed you."

A smile touched her lips as she cuddled a little closer to his body. "I remember how much you enjoy sex . . . it's a wonder you waited as long as you did." But as soon as she said it, an image of Deana popped into her head. She caught her bottom lip with her teeth, looking away from him. *Why* did she have to think of *her*? There was no question that they had had sex . . .

As if he read her thoughts, his hand gently turned her face to look at him. "It was never *just* sex with you . . . I love you."

"We just had a quickie" she teased.

"That we did." His mouth moved toward hers. "We'll have to slow it down this time . . . if you're ready."

"I'm ready" and her lips opened for him.

The kiss was slow and tender . . . and interrupted by baby noises over the monitor.

"Is she awake?" Ricky asked, hoping she wasn't.

"I don't think so." "It's a wonder she slept through her mom crying out in pleasure" Ricky teased with a smile, tracing her bottom lip with his forefinger. "You still have a tendency to be loud."

With a soft chuckle, Amber replied, "She sleeps through the TV and stereo . . . she'll have to get used to that, too."

Ricky's mouth covered Amber's, kissing her . . . long and slow. He pulled back long enough to whisper, "That waste basket will be filled by the time I leave . . ." and took her mouth again. They stopped to listen when a soft cry came over the monitor. Waiting a few moments and not hearing any more sounds, they looked at each other. "There will be times she will interrupt us" Amber said.

He sighed. "That's something we'll have to deal with when it happens." Ricky watched as her face became sad. "What's wrong?"

"I'm so sorry" she whispered.

"Sorry? For what?"

"For leaving you . . . for taking away time that we'll never get back . . ." Tears filled her eyes. "For not letting you know that I was pregnant." A tear slid down her face . . . then another.

"*Sh-h-h-h . . . don't*" was his whispered response. "Don't cry . . . sh-h-h-h." Gathering her into his arms, he held her close. "It's okay now . . . we're together . . ." Holding her for a few minutes, Ricky felt Amber finally relax. "Okay now?"

"Yes." Raising her head, Amber's mouth moved toward him and her lips parted as they met his.

Kissing her slowly, Ricky lay her on her back and his hand rested on her stomach. Moments later, his fingers stroked her skin. As her body started to respond, Amber sighed against his lips. Pulling back, he saw that her eyes were closed. There was a slight smile on his face as his hand slid to her breast and he watched the tip of her nipple harden.

"You like that, don't you?" His voice sounded husky.

"*Yes*" she purred

In a matter of seconds, his mouth was on her nipple, sucking and licking . . . causing her body to ache again for him. Amber opened her eyes to watch him work his magic . . . till she couldn't take it any longer. Arching her body, she pressed her breast against his mouth and he suckled a little harder . . . before pulling back. "Let's take it a little slower" he panted.

"Why? We have the rest of our lives to take it slower."

He chuckled softly. "We don't have to make up for lost time in one afternoon."

"Why not? You've had . . ." Amber stopped. She came close to saying that he had had sex while they were apart . . . and she didn't. She looked at him, afraid that he knew what she was going to say.

But he did. "Oh, Amber . . ." Ricky crushed his mouth against hers. When he pulled back, he said, "I want you, babe . . . I want *you*." Taking her mouth again, he also grasped her hand to guide it to his erection . . . and moaned into her mouth as her hand closed around him.

Amber placed it against his chest and pushed him onto his back. With her mouth next to his ear, she quietly told him, "It's not the same with you wearing a rubber. You don't feel the same." Her teeth gently grabbed his earlobe before her tongue stroked inside his ear. "I can't wait till I can feel the real you inside me . . . you and nothing else."

This time wasn't rushed. Their hands and mouths were always moving . . . always touching. They whispered their love, what they liked done and what they were going to do to the other. When Ricky entered her, he was able to take his time, unlike the time before. When Amber cried out, he joined her before she was finished.

She lay in his arms as they waited for their breathing to return to normal. Ricky then asked, "Are you sore?"

"A little . . . it's not bad."

"We'd better back off for awhile."

"Ohhhh . . . maybe." And she smiled at him.

Ricky pulled her against him. She lay with her head against his chest and his arm around her. Looking up at the ceiling, his fingers stroked her arm. As he listened to her breathing, he wondered if she had fallen asleep. Ricky thought about their love-making . . . how Amber had always responded to him. She was always ready. Amber had been hungry for him that day . . . he couldn't imagine going that long without sex. With Deana, it had only been sex. If she had known how often he had thought of Amber when they were together . . . He pushed Deana out of his head. Amber was back . . . their time apart never diminished his love and need for her.

He was amazed when he became hard again. "Give her a break" he mentally told himself.

But then, with a small sigh, Amber rolled on her back. Taking it as an invitation, Ricky closed his mouth over her breast. Her fingers were in his hair as her body arched to press herself into his mouth. He wondered if Becky would be getting hungry because he could taste Amber's milk this time. Raising his head just enough, his tongue licked over the hard nipple. Amber moaned and he did it again.

Becky's soft cries were heard over the monitor.

Sucking on one nipple, his fingers teased the other, causing it to become hard.

Amber moaned low.

Ricky's head raised to cover her mouth with his. Their tongues mated.

Becky's cries grew louder.

Amber opened her legs and his hand slid between them.

The cries continued.

Pulling her mouth from his, Amber gasped, "I have to go to her."

Rolling onto his back, Ricky tried not to show his frustration. "Okay."

* * *

After Becky was changed and fed, Amber took her to the kitchen and put her in her 'seat' on the table. "I wonder who called" Amber chatted, as she secured Becky into her seat. "The red light is flashing on the answering machine." The ringer had been shut off on the phone in the bedroom and the volume turned turned down low on the kitchen phone. There were four messages.

The first was from Jake, wondering what time they were starting out to his place the following weekend. Amber smiled, shaking her head. "Don't be so impatient, Jake!"

Sara had called next: "Hi, it's me . . . Sara. Um . . . give me a call when you hear this, okay?" And Sara called again: "It's me! A.J. and I were wondering if Ricky's with you and what you are doing for dinner, either today or tomorrow." Amber glanced at the clock to see the time was after noon. "It's been awhile since we've gotten together and we would like you to join us. Call me!"

The last call was from Deana: "Ricky, are you there?" There was silence, and then the sound of her hanging up the phone.

Staring at the phone, Amber couldn't believe she had the nerve to call her home and ask for Ricky. A noise behind her caused her to turn . . . there stood Ricky, also staring at the phone. When his eyes met Amber's, she saw the anger.

"That was Deana?" he quietly asked.

"Yes."

"*Damn* her!" He started toward the phone but Amber stopped him.

"Don't, Ricky! Calm down first!" He looked at her and she realized that she had never seen him that angry. Putting a hand on his stiff arm, she tried, "*Ricco*, we had a beautiful morning. Don't allow her to spoil it."

"She did already by calling!"

"Don't let it get to you. Come here . . ." Her hand caressed his cheek. "That was probably her intent by leaving a message on my answering machine . . . come on, don't let her win."

Moments later, she felt his body relax. His eyes turned from black and stormy to dark brown. The hardness left his jaw as he looked at Amber. Suddenly, he reached out and roughly pulled her to him, hugging her to his body. "I know . . . you're right. I'll deal with her at work on Monday."

Their attention was drawn to the kitchen table by baby noises.

"I'm gonna see my other girl." He stepped away from Amber after kissing her forehead. As he walked toward the table, Amber noticed he was wearing only his boxers. She smiled, enjoying the view.

"I have to call Jake and Sara back" she told him.

"They called, too?" "Yep . . . Sara left two. She wants to know if we want to have dinner with her and A.J. either today or tomorrow."

"Do you want to?" He took Becky out of her seat.

"Yes . . . don't you?"

Turning toward her, he answered, "Yes . . . but today or tomorrow?"

Her eyes slid down his body then back to his face. "Tomorrow."

A smile touched his lips as he briefly nodded his agreement. He then asked, "What did Jake want? Anything important?"

"Not really . . . he's just being my pesty brother about next weekend."

Ricky chuckled, cuddling Becky.

"I just remembered, seeing you two together . . . I used the breast pump."

"Without my help? I'm crushed." He tried to look forlorn.

Amber couldn't help but laugh.

"How did it go?"

"Not bad once I got the hang of it. It'll come in handy . . . like next Wednesday when I go for my doctor's appointment."

"Who's watching her?"

"Maggie. I'll stop over at the shop on the way to the doctor's."

"She'll be okay there?"

"Of course . . . I wouldn't leave her there if I didn't think so. Remember, Maggie and Matt have two kids of their own."

"That's right . . . I forgot. Well, I'm going to spend some quality time with my daughter, if you'll excuse us."

"You're excused" Amber said with a laugh, as she watched them go into the living room.

But she was still bothered by Deana's call as she dialed Jake's number. But instead of Jake, she got his voice mail, so, she left him a message: "Just a call to let you know that I will let you know when we know we are heading up to your place. Love ya!"

After dialing Sara's number, Sara answered on the third ring. "Hi, Amber!"

"Hey! Sorry I haven't called you."

"Don't apologize . . . I understand. You have a baby to take care of now. How is she?"

"She's doing good . . . and I see changes in her already."

Sara laughed. "A.J. is worried she'll be walking by the time we see her again!"

"Oh, Sara . . . I'm sorry! I . . ."

"No! It's not your fault. We can come see you easier than you can take her out."

"But I don't mind taking her out."

"Good! What about dinner tonight?"

"Um . . . well, I . . ."

"Would tomorrow be better?"

Amber had to keep from sighing out loud in relief. "That would be better . . . if it is for you."

"Oh, yes! We're anxious to see you! Have you seen Ricky?"

Her morning with him flashed through her, heating her body. "Um . . . yes. He's here now,as a matter of fact. We've been . . . um . . . we . . . I . . . um, we've been getting to know each other again."

"Oh." Then, after a pause, "Oh-h-h-h!"

Amber didn't hear Ricky step come up behind her. His arms moved around her and his hands slid inside her open robe to cover her breasts. With his mouth against her other ear, he said in a quiet voice, "I want to make love to you right now."

Her breathing came faster. Trying to concentrate on her conversation with Sara, she said, "We will see you tomorrow. What time?"

"Any time between one thirty and two, okay?"

His mouth was on the back of her neck, with his lips partially open and his tongue doing erotic things to her skin. Amber had to will herself not to moan out loud at what he was doing to her. She had to stay focused on Sara: "What do you . . ." She had to lick her lips and swallow before continuing: "What do you want us to bring?"

"Nothing . . . we're all set."

Amber had to lick her dry lips again. "Are you sure?"

"Yes." Sara chuckled as she quietly asked, "Is Ricky right there getting to know you some more?"

"Uh-huh." Amber's eyes closed as her head dropped forward to give him more room to work.

"See you tomorrow" Sara told her, still chuckling.

It took a moment for Sara's comment to register. "Oh . . . okay, Sara. Thanks for calling." It took another moment to remember how to shut off the phone. "Where's Rebecca?" she thought to ask Ricky.

"In her bassinet. I must have bored her . . . she fell asleep."

Her hand reached out to put the phone on the counter, almost dropping it on the floor when it didn't quite reach the first try. "She'll sleep fifteen minutes at the most" she murmured, then inhaled sharply when he suddenly yanked her body against his.

"That's enough time." His arousal pressed against her lower back. Ricky breathed hard in her ear while his fingers fondled her breasts. "I feel sixteen again . . . I'm a horny teenager with his testosterone level gone sky high. See what you do to me?" His mouth kissed her ear and his tongue slid in a couple of times. "Do you remember those times we made love everywhere in your apartment?"

It was hard for her to breathe. "*Yes!*" she hissed, pressing her butt against his erection.

"I need you . . . now" he murmured in a husky voice.

Amber's words and movements didn't correlate with each other as she continued to press back against him: "We can't . . . not here . . . you don't have . . ."

"Yes I do . . . I'll be prepared for this as long as I need to be . . . and let's get rid of this." He pulled her robe over her shoulders and it slipped down her arms to the floor. His hand moved between her legs and Ricky smiled. "*You are so ready for me*" he whispered in her ear.

Turning to face him, Amber raised her mouth for a long, deep kiss. Reluctantly stepping back, she watched as he tore open a condom and slid it over his erection. Backing her against the counter, Ricky told her, "Put your arms around my neck." As she did so, he lifted her onto the edge of the counter. "Hold onto me." His voice sounded huskier and just as he finished speaking, he slid inside her. His hands held her bottom to keep her from sliding backwards with his thrusts. It wasn't long before he came and Amber cried out as she clung to him.

In the few minutes it took for their breathing to return to normal, they held each other. "It's a good thing I don't have any kitchen windows." Amber murmured.

"And I'm going to have to control myself as Becky gets older." Ricky kissed her gently before helping her off the counter. "Are you okay?"

"Oh, yeah . . ." she sighed with contentment, looking up at him.

With a smile, he softly replied, "Me, too."

* * *

Dinner at Sara and A.J.'s was good. Sara made roasting chicken, mashed potatoes,stuffing and gravy, carrots and corn. For dessert there was a Banana Split cake. Amber groaned with her first bite, savoring how good it tasted. "Let me tell you . . . between today and next weekend, I'm going to gain back what weight I've lost!"

"What's next weekend?" A.J. asked.

"A weekend at Jake's. He's having a party slash cookout . . . and he always has a lot of good food!"

"Sounds like fun . . . and you get to see Jake again. I can't get over what a good brother you have" Sara commented.

Amber smiled. "Yeah . . . I think so, too." The smile disappeared when she said, "But for some reason, his girlfriend doesn't like me."

"You two are too close for her liking, must be" Ricky remarked.

"Must be."

"Well, hopefully you two can resolve things while you're there" Sara said. "I can't see Jake putting up with somebody that doesn't like his sister."

"I can't either."

While the women stayed in the kitchen to wash dishes, A.J. and Ricky took the baby into the living room with them. "She's getting bigger" A.J. commented, holding Becky. "And she looks more and more like you every time I see her."

"I hope that's a good thing."

A.J. chuckled but then said, "Okay, tell me what's been bugging you. I've been around you long enough to know when something is."

Ricky was silent for a long moment before telling A.J., "Deana . . . she called Amber's yesterday and left a message on the answering machine. Can you believe she did that? *I can't*!." He looked at A.J. after glancing toward the door to the kitchen "What is so hard for her to understand that it's over between us?"

"She doesn't want it to be over."

"But *it is*!"

"We know that."

Ricky shook his head in disgust. "I have to have another talk with . . ."

"Hey! Do you guys want any more coffee?" Amber asked from the doorway.

They both answered, 'No".

Returning to the kitchen, Amber said to Sara, "Sounded like some deep conversation going on in the other room."

"Probably something to do with work."

* * *

Ricky was waiting at Deana's desk when she srrived at work Monday morning. She smiled when she saw him but it quickly disappeared when she noticed the look on his face. Motioning with his head toward the door to an interview room, he walked toward the door. Deana tossed her purse into the bottom drawer of her desk before following him. Waiting at the door, Ricky closed it noisily behind Deana.

"What in hell were you doing calling me at Amber's Saturday?"

She made sure the table was between them before answering. "I . . . I . . . I wanted to talk to you."

"About what?"

"I . . . I wanted to hear your voice . . . I was thinking about you and missed you being at my place on the weekends. Does *she* know you spent a lot of nights with me?"

Ricky worked at controlling his anger . . . he was at his job. His hands clenched and unclenched . . . he had never hit a woman before but he was tempted right then. "That was then and this is now. *Do not* call me at all at any time, do you hear me? Especially at Amber's! What ever possessed you . . . ?"

"You never answer your cell phone when I call! I can't believe you're just dropping me."

"Well . . . news flash! Didn't it ever occur to you *why* I never answer? No matter what you do, you won't get me back, Deana . . . especially after the shit you're pulling. Back off . . . *now*." He glared at her a moment before he turned and left the room.

Deana wanted to cry but held her head high. *Damn that Amber for coming back.*

* * *

"So, what did the doctor say?" Ricky asked, after giving Amber a 'hello' kiss.

"I told him that I didn't think that Wednesday would ever get here . . . and that my baby is now six weeks old."

"Did you tell him that we didn't wait the whole six weeks?"

"Yes . . . after he asked if I was having, quote unquote, . . . *intercourse* . . . and I told him we were. I am now back on the Pill but have to keep using extra protection for another month."

"Did you tell him that the Pill failed you last time . . . and now we have Becky?"

"I did and he suggested that maybe I forgot to take the Pill on time every day . . . or I was on antibiotics or some kind of meds to throw off the balance of the Pill and it's ability to keep me from getting pregnant."

Pulling her into his arms, Ricy said, "Okay, no more doing what you did or didn't do then . . . not until we're ready to have another one."

"Oh, you know how to turn a girl on" Amber teased, sliding her arms around his neck. But she was happy that he was talking about having another baby!

"You always turn me on" he drawled, before his mouth took hers in a kiss that left them both breathless. "Damn! Can't I ever give you a plain ol' kiss?"

"What fun would that be?"

Smiling, Ricky caressed her bottom lip with an index finger. "I'm taking off this Friday and Monday."

"A four day weekend?"

"Thought you might like that. I have vacation time to use so I'm taking two this weekend and an extra day for Labor Day weekend."

"Two long weekends in a row . . . I like the sound of that."

"Me, too" he murmured before kissing her again.

* * *

Chapter 23

The sky was gray when they started out on their trip to Jake's. The 7 a.m. traffic was nowhere as busy as they knew it would be in another hour. They made their way out to Rt #87 and headed north. Becky was strapped into her car seat behind her mother.

Sprinkles wet the windshield at times. The closer they drove to Albany, the sprinkles turned to rain. "Jake will be devastated if his party gets rained out" Amber commented, as she watched the wipers swish back and forth.

"We have awhile to go before we get to Jake's . . . it's probably not raining there" Ricky said.

"You're right" she agreed, reaching over to pat his knee. "And the party isn't till tomorrow."

His hand covered hers and brought it to his lips. "I'm glad we're getting away for a few days."

"Me, too." Amber sighed. "But I have issues to hopefully iron out with Lisa."

* * *

It wasn't long after twelve noon that Ricky turned into the long driveway to Jake's. The two-story dark brown house rose up at the end of the drive, with it's screened-in porch on three sides and the four steps to the open porch at the back door that led into the kitchen. Behind her sunglasses, Amber's eyes scanned the house and the 3-car garage and all areas in-between for Jake. She smiled when he stepped out of the garage and looked their way. A big grin spread across his face and he raised a hand in greeting before motioning Ricky to park by the garage.

Amber had her seatbelt unhooked and her door open before Ricky had shut off the motor.

"Jake!" She threw her arms around his neck and he picked her up off the ground, twirling her around once before setting her back down.

He turned his attention to Ricky, who came around the back of the Durango to join them. "Hey, man!" he greeted, shaking his hand. "How was the trip up?"

"We ran into rain going to Albany but once we got off 87, it cleared up . . . which made your sister happy."

Jake looked at Amber, who shrugged her shoulders. "I was worried about the party getting rained out."

"But the forecast for tomorrow is good . . ." Grinning, he reached out to ruffle her hair. "Okay, where's the munchkin?"

Opening the back door, Ricky unhooked her seat and brought it out, with Becky still in it.

"That's quite the contraption" Jake commented.

"It's great while she's little" Amber said, unhooking the straps holding Becky in. "I think your Uncle wants to hold you, baby girl."

As Jake took Becky from her mother, they all heard a door slam shut from the direction of the house. Turning, they saw Lisa standing on the back porch, looking their way, wiping her hands on a towel. Waiting a moment, Amber called out, "Hi. Lisa!"

She responded with a wave.

"Come on and see the baby!" Jake yelled to her.

Lisa seemed to hesitate a minute before going down the steps and walking toward them, taking her time.

"Is she going to have an attitude with me?" Amber quietly asked Jake.

"She'd better not."

"Hello, Amber." Lisa stood beside Jake and acted like she didn't want to look at his sister. But when she turned to Ricky, she turned on the charm. "Well, hi, Ricky! Haven't seen you in a long while! Where have you been keeping yourself?"

Amber wanted to throttle her. She knew damn well what had happened.

But all Ricky said to her was: "Working . . . keeping busy. How have you been, Lisa?"

"Fine. It's good to have some company up here."

"Lisa, look at this baby! Isn't she just the most beautiful baby?" Jake said. "Uncle Jake is so happy to see you!" he cooed to Becky. "I was afraid you'd be starting school by the time I saw you again!"

Nobody noticed Lisa rolling her eyes.

"Come on, Jake . . . it hasn't been six weeks. You left when she was a week old" Amber informed him.

"Has it only been that long? She's grown since then! Lisa, I ask you again, isn't she just one beautiful baby?"

"She looks a lot like her daddy." Lisa looked up at Ricky and smiled.

Jake didn't notice but Amber did.

"We're taking our things up to my room" she said. "I'm ready to kick back for awhile after that long ride."

"What took you so long to get here?" Lisa asked.

"We made a couple of stops to stretch and a couple more so Amber could fed Becky" Ricky replied, looking at her through his sunglasses, wondering why the way she asked that question irritated him.

"Oh . . ." Lisa turned away from him.

Amber reached to take Becky from Jake. "She might be due for a diaper change."

Jake pulled Becky back from her mother. "Can't I keep her with me?"

"Sure . . . just don't spoil her any more than you already have!" Amber laughed.

Ricky opened the back end to take out the luggage. "It's going to take a few trips to get all this inside."

Lisa stepped beside him. "Geesh . . . and you're only here for the weekend?"

"Believe it or not" Ricky muttered, irritated by her once more.

"I put the small A.C. in the baby's room" Jake said.

"What do we have in my room?" Amber asked.

"The two window fans. I figured you two can handle the heat at night better than the muchkin, right? Unless she sleeps in your room."

"Okay, Uncle Jake" Amber replied. Opening the passenger door, she pulled out a small diaper bag and handed it to him. "Inside you will find . . . if needed . . . a receiving blanket, a pacifier, bottle, diapers and wipes. I hope you remember how to change a diaper."

Assuring her that he did, Amber then helped Ricky with the luggage, which they managed to carry in one trip. They each carried a suitcase and a diaper bag, plus a couple of smaller bags. He followed her up the back steps into the large kitchen, past the center island, through the dining room to the staircase just going into the living room. Amber glanced at the door to her right before going up the stairs. The banister smelled of fresh polish. Smiling as she climbed the stairs, she remembered the times she and Jake had slid down the same banister after their mom had polished it.

Her room and the guest room were off to the left of the hallway. The upstairs bathroom and Jake's former room were to the right. The larger bedroom at the end of the hall had been their parents . . . and now Jake's.

The three windows in her room were open, the screens in them and a breeze slightly blowing the curtains. The window fans were there, on the floor, under the windows.

"It's been awhile since I've been in this room" Ricky commented, setting the suitcase and bags on the floor. "You've changed it around."

"Yeah" she said, with a weak smile. "I had plenty of time with nothing to do for awhile." Putting what she carried on the bed, Amber looked around the room where she had spent plenty of alone-time while pregnant. Closing her eyes for a few moments, she didn't want to think about her self-imposed isolation. When she opened her eyes to find Ricky watching her, she smiled. "I was surprised my dad allowed us to sleep together when we visited."

"Me, too. I was sure I would have to bunk with Jake the first time we stayed" he said with a laugh.

Amber's laugh joined his. "Naw . . . there's a guest room" she teased.

"I guess he realized how we felt about each other." Ricky reached for her, pulling her into his arms.

"He did. That's why he never gave up on trying to get me to call you . . ." Amber slid her arms around him and lay her head against his chest. "I miss him *so* much. It was hard walking by his office on the way up the stairs . . . I'm glad Jake closed the door. I guess I half expected Dad to come walking out to greet us." She blinked back threatening tears.

Giving her a gentle squeeze, Ricky softly said, "I love you."

She looked up at him. "I know . . . I love you, too."

His mouth lowered to meet hers. The kiss started gentle but left them breathless by the time they parted. With a smile, Amber said, "They do have what they need for Becky for awhile. It wasn't that long ago that she last ate."

His thumb stroked her bottom lip. "Tempting but we should get her things ready. You never know . . ."

"Good idea" . . . though it wasn't what she really wanted to do at the moment.

Amber gasped when they walked into Becky's room. "Will you look at this!" Jake hadn't been kidding when he told her what he had bought for Becky to use. And everything looked in great shape.

Between the two of them, Becky's bags were emptied and everything had a place to go. Wipes and diapers were put under the changing table and clothes in some of the dresser drawers. Her bath supplies were placed on top of the dresser and a couple of light blankets went into the crib, where a set of baby monitors were found, laying on a thin quilt.

"He did think of everything" Ricky commented.

"I guess so."

Amber walked to the corner of the room to the windows that looked out onto the back yard. Looking at the in-ground pool, she said, "We'll have to be sure to use that while we're here."

Stepping behind her, Ricky looked out. He spotted the big rope hammock between two tall maple trees. "Have to check that out, too."

A huge maple tree dominated an area of the lawn. They saw Jake and Lisa with the baby at the picnic table beneath it. Jake still held Becky and from where Amber stood, it looked like Becky was hanging on to every word Uncle Jake was saying to her.

"He just loves her."

"He got to see her born. That makes her more special to him."

Amber heard the catch in Ricky's voice . . . touched with hurt. Pressing the side of her face against his arm, she softly said, "Don't hold it against him."

"I don't." He slid an arm around her shoulders.

"He didn't want to be there. I made him go with me."

With a chuckle, Ricky said, "I know. I heard."

They were quiet a few moments while watching Jake and Lisa with Becky. Amber noticed that Lisa made no move to hold Becky . . . but then, maybe Jake wouldn't let her!

"I used to be so jealous of Jake because he had such a good view from his room."

"I can see why."

"Want to go out and join them?"

Ricky paused a moment before answering, "I don't know why Lisa irritated me when we got here . . . but she did. And I know we can't avoid Jake because of her." He sighed. "Let's go." "It's going to be a long weekend if we let her get under our skin."

"Yeah."

"But . . ." Amber turned to face Ricky smiling. "I don't think Lisa minds having *you* around."

"Ha-ha." He abruptly pulled her against him. "You're the only one I want" he softly told her, as he lowered his mouth to capture hers.

When he pulled his mouth from hers, Amber's eyes met his, looking a bit glazed. "What is it about the way you kiss that leaves me so weak at the knees?"

"Because I just *love* to kiss that mouth of yours." His voice sounded deeper and husky.

Her eyes slid to his mouth and her fingertips caressed his lips. The sound of his last statement caused her breathing to quicken and her heart to pound harder. "Do you have any idea how *hot* that made me?"

"Oh, yeah . . ." His hand scupped her face as his mouth slanted over hers again and again before his tongue slid inside for more play. He pulled back long enough to whisper, "Press against me."

Amber needed no more urging. He was hard. When his hands slid inside the back of her shorts and kneaded her bare skin, she groaned into his mouth.

"Let's go" he whispered against her lips

And they didn't go outside. They made it to their room . . . but not to the bed . . .

* * *

Amber sat on the screened-in side porch nursing Becky later that evening. Ricky was in the shower and she didn't know where Jake and Lisa were. "You're going to love it up here, little girl" she spoke softly to her daughter, who was covered by a receiving blanket. "You'll be here as often as possible, loving and enjoying the country as much as I do. We live in the big city now because that's where your daddy lives and works. But Uncle Jake will have you up here as often as he can."

"You've got that right" Jake said.

Turning her head, Amber saw him standing in the doorway. With a smile, she greeted, "Hi."

"Can I join you?"

"Of course!"

He sat at the opposite end of the couch from Amber. "Days are getting shorter."

"I know but at least it's still warm out."

"I'm so glad you came up, sis."

"Me, too. Um . . . where's Lisa?"

"Finishing double-checking the food supply for tomorrow. It's nothing fancy, just hamburgs, hot dogs and chicken legs."

"Sounds great to me. I don't get to cook-outs in New York."

"Get Ricky to move up here."

She flashed a smile at him. "I don't think so."

"Have you asked him?"

"I haven't come right out and asked . . . no."

"Don't you want to?"

"Yes . . . but only if he's with me."

"It's a better place to raise a kid than in the city."

"Oh . . . I agree with that."

"Hey, Jake! I can only find one bag of salt potatoes and I know I bought two." Lisa came out on the porch.

Jake was irritated with the interruption. "I know you did. The bags should be together."

"Well, if they were, I wouldn't be asking you where it is." She stood on the other side of the coffee table. Glancing at Amber, Lisa did a double-take when she realized what Amber was doing. "Geesh . . ." she muttered with a scowl.

"Is there a problem?" Amber asked her.

Looking at Jake, Lisa demanded, "Help me look for the potatoes."

He jumped up off the couch. "Amber asked you a question."

"What am I supposed to say? She's sitting out here with her brother and *nursing* her baby!"

"And do you see anything?" Amber struggled to hold her temper. "The baby and I are covered, can't you tell?"

Lisa looked at her then. "But he's your *brother*!"

"*So*? Women nurse in public places!"

"*So*? And that makes it okay?"

Grabbing Lisa's upper arm, Jake angrily walked her toward the door as she muttered, "It's not right . . . it's not normal!"

"What the hell are you talking about?"

Lisa stopped, yanking her arm out of his grip. "You're her brother and she's nursing her baby with you sitting only three feet away!"

"Lisa! I couldn't see anything!"

"*That's* not the point!"

"Then what the hell *is* your point?" He hurried her into the house.

Becky started to fuss. Removing the blanket, Amber gently hushed her and rocked her slightly. Moments later, Becky's little mouth found her mother again and she quieted.

Amber tried to ignore the loud voices from the house.

Ricky's voice startled her. "What's with them?" he asked, sitting next to Amber.

"She doesn't think it's *proper* for Jake to be anywhere near me while Becky is nursing, doesn't matter whether we're covered or not."

"You're kidding me."

"Wish I was." Looking down at her daughter, she gently brushed her hair back from her face. with her fingers. "She thinks it's wrong because we're brother and sister." Amber grasped the blanket that was between her and Ricky. "I had this over us."

With a loud sigh, Ricky said, "Jake will only put up with so much of her crap."

"To tell the truth, I'm surprised he's put up with it as long as he has. He must really care about her . . . hoping she'll get over whatever."

Sitting back, Ricky said, "You didn't say much about the problems with Lisa."

Her eyes met his. "We had our own to deal with."

"But we're okay now . . . right?"

She smiled. "I think so."

They sat on the porch to enjoy what they couldn't in the city: sitting in a screened-in porch in the country with trees and flowers and no noisy vehicles or horns blowing. But the loud voices from inside the house wasn't enjoyable. Very few words were understandable. At one point, Lisa was crying but Jake didn't let up on her.

"So much for coming up a day early" Ricky commented.

"Who knew this would happen?"

"As much as I don't want to, let's go up to our room and leave them to their fighting" Ricky suggested.

"Sounds good."

Ricky stood then reached to take Becky from her mother. They heard Lisa very clearly when she shouted, "Fuck you, Jake!" They then heard her run up the stairs, down the hall and then a loud slam of a door. Ricky's eyes met Amber's. "Well, that shot down that plan."

Amber wondered why the argument had escalated so. She knew Jake could be stubborn and had a temper but she had never known him to get so angry. Wanting to go to him, she didn't know if she should. But then her head spun around as Becky was being taken from her arms. "Go to your brother" he quietly said.

She felt frustrated as she searched the rooms downstairs and couldn't find him. Thinking maybe he had gone out to the garage, Amber started the push open the screen door out of the kitchen when she saw him. Jake was seated on the top step, his back to her.

"Jake" she softly said.

"Not now, Amber." His voice sounded strange . . . harsh.

Her mouth opened to say something but nothing came out. His words stung . . . and tears filled her eyes as she watched him stand and hurry down the back steps. Amber wiped at her eyes as she turned to go back to Ricky.

He sat on the couch with his bare feet braced against the edge of the coffee table and Becky asleep beside him. Looking at her when she sat next to him, he saw how sad she looked. "What happened?"

"He didn't want to talk to me."

Sliding an arm around her shoulders, Ricky gave her a squeeze. "He's pissed off . . . you heard how they were arguing. Give him time to cool off."

"I know but . . ."

"But it still hurt when he wouldn't talk to you."

She nodded her head while fighting the next wave of tears. Amber then attempted a smile as she looked up at Ricky. "You can tell, huh?"

"Yeah . . . it's pretty obvious."

Dusk was setting. The peepers culd be heard outside. "Oh, listen to that! I miss hearing that sound!" Amber cuddled next to Ricky and closed her eyes as she listened to the outside music.

"That is neat" he said.

They listened for about five minutes before Amber said, "Let's go to bed. It was a long ride up and will be an even longer day tomorrow." Another thought struck her and she sat up. "I hope they're talking to each other tomorrow! Some party that will be if they aren't!"

"I hope the arguing is done. I didn't plan on spending my time off listening to them fight."

"I agree with you." Amber gently kissed his mouth before standing. "Ready to go upstairs?"

* * *

The sleeping Becky was put in the bassinet in her room. The AC ran quietly, keeping the room a little cooler than the rest of the house. Making sure she was covered well, Amber gently kissed Becky's forehead before setting the baby monitor on the dresser and taking the other one with her.

The door to Jake's room was closed and no light showed beneath the door.

Ricky was just pulling back the sheet and light blanket on the bed when Amber entered the room. She appreciated the view when the boxers he wore dropped to his feet. "Becky sound to sleep?" he asked, as he got into bed.

"Sure is. Must be the fresh air . . . she was outside quite awhile with Jake and Lisa earlier." Setting the monitor on her nightstand, Amber then pulled her tank top over her head and smiled seeing Ricky watching her. As she unbuttoned and unzipped her shorts, she asked, "Like what you see?" Her shorts dropped to the floor.

"You know I do."

When she started to unhook the front of her bra, Ricky said, "Let me."

Getting onto the bed on her hands and knees, Amber slowly made her way over to him on the queen-size bed. "Good thing it's early yet."

"Why is that?" His fingers unhooked her bra and her breasts fell free. His hand then slid down to rest at the top of her panties.

"We need a good night's sleep." She sat up for a brief moment to remove her bra before kissing him. "Tomorrow will be a busy day." Another kiss. "Jake loves to have parties . . . he throws good ones." Amber inhaled sharply when his hand slid inside her panties and her voice became softer.

"So, with it being early, we have time to do this . . . *again* . . . *and* get a good night's sleep."

"I like your way of thinking . . ."

Her eyes closed as his hand slid smoothly over her butt . . . and she moaned softly when his fingers slid further and found her damp folds. "You are always *so* ready . . ." he whispered.

* * *

Chapter 24

Amber quietly went down to the kitchen at 7:40 the next morning. The sun was shining and she smelled coffee! What a beautiful way to start the day! Somebody had remembered to set the time for the coffee maker. A look into the living room showed the couch was empty but a pillow and rumpled blanket told her that that was where Jake had spent the night.

A look at the door of her father's den saddened her, too. "Oh, Daddy . . ." she whispered but then shook her head. She wouldn't let that room depress her . . . she knew her father wouldn't want that.

Heading toward the kitchen, Amber wondered where Jake was. Hearing a noise on the porch, she looked to find out what it was. Jake was quietly talking to Lisa, with his back to the screens. All of the sudden, her cupped her face with his hands and kissed her passionately.

"*Yes*!" Amber silently shouted, pumping her hands once in the air in glee. Forgetting about the coffee for the moment, she hurried upstairs to let Ricky know that Jake and Lisa were no longer fighting.

* * *

"About time you two got up" Jake commented as Amber and Ricky walked into the kitchen an hour later. Amber didn't tell him that they just wanted to give them more make up time. Ricky carried the baby in her car seat/chair and sat her on the center island. Jake got up from the chair at the table where he and Lisa had been sitting. "There's my litle girl!" he cooed, zeroing in on Becky.

"Morning" Amber greeted. "Is there any coffee left?" Opening the cupboard door by the sink for cups, she didn't see the look Lisa gave her.

"Should be" Jake replied.

As Amber poured coffee into two cups, Jake cleared his throat before saying, "Sorry about last night, you two. You didn't need to hear any of that."

"Shit happens" Ricky commented, taking the cup Amber held out for him.

Amber leaned back against the counter and raised her cup to her lips. Over the rim, she cast a look at Lisa. Happy that she and Jake had made up, she was still ticked off at Lisa's remarks about breast-feeding around Jake. It wasn't like she sat there fully exposed when he was around!

"Yeah but I didn't invite you up here to listen to us fight" Jake continued.

Walking over to Jake, Amber put an arm around him and kissed his cheek. "Don't worry about it. It's over and done. Now, there's a party we have to get ready for."

If looks could kill, Amber would have been dead from where Lisa sat.

"What time do things start?" Ricky asked.

"Around noon. We don't party like we used to so things don't last long into the night like once upon a time."

Amber made a mock shocked look. "Is old age getting to you all?"

"Haha!" Jake playfully put his sister in a headlock, where she giggled and tried to get away.

Lisa set her cup down a little too hard, which caused Jake to let go of Amber to look toward the noise. "Oops . . . sorry." she said a touch too brightly.

"Want some breakfast? We have doughnuts and cinnamon buns" Jake offered.

"A cinnamon bun sounds good" Amber replied.

"They're over there on the table."

Amber started over but stopped short when her eyes met Lisa's. Ricky noticed and said, "How many would you like, babe? I'm buying." He walked to the table.

"Just one for now, thanks." She watched Lisa smile up at him from her chair.

"So, what can I help you with to set things up, Jake?" Ricky asked, as he handed Amber her breakfast.

"I have lawn chairs and two canopies to start with."

"I can help with the chairs" Amber volunteered. A little voice told her that she should ask Lisa if she needed any help but she couldn't bring herself to ask.

"You don't have to, sis. We men can handle it."

"But I *want* to help." She tossed a look at Lisa. "I want to enjoy as much of the outdoors as I can while we're here."

Ricky grabbed the handle of Becky's seat. "Will she need a hat out there?"

"Um . . . I don't think so, just as long as she stays in the shade."

"Are you all set in here?" Jake asked Lisa. "How are you doing with the salads?"

Lisa got out of her chair. "They're all set."

He smiled. "That's my girl." After placing a kiss on her cheek, Jake went out the door.

Amber caught the look on Lisa's face after Jake's praise and the kiss. She just *glowed.*

"Doesn't he give her enough attention?" Amber wondered to herself as she followed Jake out the door.

* * *

Amber helped Lisa place plastic tablecloths on eight picnic tables. Lisa didn't ask for help but Amber pitched in anyway and received a quiet "Thanks" before Lisa went back to the house. Ricky followed shortly after to change Becky's diaper. Spotting Jake just as he disappeared into the garage, Amber hurried to catch up with him. He had just taken four badmitton rackets off the wall over some tires. "Looks like they haven't been used in awhile" she commented as he wiped a large cobweb off one of the rackets. He looked at her and grinned. "I think we were the last ones to use these and how long ago was that?" He wiped another racket.

Laughing, Amber replied, "*Too* long ago! Are there any birdies to use?"

"Look in the cupboard to your left."

"Is the net still around?" she asked, opening the cupboard.

"Ricky and I already set it up on the other side of the pool."

"Hey . . . you guys are good! Oh! Here's a couple birdies but one is missing a rubber tip. We'll need a couple more, anyway."

"Keep looking."

Moving aside some old cans of spray paint, Amber listened as Jake talked: "I really am sorry about the arguing last night. I didn't want to do it while you were here."

Amber found an unopened package of three birdies that was covered with dust. Closing the cupboard door, she asked, "Don't tell me that you fight like that a lot."

There was no reply.

Amber turned to give her brother a look that clearly asked, "*Well*?"

"Not all the time."

"Oh, Jake . . . why? What kind of a relationship is that when you argue all the time? If you're not happy . . . *get out*!"

"I love her" he quietly replied.

"*Love*? You call a relationship with somebody you argue with all the time *love*?"

"You and Ricky were arguing a lot."

"Well, yeah . . . but the circumstances were a little different!"

"Amber, this isn't the time for this conversation."

"So . . . when, Jake? Will she let you and I have the chance to talk alone? I didn't realize things were so bad. I love you and want you to be happy . . . but after hearing you two argue . . . and it happens often? Well, I guess she won't mind if we talk *if* I'm not breast-feeding your niece!"

His head snapped around to look at her. "Look, Amber . . . she has issues with you . . . and us. I had hoped this weekend we could iron them out."

Waiting a few moments to calm herself, Amber then softly asked, "How often do you talk nicely to her . . . pay her a compliment? I saw how her face lit up when you asked her about the salads, Jake."

Before he could answer, they heard vehicles coming up the driveway. Jake and Amber looked at each other before he turned toward the door. "I wonder who . . ." Two pick-up trucks stopped in front of the garage. "It's Jeff and Marty" he told Amber.

Jeff Hardwell and Marty Tripper . . . childhood friends of Jake's.

"We'll talk later, Jake" Amber said, as she heard truck doors open and close.

"Yep" he replied, then walked out of the garage. "Hey, you're early, as usual, you two!"

* * *

Ricky had just picked Becky up from the changing table when he sensed someone in the doorway. He knew it wasn't Amber . . . she wasn't that quiet. Turrning, he saw Lisa standing there. "Hi" he greeted.

"You're such a good father. How did Amber get so lucky to find someone like you?"

"We were lucky to find each other" he told her.

Stepping into the room, Lisa said, "I was wondering if you would do me a favor."

He was instantly wary. "Like what?"

Walking toward him, she asked, "Would you show me how to hold a baby? I'd like to show Jake that I can hold his niece."

Ricky was surprised to hear that. He hadn't known how to hold her, either, till Amber showed him . . . and now it seemed like something he had always done Figuring it wouldn't hurt, he told Lisa, "Sure . . . you just have to be careful with her head . . . here, put your hand under her head and hold her body with your other hand . . . usually at her butt or under her legs."

"Um . . . maybe you had better put her in my arms this time . . ."

Just as he moved to place Becky in Lisa's arms, Lisa stepped closer . . . and his fingers on one hand touched her breast. Ricky's eyes moved quickly to her face but Lisa was smiling at Becky. He couldn't shake the feeling that that wasn't an accident on her part.

"Oh, Ricky . . . she's beautiful!"

"Thanks. Now, if you'd rather . . . you can put her head in the crook of your arm . . . there you go."

Lisa smiled. "This feels wonderful . . . no wonder Jake loves to hold her!"

"Yeah, he does love his niece."

"Um . . . would you show me how to pick her up out of her seat . . . or even just off the changing table . . . or a bed."

"Okay but then we have to get outside . . ."

* * *

Amber chatted with Jeff, Marty, and their wives for awhile before wondering what was taking Ricky so long to get back with Becky. Everybody wanted to see her. Jeff and his wife, Patti, had two boys, ages three and four. Marty and Jill had a two year old daughter . . . and another on the way. Amber kept glancing toward the house, wondering where

Ricky was. Then, she remembered that Lisa had gone into the house, too. "I'll be back. I have to find my daughter" she said to everyone before starting toward the house.

She smiled as she heard Jake's buddies picking on him: "When are you going to settle down and start a family with Lisa, huh, Jake? Don't wait too much longer . . . we'll be hitting the big four-o in a few short years!"

Jake laughed. "Not for another four years, anyway!"

Amber made it half-way up the drive from the garage to the house when Ricky came out the back door with Becky. Stopping, she waited for them.

"Miss me?" Ricky asked with a smile.

"Yes . . . I was beginning to wonder what was taking so long." She looked toward the back door but Lisa didn't come out. "You probably won't believe this but Lisa wanted to learn how to hold Becky . . . and how to pick her up."

"What? You let her hold Becky?"

"Do you really think she would hurt her . . . especially with me right there?"

"Yeah, you're right . . . you're right. But why would she want to *learn* how to hold her now . . . unless it was because you were alone with Becky."

"Don't start that." But the thought of touching Lisa's breast when she stood so close flashed through his mind. "She said she wanted to be able to show Jake that she could hold Becky."

"Okay . . . I can deal with that." Taking a step closer, she said softly, "And I *did* miss you."

He smiled. "Did you?" Setting Becky's seat on the ground, Ricky cupped Amber's face with his hands to kiss her. "Do you think we'll be able to sneak away when the party's going strong to be by ourselves for awhile?"

"We might . . ." she chuckled, then raised her mouth for another kiss.

"Hey, you two! That's how it all started to make my niece!" Jake yelled.

* * *

Better weather couldn't have been chosen for the day. Fifty-five people, big and little, roamed and ran around Jake's yard. Swimming, volleyball, badmitton and even a softball game were fun for everyone . . . whether one participated or watched from the sidelines.

Amber played two games of badmitton with Jake as her partner against Ricky and Jeff. The brother and sister won both matches. The two celebrated with high-fives and then Amber hugged him. "We did it! We still have it!"

Jeff looked at Ricky with a twinkle in his eyes. "Should we tell them that we let them win?"

"Yeah . . . right!" Jake retorted. "You never could beat us before!" He put an arm around his friend's shoulders. "We're both hot and sweaty. Come on . . . I'll buy you a cold beer." With a laugh, they walked toward the coolers.

"I'm beat! Those games wore me out!" Amber groaned to Ricky.

"That was a part of you I didn't know about! You and Jake make a good team."

"We played badmitton a lot while growing up, either against each other or when our friends came over. But it's been awhile!"

"I want you on my team next time!" Ricky kissed her. "Want something to drink?"

"Water or iced tea sounds good."

After another kiss, he whispered in her ear, "You know what sounds wonderful right now? If we strip and go skinny dipping in the pool."

"That does sound great . . . but what do you think Jake's guests will think?"

Ricky laughed.

Her reply was a smile.

Ricky then looked over at where most of the party was, under the large maple tree. "Do you have any idea where our daughter is?"

"I left her with Jill. She offered to watch her so I could play."

"Look . . . Lisa has her."

Amber turned in time to see Lisa carefully hand Becky to Uncle Jake. Amber smiled when she saw Jake grin at something Lisa said then leaned to kiss her.

"Come on" Ricky said. "Let's get something to drink . . . I'm dying for a cold one!"

* * *

Amber was happy that Jake's friends treated Ricky like an old friend. Even as she chatted with those she hadn't seen in awhile, she'd look around to see Ricky talking and laughing with others. A few times she saw Lisa around Ricky, standing either beside him or not that far away. Amber didn't think much about it because Lisa had known most of these people for a long time, too.

Becky slept in the bassinet next to the maple tree. She was oblivious to all the noise. Many checked on her, young and old alike. Sometimes younger hands had to be removed when they reached in to touch her.

Getting away on her own, Amber retired to the hammock. The kids had had fun on it earlier but now most of them were in the pool. Amber lay down, closing her eyes and letting the breeze slightly swing her.

"Hey . . . you got room for one more?"

"Do I know you?" she teased, not opening her eyes.

"Ha-ha." Ricky lay beside her.

Smiling, she moved over a bit to give Ricky more room.

"Tired?" he asked, after getting comfortable with his arm around her.

"Yeah but I'm okay." She was quiet for a few minutes, then asked, "Are you having a good time?"

"Yes! They're a good bunch of people."

"We grew up with most of them."

They lay for a short while, not speaking, just enjoying being next to each other and listening to the noises of the party. "This is nice" Amber purred, turning toward him.

"Yes." Turning toward her, Ricky nuzzled her neck. "This is *really* nice."

"Kiss me" she whispered.

His mouth took hers. The party clatter became dim as they forgot they were not totally alone. Ricky's hand slid up her leg, over her hip and under the back of her tank top. Their bodies pressed closer as their kisses meant business.

"Don't try anything on that hammock. Jake and I did once and it was almost a disaster. I don't want either of you to get hurt."

Pulling their mouths apart, Amber and Ricky looked at one another before he rolled onto his back. "Thanks for the warning, Lisa." A hint of sarcasm could be heard.

"Is Becky still asleep?" Amber asked, not knowing whether to be angry or embarrassed at the interruption.

"Yes. She's such an angel! You two made such a beautiful baby!"

"Where's Jake?"

"I don't know . . . he's around somewhere."

Not wanting her around, Ricky suggested curtly, "Then why don't you go find him?"

Lisa's body stiffened at his tone. "Why should I?"

"Because I want to be alone with Amber."

She glared at him, then huffed, "Fine!" and walked off.

"What was that all about?" Amber asked.

Tucking her against him, Ricky mumbled, "Nothing much."

As Amber snuggled against his body, she wondered what Lisa had done to make him angry.

* * *

It was almost 9 o'clock when the last of the guests left. Becky slept in her seat on a picnic table while the adults did some last minute cleaning. The badmitton equipment, as well as the softball bat and ball were put back in the garage. Wet towels were hung over the fence around the pool and the few soda and beer cans that didn't make the designated bins were picked up. Most of the lawn chairs were put away but four were left out. Jake pulled a bottle out of a cooler, twisted the cap off and took a long, cold drink of beer.

"Nice party, Jake! It was good to see everyone . . . and they all seemed to have a good time!" Amber said, sitting opposite him.

He smiled, laying a hand on Lisa's knee. "We do have good parties, don't we?"

"Yep, we do."

Amber saw the brief look Lisa gave Ricky. She wondered what had happened between them. She sighed, sliding down in her chair to look up at the sky. "I'd forgotten how nice it is to sit out here when it's warm. The light on the garage gives off just enough light, Jake. Good idea."

"It is nice out here" Ricky agreed. "It's quiet, you can hear the peepers . . . and you don't hear horns blowing or squealing tires . . . people yelling . . ."

"You have to get out of the city" Jake told him.

Ricky finished his beer, setting the empty bottle on the ground beside his chair. "I've thought about it . . . and after being here again . . ."

"Would you move up here?" Jake asked, with a quick look at Amber.

Amber noticed how Lisa shifted in her chair.

"Man, I don't know. Times like this, it's tempting, you know?" Ricky responded. "To have a nice place in the country . . . no close neighbors and not a lot of traffic . . ."

"But the winters are frigid and usually a lot of snow" Lisa said.

"Sh-h-h-h!" Jake hissed at her.

With a shrug, she said, "I'm just giving him the whole picture."

"It's something to think about, with a baby to raise" Ricky remarked, grasping Amber's hand.

She looked at him, surprised . . . trying not to get her hopes up.

"Well, think about it" Jake said. "We'd love to have you move up here."

Ricky's response was to bring Amber's hand to his lips, kissing the back of it.

Lisa squirmed, then said, "I can't get over what a good baby Becky is. She didn't mind being held by so many people . . . strangers . . . and she slept through all the noise."

It surprised Amber to hear Lisa's praise but her next question stumped her:

"And it made it easy for everyone with all the bottles of milk you made up for her. You don't have to breast feed Becky all the time?"

"Yeah, the bottles do help a lot, especially with something like the party going on. But that's my milk in the bottles, Lisa . . . and I can freeze it, too, if I need to. That way, if Ricky and I want to go away for a night or more, Becky will have my milk to drink."

"You can? But . . ." She stopped talking and slid down in her chair. "Geesh . . ." she mumbled.

Once started, Amber wouldn't stop: "I use a breast pump, Lisa, to pump out my milk."

Jake muttered, "Amber . . ."

Amber's good mood was spoiled. Standing, she said, "I'm putting Becky to bed then I'm calling it a night. 'Night, Jake."

"Come on . . . stay up awhile longer" he quietly requested.

"No, I'm ready for bed. See you in the morning."

Ricky was out of his chair. "I'll get Becky. Good night, Jake . . . Lisa. I had a great time today . . . thanks."

As they walked to the house, Jake and Lisa watched. When they climbed the back steps, Lisa muttered, "What did I do?"

"You seem to irritate my sister."

"What did I say?"

With a sigh, Jake said, "Never mind . . ." and reached in the cooler for another beer.

* * *

Chapter 25

The night was warm. Even with the fans in the windows, the bedoom was too warm to sleep.

"Maybe we should camp out on the floor in Becky's room" Ricky teased.

"Tempting, isn't it?"

They heard Jake and Lisa go to their room . . . and they weren't arguing.

Amber and Ricky lay on the bed, with the fans blowing across their naked bodies. Every so often, the air felt cooler. "Ahhhh" Ricky sighed. "I wish the breeze outside would blow that cooler air in all night."

"Hold on a sec." She got out of bed.

"Where are you going?"

Amber made an adjustment with the angle of one of the fans. It wasn't much but she hoped it helped, even a little. Instead of walking around to her side of the bed, she straddled Ricky's body.

His hands slid up her thighs. "This isn't going to help us cool off."

"But are you complaining?" she asked with a grin.

"Never." She leaned down to kiss him. His hands cupped her breasts as they kissed, fondling and caressing until her nipples grew hard. It wasn't long before his mouth left hers so that he could take a nipple into his mouth, to suckle and lick . . . to drive her crazy. "Ohgod" she whispered, closing her eyes to enjoy what he was doing to her. But when his mouth moved from one breast to the other, she moaned, wanting more. He grew hard beneath her and she wanted him inside of her. Amber groaned in protest when he stopped what he was doing to take her mouth again. Pulling away, he whispered, "Let's go skinny dipping."

It took a moment for his comment to register and then a slow smile spread across her lips. "Okay." But the smile disappeared. "What if they covered the pool before they came in?"

"We'll just find some other place outside for me to make love to you."

"What are we waiting for?" she breathed, her body wanting what his could give her.

Ricky slid on the shorts he had worn that day and Amber only wore one of his white muscle t-shirts. Grabbing the baby monitor, she had Ricky get towels out of the bathroom while she checked on the sleeping baby. The room Becky was in was to the right of Jake and Lisa's room. Amber hoped that if Becky woke up, she would have time to get to her before Becky disturbed them. Meeting Ricky in the hall, they gave one another a long, hot kiss as a prelude as to what what was going to happen outside.

On the way out the back door, Amber flipped the switch for the light on the side of the garage.

* * *

The pool cover was nowhere to be seen. As they started down the steps that led into the pool, the water felt cool on Amber's hot skin, causing her nipples to harden. Ricky stopped to pull her into his arms and kiss her, long and sweet . . . for the moment. The kiss continued as he walked her into deeper water, to his upper thighs. "Wrap your legs around me" he whispered. Doing so, Amber felt him hard between her legs, as her arms slid around his neck. Moaning into his mouth, she pressed against his erection, wanting to feel him inside her. The fire that began in their room erupted into flames. His hands moved under her butt to hold her . . . the water made their skin slippery . . . and the sensation was erotic. Their tongues mated. His erection stirred against her and her body slid to accommodate it. Ricky stopped her, pulling his mouth away. "I need the condom I left at the top of the steps."

"I need you *now*" she hissed.

"We can't, Amber! We have to get it before I slip into you *right here*."

She slid her body along him. He was so *big* . . . so *solid*.

"*Stop*!" his husky voice growled. Without another word, he carried her out of the pool and set her feet down at the top step. Reaching down, he swiped the condom package into his hand before kissing her, hard and then led her toward a lounge chair. Grabbing a towel off a table along the way, he tossed it onto the chair and sat on it, pulling Amber onto his lap, facing him, with her legs straddling his thighs. Their eyes met as Ricky brought the condom package to his mouth to open it. But Amber took it from him. "Let me." Her eyes were still on his as she tore open the package with her teeth. The empty package fell to the cement as she looked down to place the condom over his thick penis.

Ricky watched as her fingers slid the condom over him. It aroused him even more. He throbbed, needing to be inside her. "Well, look at you" he ground out, his voice not sounding like his own.

"I've watched and learned." Amber clasped his face between her hands and covered his mouth with hers, slipping her tongue into his mouth.

His hands slid up under her thighs to lift her just enough to slide down over him. She gasped at the sensation as he slid inside her. Amber pulled her mouth from his and her head dropped back as his hands caressed her breasts . . . and she inhaled sharply when his mouth closed over a nipple. But when their rhythm increased, Ricky pulled away, placing his hands on her hips to help the motion. It wasn't long before Amber was ready . . . and Ricky, too. "*Look at me*" he ground out. Her eyes weren't focused as she lowered her head. A soft cry started and Ricky captured her cry of "*Ricco*!" in his mouth. At his release, his head fell back against the back of the lounge chair as he moaned with his final thrusts. Spent, they collapsed against each other.

Neither one noticed the curtain that moved in a window in Becky's room.

* * *

The kitchen was empty when Amber stepped in the room. After pouring a cup of coffee, she carried it to the table where the morning newspaper lay. After reading only Dear Abby and the comics, she stood, wondering where Jake and Lisa were. Ricky was just getting into the shower when she came downstairs. Noticing a few dishes on the counter from the day before, Amber took it upon herself to wash them. Filling the sink with water and dish soap, she added the large spoons that were used in the salads, aluminum containers that salads were in and a few baby bottles.

"You don't have to do that" Lisa commented, coming in from the back door.

"I don't have anything else to do."

Adding two coffee cups to the water, Lisa then picked up a dish towel. "I'll dry."

Amber didn't comment.

"Did you have a good time yesterday?" Lisa asked.

"Yes . . . it was good to see everyone."

Lisa was quiet for a few moments before commenting, "It was a warm day . . . and last night didn't seem to cool off any. I bet you were wishing you had the AC in your room."

Where was she going with this? "It was warm but the fans helped."

Another long pause, then Lisa said, "I checked on Becky while you were in the pool."

Amber's hand stopped before it reached the hot water faucet. They had the monitor . . . how come they didn't hear her? But then she remembered how hot and heavy things were between her and Ricky . . . "We hoped she would sleep. I'm sorry we weren't there to take care of her." Her heart pounded. How much had Lisa seen?

"Oh, that's okay. She didn't wake up. I needed something out of the other bathroom so I was up to get it. I just checked in on her before I went back to bed. Becky is such an angel." There was no telling Amber what Lisa had had in mind . . . she heard someone in the hall and she got up, hoping it was Ricky. Wearing only her short robe, tied loosely at the waist and open at the top, she went quietly into the hall, closing her bedroom door behind her. Seeing the door open to their room, Lisa was disappointed, knowing she must have just missed the two of them before they went downstairs. "Jake was sleeping, so I decided to look in on Becky. I realized then that the garage light was on . . . and I couldn't help but watch what was going on by the pool."

Feeling the heat from embarrassment rising to her forehead, Amber couldn't look at Lisa. And Lisa didn't make it any easier:

"Jake came looking for me. Standing behind me, he saw you and Ricky. It seemed like we stood there quite awhile, watching you two. We were hot . . . so hot . . . you two are good. Jake finally took me back to bed and we had good sex like we used to . . . something that hasn't happened in a long time. I guess both you and I got lucky last night, huh?"

"And you're telling me this because . . . ?" Amber forgot her embarrassment for a moment to look at Lisa, not liking the so-called conversation.

Lisa shrugged her shoulders. "Just making small talk." Folding the dish towel, she drapped it over the edge of the counter and walked out of the room.

"What the hell was *that* all about?" Amber muttered, looking at the doorway Lisa had just disappeared through. And then the thought that she and Ricky were being watched while . . . her own brother watched while she and Ricky made love! Wait till Ricky heard that one. With a sigh, she let the water out of the sink then wiped it down, leaving the remainder of the dishes to air dry before going off to find Ricky.

He had just come down the stairs, holding Becky. "Ah . . . just who I was looking for" Amber greeted him, reaching for her daughter.

"Why? What's up?"

"Go for a walk with me?"

"Sure."

"Maybe we should have a hat for her."

"I'll be right back." Ricky took the stairs two at a time.

"I'll wait for you outside!" she called after him, then went out to the porch and out the door.

* * *

"You told her *what*?" Jake shouted at Lisa. They stood near the steps to the back door.

"Sh-h-h-h!"

"You actually told her that we saw them at the pool last night?"

"Yes."

"*Why*?"

With a shrug, she answered, "I thought they should know that they weren't as alone as they thought they were." Lisa had wanted to say more to Amber but she figured she would go crying to her brother and Lisa couldn't afford to get Jake too mad at her. He would kick her out if she did anything to upset his baby sister too much. But Amber's reaction when she heard they had been watched was worth it. And Lisa totally enjoyed what she had witnessed out the window . . . Ricky was HOT and to see him in action . . . whoa! Lucky Amber! Lisa wouldn't mind a tumble with him . . .

"That wasn't a smart move, Lisa. How can I face my sister knowing that she knows that I was stupid enough to watch something private between her and Ricky?"

Sliding her arms around his neck, Lisa smiled as she replied, "I told her how hot they made us and we went back to bed for our own sex."

Removing her arms, Jake said, "You don't know when to shut-up, do you?" Turning, he rushed up the steps and into the kitchen, not waiting for Lisa.

Hearing her coming up the steps, he went into the dining room. Jake wasn't sure how to deal with what she had just told him. But Lisa followed him into the room. "Jake . . ."

He spun around to face her, ready to explode but the footsteps they heard coming down the stairs stopped him. Ricky appeared, smiling when he noticed them and then held up a small white cotton hat. "Needed this for Becky."

"Are you going somewhere?" Jake asked.

"Amber wants to go for a walk. See you later." And then he was on the porch and out the door.

Without a word, Jake walked away from Lisa back to the kitchen, opened the refrigerator for a beer and went out the back door. She watched him, almost commenting on it being too early for a beer but decided against it.

Ricky and Amber walked along the mowed path that was behind the house. Jake kept it mowed like their father had. It went through a large overgrowth of trees, large ferns and cattails, some wildflowers and lots of sunflowers. Her parents had decided to keep all that growth but they kept it at bay, instead of letting it grow all over the place. The path was a half a mile long, one that Amber and Jake had used often while growing up.

"This goes to the clubhouse, doesn't it?" Ricky asked.

"Yes, it does. Wait till you see it."

"Why?'

"You'll find out."

When they came to the end of the path, the clubhouse stood off to the right. Ricky stopped, and then laughed. "Look at that! Siding!"

"Jake was bored before his work got busy and he decided to put siding on" Amber said with a laugh. "He said he wanted to keep it in good condition for his niece or nephew to play in!"

Looking down at his daughter who was in his arms, Ricky said, "Your uncle's a good man."

"Want to go inside?" Amber asked.

The clubhouse was built by their father when Jake and Amber were young. It was one large room, big enough for two couches, two comfortable chairs, and a card table with four folding chairs. At that card table, there had been many card games, as well as checkers and chess. A dart board hung on one side of the room and a boom box sat on a wooden stand that Jake had made in shop class in high school. Electricity was hooked up but was shut off during the winter.

"The furniture has been changed around since I was last in here" Ricky commented, as he looked around the room. "Wait a minute . . . there's only one couch. What happened to the other one?"

"One of Jake's buddy's needed a couch for his camp and since this place is hardly used any more, Jake offered him the couch that was in here."

Jake looked at the couch, then around the room again to see a large cupboard that looked familiar. "Didn't that used to be . . ." His gaze moved back to the couch, then to the cupboard. "That was in your apartment when we first met . . . is that the couch you had there, too? The one you used for your bed?"

With a smile, she answered, "It sure is. There were too many memories of you with that bed . . . couch . . . I couldn't bring myself to totally get rid of it. Jake said I could keep it up here."

"I remember you said that you didn't get rid of it . . . will it survive the cold winters out here?"

"I made him promise to put it in the garage . . . he keeps the garage heated. The sheets and blankets for the bed are still kept in the same cupboard . . ." Stepping closer to him, she peeked at their daughter. "If Becky was asleep, we could rekindle old memories . . ." But two dark eyes peered back at Amber.

"We'll have to wait till another time." Ricky leaned to kiss her. "Maybe in a little while . . ." he whispered. "But not by the pool this time . . ."

She smiled, leaning her head against his shoulder. And suddenly, the real reason she had wanted to go for a walk with Ricky came to her. Her head popped back up. "Oh . . . wait till you hear this . . ." and she told him what Lisa had told her.

* * *

Lisa walked out to where Jake sat with his feet up on the picnic table seat. He had finished his beer and sat with his mind off somewhere else, rolling the empty bottle between his hands. But he heard Lisa approach and gave her a look before turning away.

"Don't be mad at me" she said.

"I still can't believe you told Amber . . ."

"But last night was good between us . . . I miss that, Jake."

He looked at her. "Last night was great . . . like it used to be. Why don't we make love like that now?"

Lisa looked at him like she couldn't believe what he was saying. "We don't *make love* any more, Jake! It's some kisses, a feel here and there . . . and then you're done before I've even started! You don't have much affection for me any more . . . you seem to save it all for your sister."

"*What the hell*??" Jake got off the picnic table and turned on her.

"You two touch each other all the time! You're always hugging and touching somehow! Just yesterday morning you two were joking around and you put her in a headlock . . . when was the last time you did that to me?"

"I knew it! You *are* jealous of me and my brother . . . I *knew* it!"

Neither Lisa or Jake had noticed Amber and Ricky as they walked up to them. Both of their heads swung in Amber's direction as she spoke:

"So, that's the problem you've had with me all this time? Because Jake and I are close?"

"It's not normal for a sister and brother to be that close!"

"*Who* said it's not? *You*?"

"Nobody else I know is that close! You're always talking on the phone . . . he went down to New York to be with you before Becky was born . . . and he was *in the delivery room* with you! You sit near each other when you're nursing . . ."

"I'm covered, Lisa!"

"That's not the point! He shouldn't sit so close to you then . . . or whenever!"

Amber looked at her, dumb-founded, not believing what she was hearing.

Ricky spoke up: "Lisa, now that I'm back in Amber's life, she won't feel she needs to be on the phone with Jake so much. But if she wants to talk to him, I won't deny her. They've had each other around their whole lives . . . who am I to tell her she can't still be close to him?"

Amber looked at Ricky, as he held their daughter and said what he did to Lisa. Her heart swelled even more with love for him. "Listen to what he said, Lisa" she gently told her.

"But she comes here, acting like she still lives here! She gets into the cupboards, the 'fridge . . . wherever she pleases! It's *our* home, Jake . . . not hers!"

"It's still her home . . . she grew up here . . . and she was just here for eight months" Jake argued.

"If that has been bothering you, too, Lisa . . . why didn't you say something before now? Like Jake said, I grew up here . . . and he's still here . . . I still think of it as my home" Amber said

"I thought your home is now in New York, with Ricky and your baby" Lisa remarked.

"It is . . . but this is *home* . . . do you know what I mean?"

Lisa didn't reply . . . and she didn't look happy. Jake cleared his throat before saying, "Well, since it's confession time . . . I . . . um . . . Amber and Ricky, I'm sorry . . . I . . . *we* . . . had no business watching you two last night. I am *really* sorry this whole mess happened . . . I really wanted you two to have a good time this weekend."

"It is weird knowing you saw your sister and me doing what we shouldn't have been doing by the pool . . . but we figured you two were asleep and we would be alone" Ricky said.

"No . . . it's okay you were out here. We shouldn't have watched . . . no matter what." Jake sighed. "And if Lisa had kept her mouth shut, we wouldn't be having this conversation."

"Well, at least I know now why she's had it in for me lately. I never realized how much you resented me, Lisa."

"Now you know" Lisa quipped, sitting in a lawn chair.

Jake glared at her before turning back to Amber. "I *am* sorry."

Not caring about Lisa, Amber hugged her brother. "I should be mad at you but your seeing us was a chance we took by being out here." She stepped back . . . then slapped his arm. "*How dare you watch us*?"

"*Ow*!" Jake rubbed his arm. "How many times do I have to say how sorry I am? How do you think I felt after I finally realized I was watching *my sister and her boyfriend*?"

Amber had to laugh at how red Jake's face had become. "Okay, enough of this topic. It's been enough embarrassment for all of us."

"Hey! How about some alone time for you two?" Jake suggested.

"*Alone* time?" Amber repeated.

"Give me the munchkin to watch for a few hours while you and Ricky go off together . . . alone. Go check out the waterfalls for awhile."

She looked at Ricky, who smiled at her. "What do you think?" she softly asked.

"Let's go."

Turning to Jake, Amber said, "Becky ate before we came back from our walk, so she should be good for awhile. You know there's bottles in the 'fridge if needed." She smiled. "Thanks, Jake." As much as she loved her baby, knowing she would have some time alone with Ricky without interruptions was what she wanted.

"Go have a good time" Jake said, taking Becky from Ricky.

Sliding her arms around Ricky, Amber remarked, "How about you go on ahead while I go in to take care of a couple of things quick? Do you remember where the falls are?"

"Out behind the clubhouse."

"Yep."

"How long will you be?"

"I have to pee" she whispered, then a little louder, said, "I'll join you as soon as possible."

Not caring that they weren't alone, Ricky cupped her face with his hands and kissed her slow and deep. Then, holding her close, he whispered in her ear, "Grab a couple more condoms. I only have one with me."

With a giggle, she answered, "Okay" and stepped back from him. Starting toward the house, she said to him, "See you soon."

Lisa sat in the chair, first watching Amber and Jake walk to the house before turning her attention to Ricky as he walked toward the path . . .

* * *

Ricky walked past the clubhouse and took a right. He slowed his pace, checking the trees in front of him, not quite sure where to make his next turn. Ah . . . there it was. He found the tree with the branches that looked like something had taken a large bite out of the center of them. He had a smile on his face as he made his way past the ferns . . . he hadn't forgotten his way. Jake had mowed but the path to the falls wasn't as obvious as the one to the clubhouse. The noise of the falls became louder when he walked around the huge boulder and over some large tree roots that were above the ground. Stepping around a group of four tree stumps, Ricky saw the falls.

They weren't large, only about eight feet high, fed by a creek that ran along the property. The water ran down over rocks of different sizes and ran into another creek at the bottom. Ricky noticed that Jake had done a little landscaping, having had planted a couple of bushes near the pool at the bottom of the falls. A bench had been made out of a large piece of slate placed on two large stones was at least seven foot long. Checking it out, Ricky found it was sturdy. He walked to the falls and stuck out his hand . . . the water was lukewarm.

Hearing a noise behind him, he smiled, glad that Amber hadn't taken long to meet him. But when he turned, his smile faded away. "Lisa . . . what are you doing here?"

"To see you."

"Why?" he demanded. "It was bad enough yesterday that you rubbed up against me every chance you got."

"But you never said anything" Lisa replied, slowly walking closer.

"I didn't because I didn't want to ruin Jake's party. I tried to stay away from you but somehow you managed to be around me. Back off, Lisa . . . I'm not interested."

"I *so* enjoyed watching you fuck Amber last night . . . it was like having my own private screening of porn." She walked around Ricky to stand closer to the water.

"Amber will be here soon" he said, moving away from her.

"Oh, she's with her brother. It'll be awhile." Facing Ricky, she said, "I want somebody to look at me the way you look at Amber . . . Jake used to. But now he smiles and laughs more with his sister."

"And the reason for that is . . . ?" Ricky wanted her out of there, wanting his time alone with Amber.

Lisa looked at him for a long moment before a slight smile appeared on her lips. "I don't know why" she quietly said, before pulling her tank top over her head . . .

* * *

When Amber walked into the kitchen with a blanket in her arms, Jake turned from the counter and handed her a bag. "There's some sandwiches, small container of macaroni salad, watermelon and drinks in there, as well as napkins and plastic forks. Oh! And some of Jill's famous chocolate chip cookies." Becky was in her seat on the counter by where her uncle stood. "We'll be fine . . . just go enjoy yourself. This is my time to spend some time with my niece . . . who knows how soon I'll be able to do it again."

"Where's Lisa?"

With a shrug, he said, "Don't know."

"Thanks for the lunch." Amber started toward the back door.

"There's a small cooler in the garage to keep everything cold until you get to eat."

"I probably better grab it." But she did an about-turn and went to Becky. "Bye, my little girl. Be good for Uncle Jake . . . Mommy and Daddy will be back in awhile." Kissing her forehead, Amber then gently brushed back some of her dark hair before turning to Jake. "Thanks for doing this. See you in a few hours. If you *really* need me, you know where to find me."

With a grin, he said, "Have fun . . . nobody will bother you."

* * *

"Put your top back on."

"Don't you like what you see?" Like the day before, she wasn't wearing a bra.

Her large white breasts contrasted brightly with her otherwise tanned skin. Ricky's eyes rested on them for a moment before moving up to meet her gaze.

"Put your top back on" he repeated, quietly.

"I don't have any milk flavoring."

His eyes turned cold. "You disgust me. Jake deserves somebody so much better . . . how would he react if he knew what you've been doing? I don't want you, Lisa . . . you're *nothing* like Amber. I didn't tell her about your rubbing against me yesterday . . . but I was tempted . . ."

Amber could hear Ricky's voice but not what he was saying. Who was he talking to?

"Now, I'm only going to tell you one more time . . . put your top back on . . . and stay away from me until you tell *us* good-bye tomorrow."

Lisa looked as if she might defy him but then slowly pulled her top down over her head . . .

Amber walked into the clearing just as Lisa's top covered her breasts.

"Am I interrupting something?" she coldly asked.

*   *   *

Chapter 26

"No" Ricky said, his eyes still on Lisa. "She was just leaving."

Tossing back her hair, she walked toward the exit . . . and where Amber stood. As Lisa stepped past her, Amber said in a low but clear voice, "You take care of your man and leave mine alone."

Lisa shot her a look before disappearing. Amber looked at Ricky. "What was that all about? Did she have her top off?"

"Yes." There was no sense in lying.

"Why? And why were you looking at her?"

"How could I not? She just suddenly took it off. Besides, she's nothing compared to you." He walked toward her. "And I told her so." Ricky stopped and stood in front of Amber. But when he saw the look in her eyes, he growled, "*Damn it! Don't* be mad at me!"

"Why is it that I have to deal with these women that want you?"

"Amber . . . I love *you* . . . I don't want *them.*"

"What would you have done if she had gone totally naked? She probably would have if I hadn't shown up when I did."

Gently grasping her upper arms, Ricky softly said, "Don't go there, Amber. It didn't happen so don't torture yourself over it."

But she wouldn't let it go. "But *what* if she had? *What* would you have done?"

"I would have walked out of here."

"You wouldn't have looked at her?"

"No . . . I don't know . . . probably not . . . Oh, Amber . . . *don't.*"

"But she's so beautiful . . . she has the perfect body . . . nice ass, slender hips . . . big boobs . . . no fat on her belly . . ."

Ricky knew what the problem was by then and cupped her face with his hands. "*You're* beautiful to me in every way." He moved one hand down to lay on her stomach, (which, no matter how much she moaned, *was* disappearing), and said, "But this just shows everybody that you gave me a beautiful daughter . . . and I'll take five more."

"*What*?" Amber was shocked but after a couple of moments, smiled at him. "You really mean that, don't you?" The blanket and cooler she carried fell to the ground with a thud.

"Yes, I do."

"Not that I want five more . . ." and she laughed before hugging him. But it didn't take long for her to become serious and look up at him again. "You really think I'm beautiful?"

"Yes" Ricky whispered. "You're my love . . . my life . . ."

His mouth covered hers, his tongue sliding in as hers opened for him. Her arms slid around him and he stepped closer, his arms holding her tightly against him. There wasn't much material between their bodies, with both wearing shorts, Ricky in a muscle t-shirt and Amber in a loose-fitting tank top. Cupping her butt, his hands held her so that she pressed against his erection. With a low moan, Amber adjusted herself around him, rubbing against his hard length.

He pulled his mouth from hers, breathing fast and hard. "Let's get away from here . . . closer to the falls." Leaning down for the blanket, Ricky also grabbed the bag. "I asked for only a couple of condoms . . . not a cooler full" he commented, his mouth seeking another kiss from her.

"Ha-ha. Jake made us a lunch. The condoms are in my pocket." Amber kissed him. "Love me, Ricco . . . *I need you*."

The blanket was spread quickly near the falls. Amber pulled Ricky's t-shirt over his head before reaching for the snap and zipper on his shorts. Grabbing the condom out of his pocket just before his shorts and boxers slid to his feet, Ricky's breathing became faster as he watched her look at his naked body. Her tongue licked at her lips as her eyes focused on his erection. Reaching out, the tips of her fingers skimmed down it's length . . . and she heard Ricky groan softly as his body shuddered at her touch. Her eyes raised to watch him as her hand closed around him. His eyes closed and he moaned . . . the moan elongated as her thumb wiped at the wet on the tip of him.

"Undress for me" he ordered in an odd, thick voice, and his eyes were on her.

Looking at his face, Amber slowly unbuttoned and unzipped her shorts before pushing them and her underwear over her hips. Stepping out of them after they fell to her feet, Amber then pulled her top over her head and let it fall to the ground. Within moments, her bra was off . . . and they stood naked. Her breasts ached but it wasn't from her milk. She needed to be touched. With a hand under each breast, she raised them higher. Stepping forward, Ricky leaned toward her to kiss each breast before licking each nipple. It was Amber's turn to moan when he took a nipple into his mouth and suckled, then moved to the other one. Amber couldn't stand it any longer. She lowered herself to the blanket, opening her legs to Ricky. He knelt between them, then reached out with a finger to stroke before sliding inside her. Her breath was sucked in through her teeth. Removing his finger, he bent down to taste where it had been and used his tongue as he had his finger. Amber gripped the blanket beneath her with both hands, breathing hard and moaning with each flick of his tongue. Finally, she groaned, "*I want you inside me, Ricco.*" Sitting back on his knees, he put on the condom and then entered her in one thrust. Ricky hovered above her with his hands on the blanket at each side of her shoulders. Meeting each of his thrusts, it didn't take long for Amber to cry out as her body convulsed, with wave after wave of pleasure. He tried to watch her as he felt his release about to happen but his eyes closed and his head went back. The moan he uttered dragged out and grew louder till he collapsed against Amber, breathing hard. Moments later, she was in his arms, head against his chest, listening to his pounding heart slow down.

"This is awesome" she quietly commented. "Laying outside, totally naked, after making love."

She heard his chuckle rumble deep in his chest. "Last night and this afternoon were a first for me . . . something I won't ever forget." Ricky kissed the top of her head. "Was it as good for you as it was for me?"

"Oh, you know it was." Snuggling closer, she murmured, "I don't want today to ever end."

Ricky chuckled as he held her closer. "We have a daughter that will want you after awhile."

"I know . . . I know. Does that make me a bad mother?"

"No . . . just a mother that's been with her baby for over six weeks with no break." He kissed her head again. "We'll just enjoy this time while we have it."

They were quiet for a short time, enjoying their closeness and lack of anybody else around. But then Amber said, "I hope Lisa got an eye full if she watched us again. If she thought last night was hot, this time we burst into flames."

With a gentle squeeze, Ricky muttered, "Don't think about Lisa."

That statement caused Amber to remember something else she had been going to ask him:

"What happened with her yesterday that upset you so much?"

He was quiet for a few long moments, then said, "Let's not talk about it and spoil our time alone."

But her interest was aroused. "What was it, Ricky? What did she do?"

He let go of Amber and sat up. "Let it go."

"Ricky . . ." She sat up, also.

Not looking at her, he answered, "She spent a lot of her time following me, using any excuse to walk by me . . . close enough to rub against me with her breasts." After taking a deep breath and slowly letting it out, Ricky finished with, "And I didn't say anything because I didn't want to make a scene and spoil the party Jake had looked forward to for so long."

Amber was silent for so long that Ricky turned his head to look at her. She sat there, staring ahead, working her bottom lip with her teeth. Finally, she sputtered, "The bitch! What a bitch! How *dare* she? Oh! Wait till my brother finds out about this!"

"No! Don't tell Jake!"

"And why not? So she can rub her big tits against you ever chance she gets?" Amber's eyes met his. "Or did you enjoy it?'

"Come off it, Amber! I did not . . . forget it . . . it's not worth arguing over. I *knew* I shouldn't have said anything! She's not even here and look what she's doing to us." He rubbed his hands over his face. "I can't believe this is happening . . ." he muttered.

"How could you think that I wouldn't say anything to Jake? I can't stand by and watch him play house with her, knowing what she did behind his back!"

Ricky stood.

"Where are you going?"

"To get dressed. So much for our time alone." He reached for his boxers.

Amber watched him put them on. Without a word, she stood, pulling the blanket with her. Wrapping it around herself, she walked to the bench and sat down. Tears welled in her eyes. The love that she and Ricky had made not that long before suddenly seemed so long ago. *Damn you, Lisa*! Her tears spilled over and Amber wiped her face with her hands. She looked at the water as it fell over the rocks but didn't see it. Putting her feet up on the bench, she hugged her knees. *Oh, Ricky . . .* Wiping her face again, Amber couldn't fathom why this mess started. How would Jake react? She had a fairly good idea. *Why . . . why Ricky, Lisa*? It was bad enough that she had had to deal with Deana . . . and now with her and Ricky still working in the same squad, she found herself wondering if Deana would try anything with him again. Amber sniffed then wiped at her nose with the back of her hand, hoping the noise of the falls hid any sound she made so that Ricky didn't hear her . . .

But he did. His attention kept drifting to Amber as he pulled on his shorts. He thought she was crying but knew for sure when he heard her and then he saw her wipe at her nose.

Amber didn't hear him when he walked up next to her and was startled when he asked, "Is there room for one more under that blanket?" She looked up at him with tear filled eyes. When a tear slid down her cheek, he reached out to wipe it away with an index finger. "Don't cry."

"It's warm under here" she commented, then lowered the blanket under her arms, keeping her breasts covered. "But you can sit next to me."

"I want to hold you." Reaching for her, Ricky buried his face in her hair.

Amber turned the upper half of her body to put her arms around him, but it wasn't enough. Not caring any more about the blanket, she let it slide off as she straddled his lap,facing him, her arms around his neck, with her body pressed against his as tightly as she could. As she clung to Ricky, Amber said, "I don't want to fight. I *hate* fighting with you!"

"I know . . . me, too" he agreed, with his arms holding her tightly. "I'm sorry for being an ass."

"You're not an ass." Her body shifted as her legs wrapped around him. Turning her head, she was able to kiss his neck. Suddenly, she sat up to meet his eyes and her hands cupped his face. "Don't you see, Ricco, that I *have* to let Jake know what *she* did? He deserves to know!"

"Oh, Amber . . ."

"What if one of your sisters husbands made a pass at me? Wouldn't you want to know? I know you would want your sister to know what a slime ball she was married to!"

"My sisters have good marriages."

"That's not the point! I have to tell him! He knows me too well . . . I would never be able to hide from him that something is bothering me!" She kissed him. "Can't you see what I'm saying?" She kissed him again. "He needs to know." Amber's eyes dropped to Ricky's mouth and then her index finger stroked his bottom lip. "But you know what I need?" Amber murmured, as her finger followed the shape of his mouth.

"Tell me" he breathed as he watched her face watching her finger.

Leaning forward, her tongue slid out to lick at his bottom lip. His mouth automatically tried to capture her tongue but Amber pulled her head back and she gave him a slight smile. "*You.*" She leaned forward again to stroke her tongue over each of his lips. Ricky closed his eyes, as his body responded to the erotic sensations her tongue delivered. She then whispered, "Give me your tongue" . . . and he did. Even the way she sucked on it turned him on all the more.

He finally pulled away. "I've got to get out of these shorts."

With her arms loose around his neck, she brushed her breasts against his nipples. "You were the one who had to get pissy and put them on" Amber softly teased.

"Don't remind me" he grunted before kissing her hard but briefly. "Get up so I can get them off before I bust through."

Amber knew he was hard . . . she felt and ached for him the harder he became. Reluctantly, she got off him but she watched as what little he wore fell to the ground.

"Where are the condoms?" he asked, breathing hard.

"I'll get them." Amber hurried to snatch her shorts up where she had left them but had to reach in each pocket before she found the two she had brought.

Ricky had doubled the blanket and spread in on the stone bench. Sitting on it, he reached for Amber as she neared him. She straddled him once more as her lips seeked his. His hands cupped her breasts before he lowered his mouth to take a nipple into his mouth. Moving her lower body closer, she rubbed against his erection until neither one could stand it any more. Tearing open a package, Amber slid the contents over him. "Lay down" he hoarsely told her.

And she did . . .

They napped as they lay beside each other. Ricky woke first, wondering what the noise was he heard . . . then smiled to himself when he realized it was the falls. Looking at Amber as she slept on her back, he felt a tenderness he had never felt before. She was his world . . . with Becky to complete it. After losing Amber for close to a year, he knew he could never live without her again . . . and he wasn't going to let Lisa or anybody else ruin it for him.

Deep in thought, Ricky didn't notice when her eyes opened. Amber blinked a couple of times before her eyes focused and she saw him. She stretched and then smiled. "Hi."

His eyes met hers. "Hi . . . how was your nap?"

"Wonderful." She stretched again. "I could get used to this . . . waking up totally naked outside."

He chuckled. "We should do it more often."

"Well, before Becky gets older, anyway." She smiled again. "Or we could move to an island in the tropics and live like this . . . she would grow up thinking nothing about it."

After another chuckle, Ricky kissed her . . . then looked at her. As his fingers caressed the side of her face, he whispered, "I love you, Amber."

"I love you, too." She took another kiss from him.

"Will you marry me?"

For a few seconds, Amber stopped breathing. "What?" she was finally able to say.

"Will you become my wife?"

"Oh, Ricco . . ."

"This wasn't how I planned to do it but the surroundings are perfect . . . I planned on having a ring for you when I asked but it just seemed right to ask you *now*." His fingers came to a stop under her chin. "Well . . . ?"

"Oh, God . . . yes!" She raised her mouth to his. "Yes, Ricco . . . I will!" she exclaimed, after their kiss. "I don't care about a ring right now . . . just a simple band when we say 'I do', okay?"

"We'll see." There was already a ring at his apartment for her . . . one with Becky's birthstone. "Come here" he murmured, pulling her against him. "You just made me a very happy man."

She was going to be Ricky's wife! He had forgiven her for all she had done. He had given her another chance. "You don't know how happy you just made me!" Amber whispered.

They held each other. After awhile, a thought crossed Amber's mind and she chuckled.

"Care to let me in on it?" Ricky asked, pulling back to look at her . . . with a smile on his lips.

"If Becky ever asks about how you proposed to me . . . what do I tell her?"

"Well . . . we were in a romantic setting, with a waterfalls and green grass . . . we can eliminate a couple of facts, like how we had been making love in that beautiful setting . . . and were naked at the time I asked you . . ." He started to laugh. "It is funny when you think about it!"

* * *

They ate the lunch Jake had sent them before dressing to go back to reality.

"I hope Becky was good" Amber commented as she and Ricky folded the blanket.

"You missed her, didn't you?" he asked, taking the blanket from her.

"Yeah . . . this is the longest I've been away from her." But then Amber put her arms around his neck and kissed his mouth. "But don't think I didn't enjoy my time here with you."

"Oh, I *know* you did . . . the animals around here must have wondered what that noise was that came from you . . ." Ricky smiled before kissing her.

"Let's get back to the house . . . I can't wait to tell Jake our news!" Amber couldn't stop smiling.

* * *

Lisa spent her time with Jake and Becky while Amber and Ricky were gone. In just the short time Becky had been there, Lisa had fallen in love with her. And she knew she had better spend some time with Jake . . . Amber wasn't dumb and Ricky had most likely told her what she had done. There was no doubt that 'little sister' would tell her brother. Lisa had thought about telling him herself but couldn't get up the courage. It scared her that Jake would tell her to get out. She knew she shouldn't have done what she did around Ricky but she couldn't stop herself. And if there was that slim chance that he would forget about Amber for awhile . . . it would have been worth it all. Jake didn't pay much attention to her any more.

Becky needed a diaper change. Jake had given Lisa a lesson on how it's done. When Becky became a little fussy, Jake wondered where he had left the bottle she had earlier. "It's out on the picnic table" Lisa told him. "I'll go get it."

She dashed down the stairs and out the side door off the porch. In her hurry, Lisa never noticed Amber and Ricky coming up the path . . .

"There's the bitch. I have a few things to say to her." Amber pulled away from the arm that Ricky had around her shoulders.

"Come on, Amber . . . don't . . . don't spoil what we had this afternoon."

She spun around to look at him. "I *can't* let her get away with what she did!"

Ricky was torn between knowing she was right and not having their mini-vacation ruined any more than it already was. "Amber . . . talk to Jake first."

But she was already walking toward Lisa.

He moved a little closer, just in case things got out of hand. Ricky winced when he heard Amber ask, "Who the hell are you to rub your body on my man?"

Lisa turned on her. "How do you know he didn't like it? So, don't be blaming this on only me, Amber!"

With a harsh laugh, Amber came back with, "I doubt that! He doesn't care for sluts!"

"He loves you, doesn't he?" Lisa quietly asked.

Amber stared at her, not expecting that question. "What do you mean by that?"

"Does Ricky know how you were a few years back? How you slept with anybody?" She laughed at the look on Amber's face. "I bet he'd be interested in hearing about it . . . his *innocent* Amber who fucked just about everybody around, not caring if they were single or married?" Stepping toward Ricky, Lisa started, "Hey! . . ."

But Amber grabbed her arm. "*Don't* you dare" she hissed. "You're so jealous of me and my my brother, so you decide that you want to take my guy from me any way that you can . . . by telling him about my past, flaunting your boobs, your body and smiling so sweetly at him . . . grow up, Lisa! Do you hate me that much? I can't believe my brother *loves* you! And you do this shit behind his back? How many others have there been?"

"What *is* going on?" Jake stood beside Ricky.

Ricky sighed. "A *big* mess, Jake."

"What are they arguing about?" Jake started to walk toward them.

"If you value your life, I wouldn't get too close" Ricky warned him.

But Jake heard what the argument was about as he moved closer:

"You had better keep your boobs off my fiance . . . rub them on Jake! *He's* the one who you should be doing that to! And keep your free show for Jake, too! I can't believe you were topless in front of Ricky! You knew I was going to be there . . . did you want me to see you do that?"

"What are you talking about, Amber?" Jake demanded to know.

"Ask her . . . I want to hear her talk her way out of this one!"

Ricky stepped in, grabbing Amber's arm. "Let's go . . . it's between them now."

Trying to pull free, Amber protested: "But I want to hear this! She's supposed to be in love with my brother and she does things like she did to you?"

"Is what she saying true, Lisa? What did you do?"

"Jake . . . I . . ." Lisa stammered.

"Come *on*, Amber . . . we're out of this now." Standing behind her, Ricky took hold of her upper arms and moved her toward the house.

"No, Ricky!" Amber tried again to get away but instead felt pain. "Ow! That hurt!"

"Then quit fighting me."

"But she'll lie to him!"

"That's something that they have to work out . . . besides, I don't think he's going to believe her anyway."

They climbed the steps into the porch, to find Becky was sleeping in the bassinet, so Ricky wheeled her inside the house. Amber turned to hopefully hear whatever Lisa told Jake but Ricky returned to the porch to steer her to the opposite end of the house.

Jake and Lisa argued . . . loudly.

* * *

Chapter 27

"Tell me what Amber was talking about!"

"She's your precious sister, Jake! You believe anything she tells you!"

"*What* did you do to Ricky? Did you actually take your top off in front of him?"

"Oh, come on, Jake!"

"*Did you*?"

She wasn't good at lying . . . Jake always saw through her when she tried. "But, Jake . . . I . . ."

"*Answer me*!"

"Yes! But I . . ."

"Oh . . . this ought to be good." He folded his arms across his chest and leaned back against the picnic table.

"*You* never pay any attention to me! I wanted somebody to look at me the way he looks at Amber!"

"What do you mean I don't pay any attention to you?"

"You don't! People would think we've been married fifty years the way you are around me! I want somebody to pay attention to *me*!"

"So, you hit on my sister's boyfriend? Knowing how much Ricky loves her, did you honestly think he would take your bait?" Jake spun around once in frustration before facing her again. "I honestly thought we had something, Lisa! Do you have any idea how this makes me feel? Why didn't you say something to me instead of hitting on Ricky?" He started to pace. "You took off your top in front of him, today, when you knew I was giving them time to be alone and not have to worry about Becky . . . I guess I should have worried about *you*! Jesus, Lisa! You watch them make love by the pool and then you . . ." Jake stopped and stared at her. "You wanted him, didn't you? After seeing him with Amber . . . *shit*!" He started toward her but suddenly stopped. When he spoke, his voice dripped with ice: "Pack your things and get out of here. Do it now and do it fast. I want you out of here . . ."

It had happened. He kicked her out. The tears came. "Oh, Jake . . . please, don't! I'm so sorry! I love you!"

"You do? Well, you have a funny way of showing it. Now, one more time . . . get your things and get out of here." Jake then turned and walked toward the garage.

With tears streaming down her face, Lisa watched Jake go to the garage and disappear inside. She hadn't intended on things going as far as they had but she had gotten caught up in the thrill and wanted to find out how far she would get. It got her thrown out of Jake's house . . . Jake's life. Slowly walking to the house, Lisa knew better than to attempt to talk to him too soon. It would be better after he calmed down. But her heart was broken and it was all her fault. By the time she reached the dining room, she was sobbing and had to sit in one of the chairs at the table. When the worst of the storm passed, she went up the stairs to pack.

Amber and Ricky were in their room, on the bed with Becky between them . . . and the door closed. Neither one spoke, lost in their own thoughts.

Ricky had never seen or heard Amber so angry. He knew she was right. They were basically guests for the weekend and . . . he still couldn't believe the things that Lisa had done to him! He had thought Lisa was flirting with him ever since he and Amber arrived but certainly didn't think much of it until the time he put the baby in Lisa's arms and his fingers touched her breast. Now he knew it was intentional . . . on her part. And Jake! He felt so bad for Jake! He hoped Jake didn't think he had any part in Lisa's little scheme. There was no denying that Lisa was very attractive but she wasn't his type. Ricky now knew her beauty only ran skin deep. Lisa's beauty wasn't like Amber's, who was beautiful inside *and* out. How did Jake put up with this one?

The bitch! *How dare she go after the man I love*? Amber then thought about how Ricky had asked her to marry him. But had he asked her because he felt guilty about Lisa? Did something happen that he wasn't telling? No, that couldn't be . . . not the Ricky she knew . . . and not with Jake's woman. He had always been up front with her . . . hadn'the? And

Jake . . . if it was legal she would have killed Lisa for doing this to him! Had there been any others? Any of his friends? Some friends if they took Lisa up on whatever she offered! But the names she could think of had all been good friends with Jake for years . . . Amber couldn't imagine any of them going behind his back.

The sound of someone running up the stairs got Amber and Ricky's attention. They then heard the sound of Lisa crying as she passed by their room. Ricky sighed loudly, moving one arm up over his head. He felt terrible about this whole mess. Amber wondered how Jake was doing . . . and she had a few more words for Lisa. As she moved to get up, Ricky's hand reached over to grasp her arm.

"Don't . . . stay here."

Reluctantly, Amber lay back down. "She had no right to hurt Jake like this."

"I know but Jake's a big boy. He'll handle it in his own way."

"And she had no right to strut her stuff in front of you."

"I know that, too. Jake has to be crushed."

"I have to see him." Amber tried to get up again but Ricky's words stopped her:

"Remember what happened the first night we were here and they argued. Jake pushed you away and that hurt you."

"Right." She knew he didn't mean it but she couldn't stand if Jake didn't want her comfort again. Laying on her left side to face Ricky, Amber placed a finger against Becky's hand for her little fingers to grasp. "I was so excited about coming up here for a few days."

"I know you were. And I looked forward to it, too." Moving onto his side, his dark eyes met Amber's. "There was a lot going on that you didn't tell me about . . . problems between those two."

"I know . . . but like I said, we were working on our own problems and didn't think theirs was *this* bad."

Becky made some noises. Her head turned toward her mother and her pursed lips motioned toward her breast.

"I think she's getting hungry" Ricky said.

"I wonder when she last had a bottle."

"That doesn't matter. She's hungry now." "You're a little piggy since we've been up here, little girl" Amber teased, pulling up her top.

"Take it off" Ricky quietly requested. Her eyes met his before sitting up to pull her top over her head. When her hand moved to open one side of her nursing bra, Ricky again quietly requested, "Take that off, too."

Doing as he wanted, Amber then propped pillows against the headboard before taking Becky into her arms. "Your father wants a free show while you're eating." Settling back and getting comfortable, Amber then moved Becky to her breast before looking at Ricky.

"You're the one I want to see topless" he commented.

"And that's supposed to make me feel better?"

"Yes."

She had to smile.

Ricky watched them, as he had many times before. "I can't see why Lisa finds this so bad."

"That's Lisa. She's so jealous of anything Jake has to do with me. Why?" She looked at Ricky with tears in her eyes. "Why did she have to hurt him like this?" Lisa's threat about Amber's past suddenly popped into her head, which caused more tears.

"Don't cry" Ricky soothed, reaching to wipe away the one that ran down her cheek. "Don't be upset while nursing . . . don't be upset at all."

"I know . . . I know." After taking a couple of deep breaths, she wiped at her eyes. "I never had the chance to tell Jake you asked me to marry you."

"You will, when things calm down around here."

Amber gazed at him. "I love you" she softly said. "How did I ever do without you?"

He smiled before moving to sit next to her. "Let's not go there, either. Everything from here on in is today and tomorrow." He kissed her head. "I love you, too."

The slam of a door and feet pounding along the hall grabbed their attention. Not long after, even though they couldn't see the driveway from their room, they heard a car start and rev before it sped down the driveway.

"Lisa . . . Jake must have kicked her out."

"Where would she go?" Ricky asked.

"She still has an apartment that she kept for some unknown reason. Maybe in case something happened between her and Jake."

"Good thing she did."

* * *

An hour or so later, after all three took a brief nap, Amber and Ricky took Becky downstairs. Jake was nowhere to be seen. Looking in the refrigerator, Amber looked for something to make for supper. With all the left-overs she found, she decided they were good enough.

Finding an empty baby bottle on the counter, Amber took it to the sink to rinse it out. In doing so, she looked out the window by the sink and found Jake. He sat on top of the picnic table, his back to the house and his head down.

Going out on the porch, she told Ricky, "I'm going to try to talk to Jake . . . he's out on the picnic table." Becky was in her seat on the coffee table and Amber smoothed back her hair before leaning to kiss Ricky, who was sitting on the couch. "Wish me luck."

Amber didn't say anything until she was next to the table. "Jake?" she softly said his name. "Can I sit with you?"

He was leaning forward, with his elbows on his upper thighs and his head held up by a fist at each side of his face, looking down. When he didn't reply to Amber's question, she figured he was okay with it. Stepping up on the seat, she almost knocked over the bottle of beer that was on the table next to Jake as she sat down.

Jake didn't speak . . . and Amber didn't press him to do so. She looked around the yard as she waited, noting the changes that had occurred over the years. The garage had gone from a two car to three cars after both she and Jake had gotten their driver's licenses. An old shed behind the garage was gone and storage space had been added over the garage. The in-ground pool had only been in ten years, upgraded from an above-ground. Her eyes rested on the far back right corner, where Dusty was buried, Jake's German Shepherd. Dusty died the year before at the age of seventeen, being Jake's shadow since he was a young pup. That's what Jake needed was another dog. Amber even missed having one around when she was home.

But then, Jake's voice brought her back to today:

"I can't believe I didn't see it . . . she had me fooled, didn't she? And Ricky! Ricky of all people she had to make a move on! I am so sorry, sis. I didn't think things were *that* bad between us . . . was I *that* bad to her? *Why* didn't she talk to me about how she felt? She got so bitchy but I didn't try to find out why . . . I *loved* her . . . and I thought she loved me back." He grabbed the open bottle of beer and drank what was in it before tossing the empty bottle onto the lawn. "I was a fool, sis. Were there others that I don't know about?"

Amber remembered having that same thought. "I have no idea" she quietly replied. "I had *no* idea that she was so jealous of me. Did she set out to hurt the both of us . . . to target Ricky to get back at me? Did you ever get the chance to talk to her like we talked about when you were downstate?" Amber sighed. "I don't know,Jake . . . I still can't believe this all happened."

"So much for inviting you up, huh? You listen to us argue, Lisa gives you grief, you find out you were watched while making love outside . . . and then Lisa decides to undress for Ricky. I really did want you to come up for a good time . . . Sorry."

She reached to pat his arm. "It's not your fault."

Just then, Ricky appeared with Becky. "I thought if anything could cheer you up it would be your favorite niece" he said, standing in front of Jake.

Jake looked up to see Becky in her father's arms. "You were right" Jake agreed, with a smile. He reached for her. "Come see your uncle, little girl." After Ricky put her in Jake's arms, Jake cuddled her against his chest. "I'm so glad you came up here to see me" he said to her.

"Will you do something for me, Jake?" Amber asked, getting off the table to stand beside Ricky, sliding her arm around him. His arm moved across her shoulders, holding her against his body.

"You know I will. I'd give anything to take away all the rotten things that happened this weekend."

"Jake, would you *give me* to Ricky, since dad can't do it?"

His head came up slowly to look at her, then at Ricky. "Really? You asked her?"

With a grin, Ricky replied, "I did."

"Here." Jake handed Becky back to her father before getting off the table. His arms wrapped around Amber, holding her close. "I am so happy for you! You know I'll give you to Ricky . . . and dad will be watching us!" His voice caught. "He wanted this to happen, you know . . . but you were too damn stubborn to do anything about it then."

"Hey, let's not bring that up, okay?" Ricky cut in. "It took awhile but now she's going to be my wife."

Jake kissed Amber soundly on the forehead before letting her loose. "When?"

She laughed. "We haven't gotten that far yet." Turning to Ricky, Jake extended his hand. "Congrats, big guy! Welcome to the family!"

"Wait! Let me take her!" Amber took Becky from Ricky so that Jake could give him a hug.

"I really am happy for you" Jake said, when he stepped back.

"Thanks . . . that means a lot" Ricky replied, grinning.

Reaching for his niece again, Jake said, "Come here, little girl. You'll be going home sometime tomorrow. You have to spend some more time with me before then." He looked up. "What time are you leaving?"

"Early" Ricky told him.

"You have to go to work . . . make sure we're up when you get up" Amber said.

"That's at 5:00."

"That's good" Ricky said. "We can be on the road by six thirty if we pack tonight."

Jake suddenly looked sad. "I hate to see you go."

"I know but we have to. Ricky has to be back to work on Tuesday."

Taking Becky out of Jake's arms, Ricky said, "I'm going to take her to check out the pool. Care to join us?"

"I'll be there shortly. I want to get the camera" Amber replied.

Both she and Jake watched Ricky as he walked toward the pool, talking to Becky. Amber said, "I don't want to leave you after what happened."

"I'll be okay . . . I'm your big brother, remember?" Jake attempted a smile.

"Jake . . ."

He looked at her. "Uh-oh . . . what's wrong?"

"Lisa threatened to tell Ricky about . . ." she swallowed . . . "my wild year."

"You don't have to worry about her doing that now."

"Well, she got me thinking . . . maybe I should tell him . . . what if somehow she tells him? Either before or after we're married . . . what if he decides *not* to marry or stay married to me?"

Shaking his head, Jake said, "He loves you too much. Besides, that all happened before you met each other. It's really none of his business what went on before you became a couple."

Amber sighed, "I know but . . ."

"Does Ricky know you were married before . . . to that jerk?"

"Wow! You're being nice!" she laughed. "And yes, he knows I was married before."

"Well, I don't think he has to know about your sordid past . . . and now you'd better go get your camera before he thinks you're not joining him."

* * *

After a supper of leftovers outside at the picnic table, the men helped clean up. Jake put the dirty dishes into the dishwasher while Ricky grabbed a garbage bag to throw paper products in. It wasn't long before they were back outside, enjoying their last night together.

Jake held Becky while the adults talked. Amber joined the conversation but her talk with Jake earlier stayed in the back of her mind. She decided to tell Ricky . . . and she would rather do it now instead of waiting till a date was set and plans were started. What if he didn't want to get married after hearing about her past?

Around 9 o'clock, she said, "Ricky, I have to talk to you."

"About what? Can it wait?"

"No." She had to tell him before she lost her nerve. Reaching for the sleeping Becky who was still in Jake's arms, she added, "Let's go inside."

"I'd like to put her to bed if you're not back by the time I'm ready to go in. I think there's at least one bottle left if she needs one."

"I think so, too."

When she leaned to kiss Becky's forehead, Jake whispered, "Amber, are you sure that you want to do this?"

"Yes." After kissing his cheek, she stood and turned to Ricky. "Ready?"

"This sounds too serious. Is everything okay?"

With a smile, Amber reached for his hand. "Let's go."

Closing the door to their room behind them, Ricky quietly asked, "Amber, what's going on?" When she turned to face him, she was smiling but he could tell how nervous she was. "Amber?"

"You know I love you with all my heart."

"Yes . . . but what . . . ?"

"Lisa made a threat to me this afternoon about something that happened before we met . . . and it has been eating at me ever since."

"But if it happened before we met . . . what difference does it make now?" He looked puzzled.

Amber took a deep breath and let it out before starting: "I told you that I was married before . . . and divorced him two years later." She looked at his feet as she spoke.

"Yes . . ." *Where was this going?*

"I . . . I then starting sleeping around . . . and it didn't matter if the guy was single or not." Her hand wiped at a lone tear that slid down the side of her nose. "I was bad, Ricky . . . and it was so ironic because I was doing what Seth did to me . . . slept around with anybody. There was nobody I was serious about . . . most were one-night stands." She raised her head to meet his eyes. "And when Lisa brought that up when we argued this afternoon, she was pleased to find out that you didn't know and was going to tell you. And I was thinking after she was gone that if there was *any* chance at all that she could tell you . . . I'd rather that you heard it from me first."

Ricky didn't reply. He just stood and looked at her, which made Amber all the more nervous. She continued talking:

"I wasn't happy with my life and grew tired of what I was doing. That's why I moved down to New York City, to get away . . . but not too far from my dad and brother . . . and start over. I dated a couple of Matt's friends who were nice but they did nothing for me . . ." Her voice caught as she said, "And then I met you." She wiped at another tear. "And since you asked me to marry you, I wanted you to know this so if you . . ." Her throat tightened and she cleared her throat. "So if you decide that you *don't* want to marry me now . . ." her voice dropped to a whisper. "I'll understand."

His voice was soft when he finally spoke to her: "Amber, I love you . . . and still want to marry you. It wasn't necessary to tell me what you just did . . . it doesn't change how I feel about you." He reached for her and pulled her close, wrapping his arms around her. "I fell in love with you the very first day we met, when I bumped into you in the drugstore and White Musk became our favorite cologne. I *was* dating someone at the time but after that first night at your apartment, with our pizza supper during the snowstorm, I stopped seeing her."

Amber looked up at him. "You never told me that!"

"I didn't want her or anybody else after meeting you." His mouth was close and his lips brushed against hers as he spoke. "I love *you*." Covering her lips with his, Ricky kissed her, long and deep. Both breathed hard and fast when he pulled away. "So, your past makes no difference to me. You're with me and I *know* you love me."

"But women like I was are called *whores* and *sluts* because we like sex but guys that have a lot of *action* are known as *studs*."

"That's the way it's *always* been and people won't change."

"For a guy that's as good looking and sweet as you are, I bet you dated a lot."

"When I was fifteen, I saw one girl for three years. After I graduated, I dated another for five years but when she knew I wouldn't change my mind about being a cop, she told me that wasn't the type of life she wanted and she left me, to marry a lawyer who was just starting out in Philly. I dated on and off for years after that . . . and then I met you, the girl I want forever." He kissed her again and held her close.

Amber thought about what he told her . . . that somebody else had left him because of his job. That wasn't mentioned when he was so angry with her about leaving him . . . but then, this other girl let him know she was leaving and why. What she said next just popped out, with no thought: "What about Deana? How does she fit in there?"

Ricky let go and stepped back, looking at her. "We're being honest here, right?"

She nodded, wondering what he was going to say.

"Deana fits in because you left me. I explained to you how we got together . . . let's not go over that again."

"Okay" Amber whispered then reached for him.

Ricky's body felt stiff for a moment but then it relaxed, molding with her body as he embraced her. "I love you" he whispered, "Always remember that." He then walked slowly, steering her in reverse. When the backs of her legs met the bed, Ricky gently helped her lay down. Their eyes met and held as he took off his clothes. After she unbuttoned and unzipped her shorts, he reached to pull them off her . . .

* * *

They had fallen asleep after their love-making but Amber woke knowing when Jake was putting Becky to bed. A glance at the alarm clock told her it was after eleven o'clock. Getting quietly out of bed, Amber slipped on her robe. Looking at Ricky, she saw he was still asleep, on his back, breathing evenly. Slowly turning the doorknob, she left their room to go to Becky's.

The light was on and she walked in just as Jake covered the sleeping baby with a blanket. "Hi" she softly greeted. "Late night for you, isn't it?"

"Yeah but I was enjoying the peace and quiet of outside . . . and having Becky with me. She was good . . . and she drank that last bottle in the 'fridge. She fell asleep about an hour ago but I was too comfy to bring her inside then. But like you said, it is late and I have to get some sleep. Five a.m. comes too early!"

Amber smiled down at her daughter before taking Jake by the arm to lead him toward the door. In the hall, she hugged him, knowing this would night could be a hard one. "Are you going to be all right?"

"Yes. And are things good with you and Ricky?"

There was no stopping the smile on her face when she answered, "Yes."

"He had no problem with . . . your history?"

"Like you told me, he said it happened before we met . . . except he didn't know that that was the main reason I first moved downstate."

Jake smiled. "Good man . . . he's so good for you. I'm glad you finally got your head out of your ass and called him . . . without much time to spare before Becky came into the world. You cut it a little close there, sis." Hugging her, Jake said, "Now get back to bed. I'll see you in a few hours."

As she slid back into bed, Ricky rolled onto his side. "Is Jake okay?"

"Right now but he'll be sleeping alone for the first time in awhile . . . and if he gets to thinking about what happened with Lisa, he won't sleep much."

Reaching for her, Ricky knew just what Jake would be going through . . . he went through the same thing the first few weeks after Amber left him . . .

* * *

It was almost 6:30 when Ricky finished packing the Durango. He then strapped in Becky's seat while Jake held her. "Please don't be walking by the time I see you again" Jake pleaded to his niece.

"Oh, Jake . . . come on!" Amber begged. "You know better than that!"

"Well, will you be making another trip up here, then? Because I can't take the time to come to see you for awhile."

"The wedding, Jake. She won't be walking by then."

"You decided on a date?"

"Nothing definite . . . we just threw a few dates out there for now."

"But it must be soon if she won't be walking yet."

Amber had to laugh. "Well, within the next six months to a year."

After Becky was strapped into her seat, Ricky and Jake said their good-byes with a handshake and a brief hug. "Drive careful, man."

"I will. See you in a few months. Thanks for having us up" Ricky replied.

"I wish things had been better for your visit."

"If we had known what happened would be happening, we wouldn't have come up" Amber quipped. Hugging Jake, she said, "Stop worrying about it. For the most part, we had a good time, big brother." Giving him an extra squeeze, she added, "Call me whenever you need to talk . . . promise?"

"I promise." Jake held her for a few moments longer. "Call me when you get home so that I know you made it there okay."

"Will do." She kissed his cheek and then pulled away to get into her seat.

Moments later, they were driving down the long driveway to head home.

* * *

Jake did call at times to comment on the pictures of their visit that Amber sent to him on the computer.

But two weeks after their visit, Jake called to tell Amber that he and Lisa were talking.

* * *

Two weeks after that call, there was a letter in the mail from Lisa: *Amber and Ricky . . . I am writing to apologize for what I did while you were here. I have no excuse, other than my jealousy . . . my jealousy of your relationship with Jake, Amber, and of the relationship you and Ricky have. You have what I have always wanted and for some reason I believed my actions would give me that. I am going to counseling twice a week now, trying to get my head straight. I love Jake and want to be with him, have a life with him.*

And my counselor is making me see that Jake must care an awful lot for me if he's sticking by me through all this even after all I have done. I know he loves you, Amber and that my jealousy made you closer instead of driving you apart. I have two sisters and a brother and I don't have much of a relationship with them. We grew up together and now are all scattered around the U.S., only keeping in touch on birthdays and Christmas. And Ricky, I am ashamed at what I did to you. I have no excuse for any of it and I am so sorry I acted like that. I hope you will both forgive me. If you don't, I will understand your reasons why. Jake is trying . . . I hope you will. Take care . . . Lisa.

*   *   *

Chapter 28

"Can you believe you're getting married tomorrow?" Sara gushed to Amber, as they sat in Amber's living room.

"Did you think he would ever get around to asking you?" Maggie asked, as she handed another bottle of Smirnoff Ice to her. "I knew he would eventually but not this soon . . . not that I'm complaining!" After opening the bottle, she added, "I'm ready to be his wife." Touching bottles with Maggie's, she then took a long drink.

"You've been ready for a long time" Sara teased.

Amber smiled as she tucked her feet under her on the couch. "I have been, haven't I?" Looking at the bottle she held, she exclaimed, "*This* tastes so good! I haven't had any alcohol since I found out I was pregnant!"

"And that's only your second bottle!" Maggie laughed.

"I would be a cheap date!"

"Are you going to take a longer honeymoon some other time?" Sara asked.

"Maybe."

"And what, pray tell, are you two going to do in a fancy hotel like the Hilton for three nights?" Maggie teased.

Amber smiled but a deep blush of red spread over her cheeks. "Oh, I have a pretty good idea of what we'll be doing after I foolishly told Ricky no sex all this week! I'm surprised he's held up on his end . . . this having no sex is killing me!"

All three women laughed and then Sara said, "Well, the wait will be worth it."

A rush of heat traveled to Amber's groin as she thought about Ricky's love-making. Her eyes closed as she gushed, "Ohmygod . . . I know it!"

"He's good, isn't he?" Maggie asked.

"Maggie! I would never ask that about Matt!" Amber laughed.

"And why not? I'd tell you that he is!" She then pointed a finger at Amber. "And if it bothers you so much not having him for a week . . . that tells us he *is* good!"

"No, not *good*!" Amber's voice then dropped to a whisper: "He's *great*!"

The three women sounded like high school girls with their giggles.

Sara went into the kitchen and brought back another bag of potato chips. As Maggie scooped a handful, she asked, "So, Jake and his girlfriend are watching the baby while you're gone?"

"Yes, they're staying here at the apartment. Jake can't wait . . . and Lisa seems excited about it, too." Amber sighed. "I probably should have asked Lisa to join us tonight but I still haven't forgotten what she did at Jake's when we were there . . . I don't think I can be around her yet without Jake." She took another long drink. "I better be careful. My baby might wake up and need me during the night, even though she's been doing so good lately and sleeping all night." With a smile, she tipped the bottle to her lips again. "Jake wanted to keep her at Ricky's tonight but I couldn't let her go when I won't have her for three nights after tonight!"

Sara commented: "I'm surprised that Ricky didn't move in with you before now."

"He might as well have . . . he's been here so much. But for some reason, some nights when he had to leave here because work called . . . he went back to his place if it was closer and really late."

Sara watched Amber as she spoke then quietly asked, "Are you okay with this now?"

With a smile, Amber nodded her head. "Yes I am. I have to be . . . for Ricky." But then she sighed. "Oh, Sara, how do you stand it after all these years?"

"It's one of those things, Amber . . . either you do or you don't. I love A.J. too much to let go . . . and I know that's how you feel about Ricky." She held up her bottle. "Cheers to you and Ricky!"

All three tapped bottles and chorused, "Cheers!"

Becky made some noise over the baby monitor. The women all became quiet and listened for more . . . but Becky must have gone back to sleep.

"We must be getting too noisy!" Maggie said in a loud whisper.

"We aren't *that* loud!" Amber laughed. "And her room is down the hall. Sometimes she does that . . . I wonder if she's dreaming."

"Could be" Maggie agreed.

"So, what time do you want me to pick you up in the morning?" Sara asked Amber as she and Maggie prepared to leave.

"Let's see . . . the wedding's at one . . . I have a hair appointment at nine . . ."

"Me, too" Maggie put in.

"I don't know . . . how about 11:30? Remember, I'm taking a port-a-crib for Becky."

"That's okay . . . 11:30 sounds good. I'll help you load up the car. It's great where you're having the wedding because we are dressing there . . . and the reception is in the same building . . . *how* did you find that place?" Sara asked.

"Um . . . your hubby knows the guy who owns it."

Sara giggled. "Oh! That's right!"

Amber hugged her. "It's a good thing A.J. is coming to pick you up. There's no driving for you tonight, girlfriend!"

"Are you sure it's okay with A.J. to take me home? I can call Matt" Maggie said to Sara.

"No, you're fine. He said no problem when I called."

"Thanks so much for spending some time with me tonight" Amber told them. "I really enjoyed myself."

"Oh! Me, too!" they chorused.

"Just think . . . your last night as a single woman" Sara commented.

"Please tell me why you aren't having a spring or summer wedding instead of in October" Maggie said

"October 25th was my parents anniversary. We were lucky that date fell on a Saturday this year . . . because we didn't want to wait any longer!"

The intercom buzzed. Amber answered it: "A.J.?"

"Who else? I left your hubby-to-be at his place."

"Come on up!"

"Well, I take it you girls had a good time" A.J. greeted, when he stepped into the apartment.

"Oh, we did" Sara replied but then all three started to giggle.

"And you're all set for a wedding tomorrow?"

"Nothing will keep me from that" Amber declared.

"Good! Now, are you ladies ready to go?"

"Are you sure you don't mind giving me a ride home?" Maggie asked A.J..

"I don't mind at all."

"See you tomorrow." Sara hugged Amber.

When she hugged Maggie, Amber said, "I hope you're okay with not being in the wedding."

"Don't worry about it. I know you and Ricky are keeping it small. Hey! I get to take pictures!"

"Take a whole bunch!

"Have you talked to Ricky yet?" A.J. asked.

"I'm calling him before I go to bed. How was your get-together at his place?"

"Not bad. I had a nice conversation with your brother and got to know his girlfriend a little bit. She didn't move too much from Jake's side the whole time I was there." A.J. hugged Amber. "I just wanted to let you know that Ricky misses you."

"I wouldn't let him see me tonight."

"I know . . . I heard." A.J. chuckled. "You've tortured the poor guy for a week!"

Amber grinned. "I know . . ."

"He still loves you . . . and he knows the torture will be over with tomorrow night!"

* * *

"*Hey, Ricco* . . ." she purred when he answered the phone.

"Hey, yourself! How was your party?"

"We had fun. How was your's?"

"We sat around and bull-shitted."

"That's about all we did. How was Lisa?"

"Good . . . had no problems."

"That's what I like to hear. Are they still up?"

"No . . . we're all in bed. Well, they're in my bed and I'm on the couch."

"I'm heading to bed. Becky's been sleeping . . . hope she does for the rest of the night. I had a couple of drinks."

"I hope there's no hangover tomorrow" Ricky teased.

"Nope . . . didn't drink enough for one of those!"

He was quiet for a moment before saying, "I miss you. It's been rough without you beside me at night . . . I haven't slept much."

"Oh, don't try to make me feel guilty! It's only for one more night, you know!" Then Amber sighed. "I miss you, too, Ricco."

With a moan, he said, "You know how it affects me when you say my name like that . . . and you aren't here with me . . . my body misses you, too."

Her body felt the same way. Lowering her voice, Amber asked, "Are you sleeping in your birthday suit?"

"I can't . . . I have company, remember? I'm wearing sweats. How about you?"

"My birthday suit misses yours."

Ricky softly groaned. "*Don't*, Amber! It's been too long of a week!"

"What *was* I thinking?"

"And *I* agreed to it! Can I come over now?"

"That is *so* tempting . . . but no."

"I love you, anyway."

Amber chuckled. "I love you, too."

With a groan, Ricky muttered, "I am *so* horny for you! Just wait till tomorrow . . ."

"Where? The broom closet at the reception?"

"Is there one?"

They both laughed.

"What time will you be there?" Ricky asked.

"By noon. How about you?"

"Well, since I can't see the bride before the ceremony, probably by quarter to one."

"Are Jake and Lisa riding with you?"

"Yep . . . and taking a cab back to the apartment whenever they leave the reception."

"I'm going to try to get some sleep" Amber told him.

"I should, too."

"Talk to you in the morning?"

"Probably not. But I will see you at one o'clock."

"I'll be the one in the white dress . . ."

With a chuckle, Ricky said, "I'll be looking for you."

* * *

Chapter 29

"You look gorgeous" Sara gushed after helping Amber with her jacket. The short white jacket complimented the white A-line, calf-length, sleeveless dress she wore. Small silk white roses and baby's breath enhanced her stylish new hair-do, as well as a gold hair clip borrowed from Sara. A gold heart shaped locket that was her mother's hung around her neck. Jake had found it one day and had brought it for Amber to wear on her special day. A picture inside the locket was of their parents on their wedding day. Sara and A.J. had given her a gift of a gold wrist bracelet and a matching ankle bracelet. And last but not least was the blue garter. Amber had forgotten to put it on till Sara reminded her. Amber slid off the white sandal on her right foot and pulled the garter up her leg and over her knee. She noticed that Sara was making upward hand motions. "Higher?"

Sara laughed. "Why not?"

Becky lay on the double bed, wearing a fresh diaper, a yellow dress with yellow socks, and a white headband with a small yellow silk butterfly attached to it.

At ten minutes to one, there was a knock on their dressing room door. Amber looked at Sara, hoping it wasn't Ricky. Sara opened the door to find Jake and Lisa standing there. "Is the bride ready?" he asked.

"Come on in" Sara invited.

Stepping into the room, Jake took one look at Amber and whistled softly. "Well, look at you."

"You look so beautiful, Amber" Lisa said.

With a smile, Amber thanked her. Her attention was then drawn to Jake as he walked toward her. "You don't look so bad yourself, big brother."

She reached to straighten his tie, which didn't need straightening but she had to do something with her hands. "You're pretty spiffy looking in that tux." Her eyes filled with tears.

"Don't do that" he warned, taking her hands in his. "You'll ruin that make-up that you so rarely wear." Jake wanted to hug her but was afraid of wrinkling her dress so he gently squeezed her hands. "I was going to ask where my sister was when I came into the room but when I saw the tears in your eyes, I knew I found you" he teased. Stepping back, he said, "You are beautiful, sis. You really are."

"Thank you" she whispered, afraid to cry. "I wish Dad was here."

He smiled but blinked back the tears that had suddenly filled his eyes. "Me, too."

Clearing her throat, she asked, "Is Ricky here?"

"He and A.J. are talking with the minister."

"Reverend Jenkins is Maggie and Matt's minister. He was nice enough to do the ceremony."

"Are you nervous?" Jake asked.

"Can you tell?"

"Yeah . . . you keep chewing on your bottom lip. You won't have any lipstick left on it."

"I'm nervous *and* excited." Glancing at the clock on the wall, she said, "Five more minutes."

"Would you like me to take Becky down to see her father?" Lisa asked.

Amber hesitated at first, not liking the thoughts that ran through her head. *But Lisa will be good . . . there's too many people around . . . Well, there was a lot of people at the picnic, too . . . but she'll be good if she wants to stay with Jake . . . and besides, it's our wedding!* "He would love that, Lisa. He didn't get to see her much this week. Thanks for thinking of it." She picked the diaper bag up off the floor and handed it to Lisa, who slung the strap over her shoulder. "She ate not too long ago and has a clean diaper." Amber scooped Becky off the bed and kissed her cheek before handing her to Lisa. "See you in awhile."

Jake kissed Lisa on her way out of the room. Turning back to Amber, he pulled his phone out of his pants pocket. "We have time for a couple of pictures . . . I want one of you . . . I probably won't see you look this pretty again until Becky gets married." He grinned at the face she made at him. "And I'd like one of you and Sara together. Sara, you've been a good friend to my sister and for that I'll always be thankful." He held up the phone to snap the pictures. "You both look beautiful." Sara's dress was a slightly shorter version of Amber's and the color was peach.

Suddenly, it was time. The wedding music floated up the stairs. Jake and Amber looked at one another. "Well, it's time, sis." When she slid her arm through his, he said, "I am so happy for you and Ricky." He gently kissed her cheek.

Smiling through the tears that threatened to fall, Amber told Jake, "Take me to Ricky."

"Oops! Wait!" Sara exclaimed, turning to one of the dressers. She picked up two bouquets of silk sunflowers and handed the slightly bigger one to Amber. "*Now* we're ready." Amber gave her a quick one-armed hug then said, "After you, Sara."

Ricky looked expectantly toward the staircase. It had a railing on one side and it was decorated with white streamers and silk sunflowers. He saw Sara and looked for his bride. Moments later, she came into view. Suddenly, Amber was the only person he saw. Ricky watched as she slowly descended the stairs, smiling at something Jake said to her. But then she looked directly at Ricky and her smile was all for him.

The ceremony was short but beautiful. They had written their own vows and in minutes, rings were exchanged and Rev. Jenkins pronounced them husband and wife. When Ricky was told he could kiss his wife, A.J. worried that it lasted a little too long, knowing how frustrated his friend had been most of the week!

Maggie had taken pictures starting with Amber's walk down the stairs. Pictures were then taken of the bride and groom, alone and with the baby. Lisa held the baby while shots of the four in the wedding party were taken, of just Sara and A.J.,and last but not least, Amber and Jake. As she took Becky from Lisa, Amber said, "Let's get some pictures of you and Jake."

But Amber found her eyes drawn to Ricky more than once. When the picture taking was done for the moment, Amber handed the baby to Jake. "Give us five minutes and then we'll join the reception" she whispered.

"Where are you going?"

"Upstairs." Pointing a finger at him, she hissed, "*Shush*!"

He pointed a finger back at her. "*Five* minutes . . . that's all! And then I'll have the DJ announce your arrival."

"*Seven* minutes."

Jake rolled his eyes. "*Okay*."

Grabbing Ricky's hand, Amber started for the stairs. Realizing where she was taking him, Ricky rushed up the stairs with her. The moment they were in the room, Ricky closed the door, pulling her against him. "I've missed you!" he groaned before his mouth covered hers. They kissed as if they hadn't seen each other in months instead of days. Ricky slid her hand down over the erection that strained against the front of his pants. "I need you" he whispered needlessly.

Her hand stroked him but then pulled away. "We can't . . . not now. I know my brother . . . he'll be banging on the door if we're not downstairs when we're supposed to be."

"You're right" he sighed. "I never noticed . . . is there a closet off the reception room?"

Amber laughed. "I don't know!"

Ricky took her hands in his, kissing the backs of each. "You look so beautiful . . . you took my breath away when I saw you coming down the stairs."

"And you in that tux . . . I never dreamed you could be any handsomer than you all ready are!"

After a gentle kiss, Ricky teased, "We'll have to dress up more often."

She giggled then said, "When I got to the top of the stairs, I had this vision of tripping and falling down them . . . what a grand entrance that would have made, huh? I think I had a death grip on Jake's arm . . . but when I saw you standing there, watching and waiting for me, Jake knew that I wanted to run to you and he held me back!"

Ricky laughed with her but then became serious. "I can't wait to get you alone tonight."

A warmth flushed through her body, knowing what he could do to her. Amber stammered, "We'd better get back."

His thumb gently rubbed at the corner of her mouth. "You had better fix your lipstick. I kind of messed it up."

"One more kiss."

Ricky obliged.

* * *

"And here they are . . . Mr. and Mrs. Ricky Davis!"

The room exploded with applause, yells and whistles as the newly married couple walked through the doors. They held hands as they responded with smiles and waves to those around them. Jake was the first to approach them. He shook his new brother-in-law's hand and then finally hugged his sister.

"Good timing" he said into her ear. "I actually thought you wouldn't be back on time."

"I should have bet you!" Amber laughed.

The start of one of Ricky's favorite songs filled the room, a song titled, "Color My World". "Excuse me but I need to dance with my wife" he said to Jake.

"She's all your's!"

With an arm around Amber, Ricky walked her to the center of the dance floor. Taking her into his arms, he held her as they danced to the slow music that began with a piano and ended with a flute, with a few beautiful words in between. "I love you" Ricy told her as he expertly moved her around the floor.

The food was delicious. Baked chicken and roast beef were the main courses. Small, seasoned potatoes, stuffing, gravy, baked ziti with sausage, tossed salad, green beans with garlic and rolls were set out buffet style.

After the meal, A.J. stood to give a funny but at times solemn toast. Sara had her say and drew some laughs, too. She ended her speech by telling Amber, "You married the love of your life . . . just like I did. Happiness always."

Ricky made a production out of removing the garter from Amber's thigh. As the DJ payed the theme for 'the stripper', Amber saw the look in Ricky's eyes as his hands slowly slid up her leg. "Behave" she whispered. Out of the thirty guests, many of the men . . . and some women . . . made a lot of noise when his hands disappeared under her dress as she sat on a chair. It was difficult for Amber not to show a reaction when he reached the garter but his long fingers slid further to stroke inside her thighs near her groin before returning to the garter and slowly removing it. The men cheered when Ricky twirled the garter around his index finger. His eyes met hers as he held out his other hand to help her out of the chair. Pulling her to him, they kissed. When they parted, amid the noise of the crowd, Amber leaned toward Ricky to say, "You don't play fair."

His eyes gleamed as he replied, "And I bet you're ready for me."

She felt the familiar warmth spread up her body as she stated, "Aren't I always?"

Not wanting to toss her bouquet for someone else to have, Amber had the single women take a piece of paper with a number on it out of a basket. And from another basket, a number was drawn to pick who would get the garter put on their leg.

The man who caught the garter was Charlie Parks, a good looking, well built man of twenty-nine who was a cop at the precinct where Ricky worked. The number he drew from the basket was the number Lisa held.

Amber watched her brother as he watched Lisa sit on the same chair that she had sat on not long before. Lisa laughed as Charlie knelt before her with the garter. He slipped it over his hand before he removed Lisa's high heel and then slowly slid the garter over her foot. As with Amber and Ricky, there was a lot of laughter and cat-calls as everyone watched. Charlie said something to Lisa, who laughed and then slid her dress a little higher up her leg. Amber saw Jake's eyes narrow, a sign that he wasn't happy with what he saw. She hoped he would keep his cool. Lisa's dress moved up little by little and Jake's eyes narrowed even more. Amber made her way over to stand next to her brother. "Jake . . ."

"*I don't like it*!" he whispered angrily.

Laying her hand on his arm, she said, "It's all part of the reception, Jake. It's supposed to be fun."

He took a deep breath as he continued to watch. He let it out when the dress and the garter moved over her knee. Lisa said something to Charlie, shaking her head and placing her hand over his. He spoke to Lisa but she smiled as she shook her head again. Charlie then took her hand to help her up.

Jake's body tensed when Charlie hugged Lisa . . . and she hugged him back.

As the applause sounded, Charlie held her hand once more and bowed to their audience. With a laugh, Lisa curtsied. Letting go of this hand, Lisa hurried toward Jake with a big smile on her face. Before Amber moved away from Jake, she warned, "Be nice!"

Lisa's arms moved around Jake's neck. "I was *so* embarrassed! I couldn't stop laughing!"

He stepped back to look at her as he asked, "*Why* did you draw a number?"

Her eyes met his. "I don't have a ring on my finger, do I?"

Music started to play again, a slow song by Elvis.

Jake looked at Lisa a long moment before grabbing her arm. "Let's dance" he said, moving toward the dance floor.

Maggie took pictures of the cake. Amber stepped beside her and put an arm around her. "I do hope that you haven't been only taking pictures."

"I ate" was Maggie's reply. But then she laughed at the shocked look on Amber's face. "I also danced with my hubby a couple of times."

"I want you to enjoy yourself."

"I am! Don't you know that this is a treat for me to have something to take pictures of besides kids, a husband and the dogs?"

Amber laughed and hugged her. "Just have a good time! Where is Matt?"

"I left him at our table with a couple of guys that Ricky works with, talking about pro basketball. So, here I am, taking more pictures and loving it!" She returned Amber's hug then looked at her. "You do realize that this is our wedding gift to you and Ricky . . . taking pictures and developing them for you."

"Thank-you . . . that's the best gift we could ask for."

Maggie grinned, then asked, "How about cutting the cake? Get your husband over here to help you."

After the cake was cut, pictures were taken of the bride and groom as they fed one another a small piece, and both being good about it, to the disappointment of some. The cake was small in comparison to other wedding cakes but it had three tiers, each tier a different flavor. The bottom tier was marble, the middle was white and the top was orange . . . and that was what the bride and groom were keeping in their freezer for a year! The frosting was fluffy white, made with whipped topping . . . and decorated with small sunflowers made of frosting.

As Amber chatted with Sara and Maggie, all three were surprised to hear the DJ announce: "Hey, the new Mrs. Davis . . . please join your brother on the dance floor for one dance." When she spun around to look, there was Jake, smiling and holding out his hand to her. The DJ then said in a gentle voice, "This dance is in memory of your father."

Applause filled the room.

Amber's jaw dropped for a few seconds as she looked at Jake. She told her friends, "He's going to make me cry and ruin your wonderful make-up job, Sara."

"We can fix that. Now, get out there."

Her eyes scanned the room in search of Ricky. She saw him standing with a couple of the guys he worked with. His eyes met hers and he smiled.

Just as she stepped into her brother's arms, the music began, playing, "Butterfly Kisses." Tears threatened automatically. "Oh, Jake . . ."

"It was a toss up between this and *Daddy's Little Girl.* Dad used to sing both to you."." With one hand at her waist and the other holding her hand, Jake moved her gracefully around the floor.

"Why are you doing this?"

"Because I know that Dad wanted to dance with you at your wedding. So, this song and me are the next best thing." His voice tightened and cracked before he finished speaking.

Amber smiled at him through her tears that fell. No wonder she loved him so much. When he smiled back, she saw his tears slide down his face. Taking her hand from his, Amber slid her arms around his neck as Jake hugged her. "I love you, big brother."

"Even after I made your mascara run?"

Amber laughed. "Yes!"

After giving her a gentle squeeze, Jake replied, "I love you, too, Amber."

Becky napped awhile in the port-a-crib after her mother had taken her upstairs to nurse her. Then, after a diaper change and in her father's arms, she walked around the room with her parents, stopping to chat with the guests.

Not long after, there was some commotion behind Amber and Ricky that they paid no attention to . . . not until they heard A.J.'s voice demand, "Get back here!"

"No! I have to talk to him!"

Ricky turned as he recognized the voice. He saw A.J. trying to get a good hold on Deana's arm but she kept pulling loose as she was determined to get to Ricky.

Amber turned, starting to say, "What's go . . ." and her eyes met Deana's.

"Well, don't you make the perfect family?" Deana sneered. "*Daddy, mommy . . . and baby.*" She looked up at Ricky. "I can't believe you actually married her . . . you have to know that she won't stay with you." Deana was not steady on her feet, she swayed side to side as she spoke.

A.J. grabbed her arms from behind. "Come on, Deana . . . let's get you out of here."

"No!" She jerked out of his grasp. "Ricky! You know she doesn't really love you . . . she'll walk out on you again whenever your job gets tough!" With another quick move to get free of A.J., Deana almost lost her balance. But she straightened up, swaying a bit as she attempted to push her unruly curls away from her face. "She only married you to keep you away from me!"

Amber stood still, staring, as if in shock. Ricky gently handed the baby to her. "Here, babe, take Becky. I'll be back." His hand cupped her cheek as he kissed her lips before turning back to Deana.

Deana laughed as he grabbed her arm. "That was your goodbye kiss, Amber. He's leaving with *me* now."

Ricky walked quickly, just about dragging Deana along. Some of the near-by guests watched but with the loud music and dancing, most paid no attention. As he opened the door and pushed her through, he growled, "*What* are you doing here?"

A.J. stepped beside Amber. "Are you okay?"

She looked at the door that closed behind Ricky and Deana. "What is she doing here?"

"She's drunk, darlin'. She had to have heard about this through the grapevine at work. We did try to keep it from her but it's almost impossible with her working in the same place we do."

"How *dare* she come here?" Looking at him, Amber's eyes were filled with tears.

"Like I said, she's drunk . . . and she still has feelings for Ricky."

"And that gives her the right to burst into our reception?"

"I didn't say that."

"She ruined our day."

"No she didn't. But she will if you let her."

Suddenly, there was Jake. "Amber! Are you okay? Where's that bitch? Where did Ricky go?"

"He escorted Deana out of here" A.J. answered.

"Where were you?" Amber asked him.

"The bathroom."

A.J. then realized what song the DJ was playing. It was a favorite of his, an older favorite of many, sung by Louis Armstrong. "Come dance with me, Amber."

She looked from him to the door. "I can't." *Where was Ricky?*

Jake gently removed Becky from Amber's arms. "Go on . . . go dance."

"Jake . . . !"

"Go!"

It wasn't what she wanted to do but she did slide her hand into A.J.'s. "Sorry. Let's go before it's over."

As A.J. pulled her into his arms, he started to sing along: ". . . *and I think to myself, what a wonderful world* . . ." Amber never knew what a good dancer he was . . . and singer: ". . . *I see friends shaking hands, saying how do you do? They're really saying I . . . love . . . you.*" After kissing her cheek, he told her, "Sara and I do love you, you know. We're so glad you're back in our lives." He then finished with, "*Yes . . . I think to myself . . . what a wonderful world . . . oh, yeah.*" Giving Amber a quick squeeze, he said, "It is a wonderful world, darlin'. You and Ricky are married now and you have a beautiful little girl. Don't let anybody . . . including Deana . . . destroy what you have."

"Hey! Are you putting the moves on my wife?" Ricky appeared next to Amber, who smiled in relief to see him and wrapped her arms around him, resting her head on his chest.

Sara also appeared. "Is everything okay? Amber? I was upstairs getting my things together and didn't know anything about Deana until I came down the stairs, and heard her giving Ricky a hard time about leaving."

A.J.'s eyes met Ricky's. "She's gone?"

Ricky nodded. "*Finally.*" He nuzzled his face against Amber's hair. "I am *so* sorry, babe. I had no idea that she would show up."

She didn't respond right away but when she did look up, Amber was smiling. "It's over. Let's enjoy the rest of our reception."

As if on cue, a slow, beautifully haunting song, "Lady In Red", began to play. Ricky gripped Amber's hand and walked to the dance floor. He kissed her then held her close as he moved her around the other dancing couples . . . except his mind went back to Deana:

"Where are you . . . Ow! Will you slow down? You're hurting me!" She yanked her arm out of his grip.

Glaring down at her, he said, "I'm asking again . . . *what* the hell are you doing here?"

"Trying to save you from *her*. Do you really believe that she won't walk out on you again just because you married her?"

"You're not welcome here, Deana. Go home and sober up."

"I'm fine!" Gripping the lapels of his tuxedo jacket, she tried again: "She doesn't deserve you! Can't you see that?"

He pried her hands away. "Go home."

"I want to be in your life . . . I never met anybody else like you."

Ricky groaned in exasperation. "What don't you understand? I *don't* love you . . . I never did! I married Amber!"

Deana's eyes filled with tears. "But what we had was special."

He sighed heavily. "We had a good time, Deana . . . nothing more. You helped me out of a slump . . . that's all. I never intended to hurt you."

"I always hoped that you would love me . . . but you wouldn't give *us* a chance. You never let go of *her.*"

"How could I? I did try but Amber's been *my all* since I met her." Ricky's eyes narrowed as he looked at her. "You expected me to take you back after the way you've been acting . . . and now crashing my wedding reception? Go home, Deana." He made a sound of frustration. "How did you get here?"

"Cab."

"Well, at least you had enough sense not to drive." Gripping her arm once again, Ricky took her out the front door. He couldn't believe his luck when a cab just happed to be driving by. Hailing it, he put a now quiet Deana inside and gave the driver her address. Asking her if she had any money and she mumbled, "Yes", Ricky shut the cab door and then turned to go back inside, to his bride . . . and saw Sara standing on the bottom step of the stairway . . .

"Earth to Ricco . . ."

He blinked and looked into Amber's eyes. He realized then that the music had stopped. "Sorry, I was deep in thought."

About who? But she asked, "About what? What we're going to do in our hotel room tonight?"

"You know, I have worn this jacket all afternoon to hide the hard-on I've had for you most of the afternoon . . . and you ask me a question like that?" He kissed her, long and deep . . . and then breathing hard in her ear, Ricky told her, "Now it's *harder.*"

"Can we leave now?" Amber was very much aware of his erection.

Wild Cherry's "Play That Funky Music" began to play, as the bride and groom looked at one another. But Ricky started to move to the fast beat and Amber joined in. The other dancers sang along with the crowd-pleasing sing-along chorus. Amber and Ricky accompanied them . . . plus she got to watch his moves . . .

* * *

"I'm going to miss you much, baby girl!" Amber cooed to Becky as she said her good-byes. Jake and Lisa were ready to leave. "You be good for your Uncle Jake . . . and Aunt Lisa." She held Becky close as she said to Jake, "There's a list on the 'fridge door . . ."

"And one on the kitchen table."

Looking surprised, Amber asked, "How do you know?"

"Because I know you. I mean, look at all the stuff you brought here for her! She'll be fine, sis . . . we'll *all* be fine. If anything comes up that we can't handle, I have your cell number." Jake smiled. "It's only for three nights. Go have a good time . . . just the two of you. It's your *honeymoon*!"

Ricky took the baby from her mother. "I haven't seen much of you this week and I've missed you." He looked at Lisa. "And thanks again for bringing her to me before the ceremony."

"Amber said that you would love to see her."

"But it was Lisa's idea to bring her to you" Amber put in.

"Okay! Enough of the chatter! Come on . . . the cab's here! Tell mommy and daddy you willl see them in three days" Jake rambled as he took Becky from her father. "You two have fun . . . which I know you will. We promise . . . no wild parties to disturb your neighbors."

Amber pointed her finger at him. "You better not!"

He playfully grabbed her finger. "You've been pointing that at me *way* too much lately! Some day you're going to do that and I . . ."

"Oh, wah-wah!" Amber hugged her brother as best she could with Becky in his arms. "See you Tuesday . . . and remember to call if you need to." She gently cupped Becky's face in her hands to kiss her forehead.

"If I *absolutely* have to."

"And Lisa, thanks for taking care of her."

"No problem" she replied, with a smile.

"I'll put the port-a-crib in the cab" Ricky said.

"No . . . you're going on your honeymoon" Jake told him.

"But I'm her dad . . . and I haven't left yet."

"Okay . . . can't argue with that. Hey, Lis . . . would you get her car seat?" Jake put the sleepy baby in it after Lisa set it on a table that had brochures on it. "Would you take her out to the cab and I'll get everything else?" He then held open the door for her and Ricky.

"Lisa seemed to have a good time" Amber commented, as they watched out the glass door. The cabbie put the port-a-crib into the trunk while Ricky hooked the car seat in the backseat. Amber kept an eye on her daughter for as long as possible until the cab door closed.

"She did." He turned to Amber. "She's trying. With the counseling she had, she's been like the girl I first met. But she does slip up every so often."

"She's only human." There was a pause before she added, "Lisa did nothing wrong with the garter and Charlie. She loves *you*."

With a smile, he said, "Gotta go . . . the meter's running." Jake hugged Amber and kissed her cheek. Opening the door, he turned once more to Amber. "You looked beautiful and so happy today . . . well, except for one episode. After I found out about it, I was ready to flatten the bitch . . . but she had already left"

Amber laughed. "I think I would have enjoyed seeing that! But now . . . go! Take good care of my baby!"

Ricky walked inside after Jake got into the cab and it drove away. Pulling Amber to him, he asked, "Are you ready to get out of here?"

"After I tell Sara and A.J. we're leaving and I have to get my things out of the room upstairs."

"Okay." But instead of letting her go, Ricky's mouth covered hers, and the kiss was long and slow, as his tongue made love to hers. They were interrupted when A.J.'s voice barked, "Get a room, will ya?"

Their mouths parted but their bodies didn't, as they tried to slow their breathing. "As soon as possible" Ricky replied, his eyes looking into Amber's.

"We'll stay and make sure the bums that are still here behave" A.J. joked.

"And we'll bring the gifts to our place so you can pick them up when you get back" Sara told them.

"Thanks" Amber said. "I'm going up to get my things", and started up the stairs.

Sara said, "I'm going to see how many are still here" and walked toward the reception room.

A.J. told her, "We still have some dancing to do, don't forget!"

She turned to smile at him. "I didn't forget!" Sara disappeared through the door.

A.J. turned to see Ricky watch Amber climb the stairs. "Well, aren't you going to help her with her things?"

Ricky shook his head. "No . . . we wouldn't be leaving none too soon if I did."

After chuckling over Ricky's comment, A.J. said, "In case I didn't tell you this already, congratulations, buddy! You got yourself a good woman, one who really loves you. You got lucky . . . like I did!"

There was no stopping the grin on Ricky's face. "I did, didn't I?" But then the smile was gone as he said, "I thought I was never going to see her again, A.J.. That tore me up inside . . ."

"I know it did" A.J. replied, placing his hand on Ricky's shoulder and giving it a squeeze. "But she's back . . . and you have a beautiful baby, too."

The smile returned and he hugged his friend. "Thanks for being there for me . . . and for butting in where Amber was concerned when she first came back."

"Any time." A.J. returned the hug. "It's the least I could do." He stepped back. "If that new bride of yours ever gets down here, you can get going and spend some time together . . . Hey! Here she comes!"

"Sorry!" Amber apologized as she came down the stairs, still wearing her wedding dress plus her coat. She stopped suddenly. "I love how they decorated this railing . . ."

"I'll save the sunflowers for you" A.J. offered.

She hurried down the last few steps and threw her arms around him after setting her suitcase and bag on the floor. "Thanks for everything, A.J.! You and Sara are the best!"

"I will pass that on to her. Now, you two . . . get out of here!"

Ricky picked up her suitcase. Within minutes, they were in the Durango and on their way to the Hilton . . .

* * *

Chapter 30

After signing in at the front desk, Ricky and Amber followed the young man, Harley, who was carrying their luggage to the elevators. If they had their way, they would have taken the stairs to get to their room faster.

Ricky moved Amber to the back of the elevator. Just as Harley reached to press the button for the 44th floor, someone yelled, "Hold the elevator, please!" Two young couples rushed in, talking and laughing. When asked what floor they needed, the four chorused, "Thirty-three!" As the doors closed and the elevator started to rise, the young people continued their chatter.

Sliding the hand he had around Amber to her butt, Ricky's fingers worked the material of her dress, pulling it up. At first they both looked straight ahead but no one paid any attention to them. When Amber looked up at Ricky, he saw the gleam in her eyes and the slight smile on her lips. Thinking it was because of what he was doing to her, he thought nothing more of it until his hand discovered that she wasn't wearing pantyhose or underwear. "Ohgod . . ." he breathed into her hair. But when his fingers slid between her legs from behind, it was her sudden intake of breath that caught the attention of one couple, who looked back at them. Amber just smiled.

"How much longer *is* this ride?" Ricky whispered into her ear.

It seemed an eternity before the elevator stopped to let the two couples off, who were still talking and laughing. Now that they were alone with Harley, Amber and Ricky felt they had to behave but Ricky couldn't stop touching her . . . and Amber didn't know how much longer she could stand him touching her before having to take him on the elevator floor.

Harley kept his back to them and they could hear him humming along with the piped-in music. Ricky's fingers moved beneath her chin to raise her face so that he could kiss her. They tried not to get too wrapped up in the kiss, which was hard not to do, considering how badly they wanted one another.

Finally, the elevator stopped. "We're here" Harley announced. Hearing that, it took control not to run out of the elevator and to their room.

The walk down the hall seemed forever. Where was their suite? Four doors down from the elevator, Harley stopped, setting their luggage on the floor. Using a card to open the door, he turned and smiled. "Your honeymoon suite."

He stepped aside to let them in and Amber stepped forward. But Ricky stopped her by putting a hand on her arm. She looked at him, puzzled. He said to Harley, "Please set our bags inside. I'd like to carry my wife in over the threshold."

Harley's smile widened and then he opened the door further. After placing the luggage inside, he asked, "Is there anything else I can help you with?"

"Is there a *Do Not Disturb* sign?"

"On the inside of the door."

Looking at his watch, Ricky saw the time was a little after six thirty. "Um . . . could we have a bottle of champagne delivered in a couple of hours?"

"I believe there's a bottle already on ice in your room."

Ricky's eyes met Amber's. "We'd like another . . . it's going to be a long night."

Harley couldn't help his chuckle. "I will see that you get another bottle . . . at 8:30?"

"Yes" Ricky replied, not taking his eyes from his new bride . . . wanting to be alone with her.

Clearing his throat gently to get their attention, Harley said, "Here are your keys to your room. The door locks automatically when it shuts. If that's all for now . . ." He handed Ricky two credit size cards before walking back toward the elevator.

"Thank you" Ricky called after him. Turning his attention back to Amber, he smiled as he murmured, "Come with me, Mrs. Davis."

As he swept her up in his arms, she corrected, "Mrs. *Enrique* Davis." Amber's arms hugged his neck as they stepped into their heaven for the next three nights . . .

Ricky didn't set her down as he took the *Do Not Disturb* sign off the doorknob on the back of the door and placed it on the front. "Aren't I getting heavy?" she asked.

"Never" he answered, kicking the door shut behind them. His mouth covered hers, gently at first. "I love you" he whispered against her lips.

Her arms tightened around his neck. "Say it again" she whispered.

"I love you." But this time, his kiss was hungry . . . and she responded in kind. Pulling back, Ricky panted, "Where's the bed?" Looking around the room, they saw a beautiful rust color couch, a matching chair and a glass top coffee table. To the right from where they stood, there was a 2-chair dining set in front of of sliding glass doors. Ricky spotted a doorway to the left. With Amber still in his arms, he took her through the doorway to find a King size bed.

Placing her on her feet, Ricky held her tightly as his mouth assaulted hers. Her body rubbed against the erection that she had been aware of more than once that day. With a long moan, he pushed her away. "*Stop*!"

Breathing fast and hard, Amber stepped farther back . . . to take off her shoes and then pull her dress over her head to show him that she had been totally naked under it. His eyes swept up and down her body, causing the heat in her body to rise a few degrees more. "You're so beautiful!" he uttered, before his tux jacket fell to the floor. Amber watched as Ricky yanked his shirt out of his pants and kicked off his shoes. Unbuttoning the cuffs, he didn't bother to unbutton the shirt . . . he just pulled it over his head. Her eyes watched closely as his fingers unbuttoned and unzipped his pants. The heat in her body exploded into a fire when his erection was free, long and large. Going to the bed, Amber grabbed a handful of blanket and bedspread, yanking it back, exposing a portion of the bottom sheet. Ricky was behind her and pressed her onto the open area. "This won't take long at all" he ground out, his voice hard with passion. Amber pushed herself up off the edge of the bed and opened herself to him. In one thrust, he was inside her. And after three more, he emptied himself, thinking it was never going to stop. When it finally did, he collapsed onto her, trying to catch his breath.

Ricky rolled onto his back on the bed. "I'm sorry . . . but I'm surprised I lasted as long as I did. I was sure I was going to lose it in the elevator when I found out that you weren't wearing any panties."

"Yeah . . . I took off everything under my dress before we left the reception. I figured it would make things easier here."

"Oh, it did." He rolled onto his side to look at her. "I wanted to be inside you . . . after not being with you all week, that's what I thought about most of the time today."

"I guess it was a dumb idea, wasn't it?" Her fingers stroked his cheek.

"We survived . . . barely but we survived." His hand cupped her breast and he noticed how her body raised to press into it. "I'm sorry it happened so fast. Give me a few minutes and then I'll be ready to take care of you."

"Let's clean up . . . and check out our home for the next couple of days."

The bathroom was off the bedroom. The room was large, with the tiles on the walls and the floor the colors of burgundy and beige. A huge mirror was the length of the long counter that held two sinks. A burgundy shag runner rug was on the floor to stand on while at the sinks. There was a large tub and a separate shower. The tub looked big enough for at least four people. On the shelf along the wall beside the tub were bath oils, bath salts, bubble bath and bars of soap, as well as small bottles of shampoo and conditioner. The shower was surrounded by a glass stall. Thick beige bath mats were by the tub and shower to step out on. Large towels and matching washcloths to match the colors of the room hung on bars between the shower and tub. The toilet sat at the opposite wall of the room, to the left of the sink and mirrors. "Ohmy god!" Amber sighed. "I want a bathroom like this!"

With a chuckle, Ricky said, "I'll see what I can do."

For some reason, she checked behind the bathroom door and found two white, plush bathrobes hanging there. "Oh-h-h-h! Look at these! Oh-h-h-h! Feel these!"

"Well . . . if we ever feel the need to wear them . . ."

Amber turned to look at him. "Maybe we had better put them on now if we're going into the other room. There's lots of windows out there and nobody bothered to pull the blinds before we found the bedroom."

Ricky laughed. "Good thinking!" He reached for the one she held out to him.

"I'll be with you shortly. While I'm in here . . . I need to make use of it."

Amber found Ricky standing in front of the sliding glass doors. "See anything interesting?"

Looking at her, his eyes moved from her feet to her head. "Yes."

She chuckled. "Thanks . . . but I meant outside."

Placing her in front of him, his arms wrapped round her. "There's a balcony out there for us . . . and look at the lights of the city."

"It's quite a sight, isn't it?"

"Yes . . . but I have a more beautiful sight to look at in here." Ricky kissed her cheek.

She sighed, feeling so happy . . . so content. "Okay . . . what do you want?"

With a chuckle, he held her closer.

"This room has to cost enough. I read somewhere that the room prices start at two hundred and fourteen dollars a night! And we're here for three nights!"

"Don't worry about that. I've been saving for awhile . . . and as a wedding gift, Sara and A.J. put some towards this."

"We have wonderful friends."

"You aren't kidding."

"Jake and Lisa's gift is babysitting till we get home. I told him that we didn't need anything else."

"True." Ricky then quietly asked, "Did you forget that you have flowers in your hair?"

With a loud gasp, Amber exclaimed, "I did! Ohmygod . . . they must look a sight by now!" She laughed, stepping out of his arms. "I had better take them out now . . . before I get side-tracked again!"

"Champagne?"

"I'd love some!" She then went into the bedroom, to the mirror over the dresser. Amber had to laugh at herself.

Her hairdresser had put many small bobby pins in to hold the flowers in place. Some weren't so easy to find. "I'll have to have Ricky look" she muttered.

Minutes later, he appeared, with two full champagne glasses. "Need some help?"

"Please" she replied, taking a glass from him. He placed his on the dresser. "M-m-m-m . . . this is good" she commented, after a long sip.

"I thought so, too. It's compliments of A.J. and Sara." After pulling two pins out of her hair, Ricky took another drink. And then, he removed the robe he wore. "It's too bulky . . . and we don't have any windows in this room."

"Hmm-m-m-m . . . a naked hairdresser . . ." She smiled at him in the mirror . . . and her body responded to his return smile.

His fingers threaded through her hair. "I think I got them all."

Another long sip. "Thanks."

Their eyes met once more in the mirror. Ricky gently took her glass from her hand and set it on the dresser. His hands then tugged on the loosely tied belt of her robe and it fell free, causing the robe to open. Their gazes held as he reached for his glass and drank from it, then put it to her lips and tipped it slightly so that she could drink. After setting it down again, his hands slid inside her robe so that his fingers caressed her nipples, causing the sensitive tips to harden into tight buds. "You don't need this on right now" he quietly said, moving his hands to take off her robe. Their eye contact never broke as he tossed the robe off to the side. Amber's breathing came faster as his body pressed against her from behind. His erection prodded her. When his hands returned to her aching breasts, her eyes watched as his fingers and thumbs worked her nipples till they became almost painful as the tips peaked and became harder. "You are so beautiful" Ricky whispered, and then his hands slid down her sides to rest on her hips. Amber's tongue licked at her lips as she watched his hands slide and meet on her stomach. She watched with interest as one hand slid further down and moved between her legs. Her eyes closed as she moaned when his fingers found her wet folds. "Open your eyes" he told her, his voice husky sounding. "I want you to see what I'm doing to you." She did . . . and saw her mouth open as she moaned when his fingers slid inside. Her body pressed down, needing to feel him deeper in her. In a low voice, he said, "I'd like to think that you were this wet when I took the garter off you today."

She swallowed hard and managed to say, "Close."

He chuckled huskily as he nuzzled his face in her hair. Moving his hands up to cup her breasts, Ricky said, "I'm going to make love to you like I should have earlier."

"I'm ready" was her whispered reply, meeting his eyes in the mirror.

Abruptly, he turned her in his arms to kiss her mouth, with his hands pressing her body tight against his. Pulling his mouth away and looking at her, the thought to set her on the dresser and take her right there crossed his mind. But he couldn't . . . not on their wedding night . . . not when there was a bed in the room . . . and she wasn't Deana. "Lay down."

Tossing the covers back more than before, Amber lay across the bed. Kneeling between her legs, Ricky leaned down to take a breast into his mouth. His tongue moved in circles around the hard tip of her nipple before drawing it into his mouth. Amber gasped, arching her body for him to take more. Moments later, he slid into her ready body and she met his thrusts as her body demanded release. It wasn't long before it came. She cried out as wave after wave washed over her her. And before she finished, Ricky's cries joined with hers.

When his body slid onto the bed, Ricky managed to slide an arm across her stomach. After their breathing was back to normal, he asked, "How are you doing?"

She smiled lazily. "Hmmm . . . I need a nap." After giving him a kiss, Amber rolled onto her side . . . and within moments, fell asleep.

Ricky curled his body behind hers, with an arm around her waist, feeling happy and satisfied. It wasn't long before he slept, too.

* * *

Ricky's eyes opened and when he saw the back of Amber's head, he smiled. She was his *wife*! He lay behind her for awhile, listening to her breathe. Deciding he had to get up, he slowly pulled his arm from around her. He was surprised when she spoke: "Let's try out the tub. A nice, hot bubble bath to soak in sounds good."

"Are you serious?"

"Sure am." His hand moved to her shoulder before sliding down her body to her thigh and then to cup her butt. "You'll probably need a few of them this weekend to keep from getting sore."

"Works for me." Amber looked back at him for a kiss. "I'll start the water."

In the bathroom, she noticed how deep the tub was. "This could take awhile to fill." Turning on the faucet for hot water and then some cold, Amber then went to find Ricky.

He was filling their champagne glasses. "The bottle's almost empty."

"How much longer do we have before our two hours are up?"

After glancing at his watch, Ricky replied, "Less than a half hour." Handing her a glass, he asked, "How's the tub doing?"

"It's deeper than I thought. It'll be a little longer."

His eyes met hers and he smiled slowly. "I can't remember the last time I took a bath."

"Ohhhh . . . you will remember this one!"

"Oh, I bet I will."

After a long sip from her glass, Amber said, "I better check on the tub one more time."

"Don't be gone too long."

She smiled and left the bedroom. While the water filled the tub, Amber added some bubble bath. "I'll give it another ten minutes" she muttered.

Ricky had left the bedroom so she found him looking out the balcony doors. Standing behind him, she slid her arms around his body. "Is everything okay?"

Raising one of her hands to his lips, he kissed the back of it. "Everything is wonderful." Turning to face her, he realized that she was still naked. Ricky reached back to pull the drapes closed over the doors.

"I don't think anybody can see me" she commented.

"You never know. Bored people use telescopes to look out their windows with. I don't want anyone to see what we do in here."

"Like what?" she asked, pressing her body against his.

He chuckled. "Yeah . . . like what."

Grinning, she raised her face to his. As his mouth moved toward hers, Amber's lips parted. As their mouths met, their tongues mated. Amber opened the robe he wore and pressed her body closer . . . as their kiss intensified with hunger. It took only moments to feel his hard erection press against her. Amber took him in her hand before sliding down to take him in her mouth.

Ricky sucked in his breath. "Not now, Amber . . ." But his hands were in her hair.

Moments later, there was a knock on the door. "Room service!" was called from the other side.

"Amber . . ."

She didn't stop what she was doing.

"Just a minute!" Ricky called out before whispering, "Amber . . . stop", though he didn't want her to. Finally, he gripped her arms and gently pulled her up. "We can continue momentarily . . ."

Smiling, she quietly told him, "I'll be in the tub", then stroked his length before walking away.

Wanting to follow her instead of answering the door Ricky took a moment to compose himself before moving toward the door. Making sure the robe covered him, he opened the door. Harley had a cart with champagne on ice.

"Here's the champagne you ordered."

"Thanks, Harley." Ricky took the ice bucket he was offered.

"Is there anything else I can do for you?"

"No, thanks." It took control not to slam the door in Harley's face.

Amber shut off the running water and stepped into the deep water. After sitting, she leaned back and closed her eyes . . . the water came up to the base of her throat. It felt so good to sit and soak . . . and the bubbles smelled heavenly.

He carried their champagne glasses into the bathroom. He slowed his pace when he saw her in the tub . . . and grew harder. What was it that made him want her as much as he did? Setting their glasses on the edge of the tub, Ricky kept his eyes on her as he removed his robe.

Her eyes opened and she smiled. "Care to join me?" She enjoyed what she saw and her eyes lingered on his broad shoulders and chest before sliding to his stomach . . . then to his erection. "Did you still have that when you opened the door?"

"I couldn't get what you were doing to me out of my head . . . yes, I was still hard." Handing her the glasses to hold as he got into the tub, Ricky sat opposite her. "What an idea to put the faucet at the side of the tub instead of at the end."

"Hmmm . . . wonder what they had in mind when they designed that." Her foot slid between his legs.

He chuckled huskily. "Yeah . . . I wonder." Holding his glass toward her, Ricky said, "To my beautiful wife."

Having to slide forward a bit to clink her glass against his, Amber replied, "To my loving husband."

Raising their glasses to their lips, they watched each other as they drank.

"This is *good*" Amber purred, licking her lips.

"Drink up . . . we have another bottle to take care of."

Her eyes watched him over the rim of her glass. Smiling, she said, "Okay, I know what you're doing . . . trying to get me drunk so that you can take advantage of me . . . uh-huh . . . I know."

Ricky laughed. "What am I going to do with you?"

Still smiling, she replied, "Well, you don't have to get me drunk . . ."

"You shameless hussy!"

Laughing, he slid forward and she met him halfway. Sitting between his legs, Amber put her legs around his hips. Then, resting her left arm on his shoulder, she held her glass in her right hand.

"Tell me something." With his free hand at her waist, Ricky inched her closer.

"What's that?"

"Why are there bubbles in here?"

"What good is a bubble bath without bubbles?"

"But I can't see your body with all these bubbles."

Draining her champagne, Amber set the glass on the edge of the tub. Looking at Ricky, she whispered, "*Feel me.*"

His glass joined hers before his hands slid down her torso and around her butt. "Ever made love in the tub?"

Her mouth inched toward his. "No . . . have you?"

"No."

When she spoke, her lips touched his: "We're going to now, aren't we?"

"Yes . . ." And his mouth took hers . . .

In the bedroom, Ricky dried Amber's back. "I tasted your milk."

"I guess I waited too long to take care of it." Turning to face him, she said, "I miss nursing our baby."

Kissing her forehead, he pulled her close to him. "It's only till Tuesday."

Amber fought back the wave of missing her daughter. "I'll have to get my suitcase."

"I'll get it."

He did, placing it on the bed. Amber found the pump and looked up to find Ricky sitting on the bed, watching. "Hey, can . . ." he started to say.

Smiling, she replied, "Yes you can."

"*Finally*!"

* * *

The time was close to midnight when they went back to bed . . . and they didn't go right to sleep. During the night, Ricky woke her twice. When he woke the third time, ready for Amber again, he reached but found her side of the bed empty. The lighted clock on the nightstand read 7:35. Rolling onto his back, he thought she was in the bathroom. But as he lay there, he realized that things were *too* quiet. Ricky tried to hear where she was. A few moments later, he heard something . . . a soft sound but it was muffled. Throwing back the sheet, Ricky got out of bed. The bathroom door was open and no light was on. He stopped to listen and heard the sound again.

Was Amber crying? Where was she? Rushing out of the bedroom, he saw her, sitting at the table. He could just make out that she had her feet up on the chair she sat on, with her head in her arms that were rested on her bent knees.

"Amber?"

Her head popped up and she quickly wiped at her face.

Ricky squatted beside her. "Hey, babe . . . what's wrong?" he softly asked.

"I'm sorry . . . I didn't want to wake you." She wiped at her nose with the back of her hand.

"Hold on a sec." Sprinting to the bathroom, Ricky grabbed some tissues for her. "Here" he said as he handed them to her.

"Thanks." She blew her nose.

"Will you tell me what's wrong?" he gently asked.

Amber chewed at her bottom lip, fighting the new round of tears that threatened. But she lost and her face crumbled. "I woke up and my breasts were full . . . I miss my baby! Does she miss me at all? Does she wonder why I'm not there to feed her . . . to hold her?" She began to sob.

"Oh, babe . . ." Ricky picked her naked body up off the chair then sat with her on his lap. As he gently rocked her, he said, "She's fine . . . Jake and Lisa are taking good care of her."

"I know . . . but I still miss her."

Not wanting to leave but Ricky asked, "Do you want to go home today?"

Amber looked at him. "No . . . we're on our honeymoon. I want this time with you . . ." Her voice trailed off. Wiping at her eyes, she said, "I'm being ridiculous . . . I can't have it both ways."

"You're not being ridiculous . . . you're just being a new mom who misses her baby. We'll go home if you want."

She shook her head.

"Call Jake later, okay?" he asked.

"Okay."

"Do you feel any better?"

After blowing her nose again, Amber attempted a smile. "I must look a sight." Her fingers traced over his lips. "I love you *so* much" she whispered.

Kissing her mouth gently, Ricky then held her closer for a few moments before standing, with her still in his arms.

She kissed him back. "Take me back to bed."

* * *

Jake answered on the fourth ring. "Hello . . . you have reached the home of the newly married Mr. and Mrs. Ricky Davis."

"Is that how you've been answering the phone?" Amber asked.

"No . . . you've been my first and only call since we got here last night. And I figured it was you now because it's not even 9 o'clock Sunday morning! Why aren't you honey-mooning? Did he toss your ass out already? Your daughter is fine. If she wasn't, I would have called you by now to tell you . . ."

"Jake?"

"Yeah?"

"Are you done?"

He sighed, sounding offended. "Yes."

"She's okay?"

"Becky is fine. She got us up only once, around two. She stayed awake for about forty-five minutes before she went back to sleep."

Amber cleared her throat, hoping to get rid of the lump that was forming in it. "That's good."

Jake was quiet for a moment, and when he spoke again, his tone had softened. "Hey, sis . . ."

"What?"

"I know you miss her."

Amber wiped away the lone tear that ran down the side of her nose. "Yes, I do."

"Don't worry . . . we're taking good care of her."

"I'm not worried, Jake . . . I just miss her."

"Are you enjoying your time with your hubby?"

"Oh, yes . . ."

"Stay focused on him . . . and you'll be back home before you know it."

"I know . . . okay. Hey, give her a big hug and kiss from us and tell her that mommy and daddy love her and will be home soon."

Jake chuckled. "I will do that. See you Tuesday."

"'Bye, Jake."

Just as she tossed her phone on the bed, Ricky walked into the bedroom. "Is everything okay?"

"Everything is fine."

"Even you?"

Walking toward him, she smiled. "I think so!" Sliding her arms around his neck, Amber said, "I'm sorry that I spazed out on you earlier."

"Don't worry about it. You had good reason." His arms moved around her. "Hungry? I ordered breakfast while you were talking to Jake."

"Good . . . I'm starving!"

* * *

Their time alone flew by. No clothes, other than the robes, were worn. They made love where-ever they felt like it, watched television, ordered room service and took many baths and showers together. Extra towels were delivered when their food was brought to them.

Amber and Ricky enjoyed every moment they had to themselves . . .

And then it was time to go home.

* * *

Epilogue

Alexandria Bay, N.Y.

It was decided to spend a weekend together. They rented rooms by the water on the St. Lawrence River. Each room had a balcony and a great view of the famous Boldt Castle. The weather was warm for mid-May but it was cool enough near the water to wear a light jacket. Boats of all sizes were in the water, ranging from rowboats closer to shore, to huge tankers in the deeper middle part of the river. There were two different tourist boats, one that was local and the other from Canada. The double and triple decker boats had many people aboard each one. Seagulls cried their loud calls as they swooped the water and over land, looking for food.

Amber and Lisa sat on a bench below the large community pavillion. They watched Ricky and Jake with Becky near the water. She slowly walked with her father's help, as he walked behind her, holding her hands up over her head.

"Look at her!" Lisa exclaimed. "She's not even a year old!"

"She's ten months . . . but I think she'll be walking on her own too soon."

Jake walked ahead and then faced Ricky and Becky. Squatting, he held out his hands to her. A big smile appeared on her face and her mouth was moving . . . Amber knew she had to be babbling to her uncle. Just as Jake's hands clasped around Becky's middle, Ricky released her hands. She reached for Jake then hugged his neck as he lifted her.

"He's so good with her" Amber commented, smiling. "They just adore each other."

"I've watched him with her since she was an infant and I know he's going to be a good daddy. He's so happy we're having our own." Lisa's hands slid around her stomach. She was seven months pregnant with their son. They had been married since February 15th. Smiling at Amber, she added, "And he's excited about being an uncle again!"

Amber was four months pregnant. "They can all grow up together."

"That's good." "How are you feeling? I know you were lucky not to have *any* morning sickness . . . everything's been good?"

"I've been feeling more tired. The baby's been really active . . . especially at night." Lisa rubbed her stomach. "And I think he works it so there's always an elbow or a foot against my bladder!"

"Oh, yes . . . I remember."

"Did I tell you that I'm planning on breast feeding?"

"No . . . but good for you." Amber hadn't forgotten how Lisa had treated her concerning breast feeding.

As if reading her mind, Lisa said, "I'm sorry I gave you such a hard time about it . . ."

"Don't get into that, okay?"

After clearing her throat, Lisa asked, "How long did you breast feed Becky?"

"I stopped shortly after she turned six months."

Both women turned to watch the guys and Becky. She was in her glory, walking between them as each held a hand. Of course, the going wasn't very fast!

Lisa broke the silence. "How have things been with that Deana? Any more problems with her? Does she still work at the same precinct?"

When Amber took awhile to answer, Lisa was afraid she had asked the wrong questions. When Amber finally spoke, her eyes were on Ricky only: "About a week after we got married, Deana told Ricky that she was pregnant with his baby. He said "Fine" but wanted her to explain how that was possible since they hadn't slept together since July . . . and if it was true, why did she wait so long to tell him and not be showing?" She watched as Ricky laughed with his daughter and her love for him swelled even more in her heart. "Shortly after that, Deana transferred to a precinct in New Jersey."

"She was something, wasn't she?"

Amber gave a short laugh. "That she was." She then thought about how she had talked to Jake about what happened with Deana . . . and he didn't tell Lisa. She still had his devotion.

Jake now held Becky as the two men talked next to the water. Becky was excited as the waves crashed near where they stood, splashing up at them. Her attention then moved to her uncle's sunglasses and she tried more than once to grab at them. Jake patiently moved her hands away each time, continuing his conversation with Ricky.

"So, how does Ricky like being a small town cop compared to a big city detective?" Lisa asked Amber.

"He loves it . . . and so do I. I don't worry as much as I used to." Amber looked at Lisa. "I had my doubts that he would really consider moving. I think the opening in the sheriff's department made up his mind." She looked back to watch Ricky laugh as he walked with their daughter on his shoulders. "Thanks again for letting us stay with you while they work on our house. It should be ready to move into in another week."

"Stay as long as you want, Amber. It's nice having all of you around . . . that little Becky is quite the character! Jake was so happy when he found out that Ricky was willing to leave the city. And then when he found out that the Niles' house was up for sale after Mr. Niles died and the Mrs. had to go into a nursing home, he called Brent Niles to find out what he was going to do with his parents place. Now you'll be living only on the next road from us, instead miles away! He's happy about that . . . and me, too." Lisa watched as the two men and the baby started to walk toward her and Amber. "And I want to say again how sorry I am for how badly I treated you last year."

"Don't, Lisa. It's done and over. Things are different now." Though she hadn't forgotten, Amber decided to forgive . . . for Jake.

"No, really . . . I have to tell you this. I was jealous of what you had with Jake . . . and with Ricky. When I saw you two together, I saw what I wanted with Jake but I went about it all wrong. I was pushing him away . . . I wanted *all* of his love and attention. I never had much from my family and I didn't want to share him with *anybody* . . . especially you. But after almost losing him, and with the help of my therapist, I finally realized what family could be like . . . and that he could love me *and* you as much as he does." Lisa's voice caught and she cleared her throat. "Anyway, what I'm getting at is that I'm glad you gave me another chance and now you're my sister-in-law."

Surprised by Lisa's speech, Amber reached to grasp her hand. "Me, too."

With a laugh, Lisa asked, "Did you think you would ever say that?"

"To be honest . . . no!" Amber laughed with her.

"Don't you miss your friends in New York?"

"Yes . . . very much . . . but we talked about this move and they knew it would be easier for them to visit us than for us to go there . . . at least until the kids are older."

"You're lucky to have such good friends."

"I know . . . Sara and A.J. stayed my friends through so much. They might be only a phone call away but I do miss seeing them whenever I wanted. And that goes for Maggie and Matt, too."

"I'm so lucky that Jake gave me another chance after I smartened up . . . I came too close to losing the love of my life." She gently squeezed Amber's hand. "And you and Ricky had another chance . . . I know how it affected you thinking you had lost him. We were both pretty stupid, weren't we?"

"Yes, we were, Lisa . . . yes, we were. It was good we came to our senses when we did!"

Amber turned to find her family closer to where she was sitting. Becky's face lit up when she saw her mother. As she tried to walk faster, she stumbled but Ricky, who walked behind her again, kept a good grip on her hands. "Hey! Slow down . . . Mommy's waiting for you!" When they were about five feet away from Amber, he picked Becky up by her hands and swung her toward her mother, who caught her, setting her on her feet on her lap. Becky leaned forward, with her mouth wide open and gave Amber a wet, open-mouth kiss before putting her little arms on each side of her neck to give her a hug.

Amber laughed as she returned the hug with one arm, using her free hand to wipe her mouth. "You're such a lover-girl!"

"Just like her mother" Ricky commented, as he watched his girls.

At the sound of his voice, Becky turned to him and babbled, reaching for him. He swept her out of Amber's arms, who commented, "She loves her daddy."

He smiled as his eyes met hers. "Just like her mother" he repeated, as he watched Amber get up.

Jake helped Lisa to stand and rubbed his hand over her stomach. "How are you doing? Has our Alan Jacob been behaving?"

"For the most part, yes. He manages to get a good kick in every so often."

"Alan Jacob? You're naming your baby after dad and you?" Amber asked, then smiled. "I like it."

"I thought I told you" Jake said.

"Nope . . . but you're forgiven." Amber kissed his cheek.

"We were talking about the house and how soon they can move into it" Lisa said.

"It'll be so nice when it's done" Jake commented. "Ricky and I have worked hard over there."

"Two of the bedrooms are ready" Ricky added.

"That's good . . . at least we won't need the third one for awhile" Amber said. Her hand slid over her small belly bump.

"We're going to have so much fun raising all these kids!" Jake remarked.

"You'll lose your eight hours of beauty sleep" Amber teased.

"I will?" He looked at Ricky, who nodded his head. "Oh, well . . . it'll be worth it."

"It will . . . though you won't think so at times" Ricky told him. He then patiently removed his daughter's grip from his sunglasses.

"Oh, yes . . . she seems to know too often when mommy and daddy want some alone time" Amber stated.

At that statement, Becky's head dropped against her father's shoulder.

"Well, you must have found some alone time sometime . . . you're having another baby" Jake commented, with a smile.

"Oh, we manage . . ." Ricky said, his gaze on Amber.

Her cheeks grew warm as she smiled.

"Okay . . . I hate to break this up but are we going to catch that boat over to the castle?" Lisa managed to get in. "But first, get some ice cream?"

"She's been craving ice cream most of her pregnancy" Jake said.

"And I don't care what flavor!" she added with a laugh.

"It all sounds good . . . ice cream and a trip to the castle" Ricky said.

Starting back to the bridge they had to cross to walk back up to the pavillion, Amber grabbed the stroller and then looked at her daughter, who was still in her father's arms. Becky seemed to know what her mother wanted and scowled, shaking her head 'no' and getting a tighter grip on her father's neck.

"The Princess has spoken" Ricky laughed.

"You spoil her too much" Amber commented, as she tossed her camera into the stroller seat with Becky's bag.

"*Me*?" Ricky slid his free arm around her shoulders. "I think we're both guilty of doing that . . . even though I enjoy spoiling the both of you."

"Oh, yeah . . . I enjoy that, too." Amber smiled as he leaned to kiss her.

"Are you taking notes?" Lisa looked up at Jake.

"Thanks a lot, you two!" Jake exclaimed, teasing.

Becky joined in on the laughter, even though she had no clue as to what was going on.

"Come on . . . we have ice cream to buy and a castle to see!" Lisa said, crossing the bridge . . . deciding she wanted a soft raspberry cone.

"There's a Singer Castle, too" Amber announced, following Lisa.

"Maybe tomorrow" Jake said, moving ahead to catch up with his wife. Running up behind her, he playfully slapped her butt. "Come on! Race you to the pavilion!"

"Yeah . . . right!" Lisa laughed, hurrying the best she could behind him.

Amber and Ricky watched. "Do you think they'll ever be as much in love as we are?" she asked him, grinning.

Looking as if he was thinking it over, Ricky then shook his head. "Naw . . . not a chance!" With his free arm, he grasped Amber by the hip and pulled her against him. "But they could be a close second." Ricky kissed her mouth. "I do love you."

"I know" she whispered before kissing him.

The kiss was interrupted by a small hand on her cheek. Amber pulled back to see that Becky had a hand on both her and Ricky's cheeks, and was looking intently at them. "We love you, too, little girl."

"Hey, you two . . . come on!" Jake called to them. He and Lisa were near the stairway to the pavilion.

"We're coming!" Amber yelled.

"Let's go have some ice cream" Ricky said to his daughter.

"Mmmmmm" was her comment.

Becky's parents laughed as they crossed the bridge to join Jake and Lisa. Life was good . . . and all because of getting another chance.

The End

CPSIA information can be obtained at www.ICGtesting.com
Printed in the USA
BVOW071409190312

285318BV00001B/1/P

9 781468 523942